# ANGLING ADMONITIONS

# ANGLING ADMONITIONS

BARRY BLACKSTONE

RESOURCE *Publications* • Eugene, Oregon

ANGLING ADMONITIONS

Copyright © 2020 Barry Blackstone. All rights reserved. Except for brief quotations in critical publications or reviews, no part of this book may be reproduced in any manner without prior written permission from the publisher. Write: Permissions, Wipf and Stock Publishers, 199 W. 8th Ave., Suite 3, Eugene, OR 97401.

Resource Publications
An Imprint of Wipf and Stock Publishers
199 W. 8th Ave., Suite 3
Eugene, OR 97401

www.wipfandstock.com

PAPERBACK ISBN: 978-1-7252-6788-6
HARDCOVER ISBN: 978-1-7252-6789-3
EBOOK ISBN: 978-1-7252-6790-9

Manufactured in the U.S.A.   05/22/20

I dedicate this book to the best example I know of a fisherman and a "fisher of men," my father-in-law, Stacy Meister. You will note as you read these devotionals that his name comes up more than any other person.

## OTHER BOOKS BY BARRY BLACKSTONE

*Though None Go With Me*
*Rendezvous in Paris*
*Though One Go With Me*
*Scotland Journey*
*The Region Beyond*
*Enlarge My Coast*
*From Dan to Beersheba and Beyond*
*The Uttermost Part*
*Homestead Homilies*
*Rover: A Boy's Best Friend*
*North to Alaska and Back*
*Another Day in Nazareth*
*Sermonettes from the Seashore*
*Earth's Farthest Bounds*

# Contents

| | |
|---|---|
| Acknowledgements | xi |
| Prelude: Angling Admonitions—John 21:3 | 1 |
| 1. Wonderful Wings—Proverbs 30:18, 19 | 3 |
| 2. Curving Creek—Philippians 2:14 | 5 |
| 3. Star-Studded—Psalm 33:6 | 7 |
| 4. Hallelujah Heron—Isaiah 23:3 | 9 |
| 5. Stream Stones—Isaiah 57:6 | 11 |
| 6. Riverside Reflections—Daniel 6:2 | 13 |
| 7. Fishing Fog—Ezekiel 29:9 | 15 |
| 8. Penobscot Prayer—Acts 16:13 | 17 |
| 9. Penobscot Psalm—Psalm 137:1, 3 | 19 |
| 10. Salmon Search—Mark 1:35 | 21 |
| 11. Scott's Stones—1 Samuel 17:40 | 23 |
| 12. Heavenly Handywork—Psalms 19:1, 2 | 25 |
| 13. Eagle Excitement—Proverbs 30:18, 19 | 27 |
| 14. Satan's Snare—2 Timothy 2:26 | 29 |
| 15. Waiting Wader—Luke 5:6 | 31 |
| 16. Ghost Grieving—Ephesians 4:30 | 33 |
| 17. Tier Truth—Jeremiah 1:5 | 35 |
| 18. Penobscot Praise—Psalms 8:1 | 37 |
| 19. Special Stringer—Proverbs 15:8 | 39 |
| 20. Stacy's Sermon—Ephesians 4:11 | 41 |
| 21. Fishermen, Fishermen?—Matthew 4:19 | 43 |
| 22. Tide's Time—Ecclesiastes 3:1 | 45 |
| 23. Downdraft Disaster—Psalm 8:8 | 47 |
| 24. God's Gifts—1 Thessalonians 5:18 | 49 |
| 25. Patient Partner—James 5:11 | 51 |
| 26. Experience, Experience—Romans 5:4 | 53 |
| 27. Outfitter's Outings—2 Timothy 2:21 | 55 |
| 28. Polished Pond—Psalm 23:2 | 57 |
| 29. Restored, Refreshed—Psalm 51:12 | 59 |

| | |
|---|---:|
| 30. Billy Bass—Job 5:17 | 61 |
| 31. Lingering Lunch—1 Peter 2:3 | 63 |
| 32. Whirlwind Way—Nahum 1:3 | 65 |
| 33. Fishing Fathoms—Luke 5:4 | 67 |
| 34. Fishers-of-Men Fishermen—Matthew 4:19 | 69 |
| 35. Miramichi Messages—Romans 1:20 | 71 |
| 36. Miramichi Migrant—1 Corinthians 4:11 | 73 |
| 37. Miramichi Moon—Genesis 1:16 | 75 |
| 38. Morning Moonset—Psalms 72:7 | 77 |
| 39. Eastern Eagle—Psalm 103:5 | 79 |
| 40. Meister's Mazda—Amos 3:3 | 81 |
| 41. Meaningful Moon—1 Peter 2:9 | 83 |
| 42. Miramichi Mud—Psalm 40:2 | 85 |
| 43. Osprey Order—Job 12:7 | 87 |
| 44. Penobscot Perseverance—Ephesians 6:18 | 89 |
| 45. Creek Carving—Ezekiel 29:3 | 91 |
| 46. White Water—Job 9:30 | 93 |
| 47. Stream Song—Psalm 144:9 | 95 |
| 48. Sparkling Stream—Psalm 46:4 | 97 |
| 49. Stream Solitude—Mark 1:35 | 99 |
| 50. Stream Sunrise—Numbers 21:11 | 101 |
| 51. Stream Sunset—Psalm 113:3 | 103 |
| 52. Snow Salmon—Job 38:22 | 105 |
| 53. Stream Springs—Isaiah 58:11 | 107 |
| 54. Holy Hardness—2 Timothy 2:3 | 109 |
| 55. Canoe Catch—Luke 5:10 | 111 |
| 56. Peter's Prize—Matthew 17:27 | 113 |
| 57. Studying Stillness—1 Thessalonians 4:11 | 115 |
| 58. Window Works—Psalms 8:3 | 117 |
| 59. Five Facilities—Hebrews 5:15 | 119 |
| 60. Silence Sound—Job 4:16 | 121 |
| 61. Stream Solace—Isaiah 41:18 | 123 |
| 62. Stunted Spruce—Hebrews 5:12 | 125 |
| 63. River Run—1 Corinthian 15:58 | 127 |
| 64. Water Walk—Luke 5:10 | 129 |
| 65. Stream Statute—Romans 8:28 | 131 |
| 66. Corner Concept—Isaiah 49:23 | 133 |
| 67. Stream Storms—1 Thessalonians 2:18 | 135 |
| 68. Water Worries—Isaiah 43:2 | 137 |
| 69. Creek Cleaning—Matthew 5:8 | 139 |
| 70. Creek Companion—John 8:29 | 141 |

| | |
|---|---|
| 71. River Reflection—Psalm 27:8 | 143 |
| 72. Saucer Sipping—Psalms 23:5 | 145 |
| 73. Soaring Statute—Isaiah 40:31 | 147 |
| 74. Riverside Renewal—Ephesians 4:23 | 149 |
| 75. Updrafts Upheavals—Isaiah 40:31 | 151 |
| 76. Scraggly Shrub—1 Corinthians 3:9 | 153 |
| 77. Spotless Snow—Isaiah 1:18 | 155 |
| 78. Twin Trees—Galatians 6:2 | 157 |
| 79. Barked Birches—Colossians 3:2 | 159 |
| 80. Bonus Blessings—Ephesians 1:3 | 161 |
| 81. Canadian Call—Proverbs 25:25 | 163 |
| 82. Frozen Flow—Ezekiel 34:26 | 165 |
| 83. Home Hills—Psalms 121:1 | 167 |
| 84. Reverend Robin—Matthew 6:26 | 169 |
| 85. Special Salmon—2 Timothy 4:7 | 171 |
| 86. Silent Sun—Malachi 4:2 | 173 |
| 87. Theological Thaw—1 John 4:19 | 175 |
| 88. Wood Warmth—Isaiah 44:16 | 177 |
| 89. Wild Wings—1 Kings 19:12 | 179 |
| 90. Sudden Surprise—Psalms 8:4 | 181 |
| 91. Likable Lad—Proverbs 18:24 | 183 |
| 92. Singing Stream—Psalms 46:10 | 185 |
| 93. Icy Image—Psalms 147:17 | 187 |
| 94. Red-Breasted Robin—Matthew 6:26 | 189 |
| 95. Whipping Winds—Psalms 103:16 | 191 |
| 96. Winter Wait—Proverbs 3:5, 6 | 193 |
| 97. River Renewal—2 Corinthians 4:16 | 195 |
| 98. Miramichi Medicine—Jeremiah 46:11 | 197 |
| 99. God's Geese—Matthew 6:26 | 199 |
| 100. Bountiful Blossoms—Genesis 6:22 | 201 |
| 101. River Runoff—Hebrews 12:6 | 203 |
| 102. Vespers Vista—Psalms 148:7, 9, 10 | 205 |
| 103. Morning Mist—Genesis 2:5, 6 | 207 |
| 104. Pasture Precepts—Psalms 23:2 | 209 |
| 105. Materialism Magnetism—Luke 12:15 | 211 |
| 106. Squirrel Tail Stillness—Psalms 23:2 | 213 |
| 107. Winged Walk—Isaiah 40:31, my emphasis | 215 |
| 108. Always Ahead—Colossians 3:2 | 217 |
| 109. Fine Fishing—1 Corinthians 9:22 | 219 |
| 110. Grand Goodbye—2 Thessalonians 3:17 | 221 |
| 111. Special "Sports"—2 Timothy 2:2 | 223 |

| | |
|---|---|
| 112. Teaching Tactics—Ephesians 4:11 | 225 |
| 113. Spiritual Season—2 Timothy 4:2 | 227 |
| 114. Boy Barry—Matthew 18:3 | 229 |
| 115. Hallowed Holes—Titus 1:5 | 231 |
| 116. Tremendous Trips—Matthew 25:14 | 233 |
| 117. Fly Fishing—James 5:11 | 235 |
| 118. Master Maker—Psalms 95:6 | 237 |
| 119. "There" Truth—Matthew 6:21 | 239 |
| 120. Fishing Friends—John 15:14 | 241 |
| 121. Fireside Five—Hebrews 10:25 | 243 |
| 122. Gauntlet Game—Ephesians 6:12 | 245 |
| 123. Angling Anglers—Luke 5:10 | 247 |
| 124. Slippery Salmon—Numbers 32:23 | 249 |
| 125. Comparison Concepts—John 21:3 | 251 |
| 126. Hampton Harvest—Mark 1:17 | 253 |
| 127. Fabulous Find—John 1:45 | 255 |
| 128. Writing Water—Revelation 1:19 | 257 |
| 129. Daybreak Dawn—Hebrews 13:8 | 259 |
| 130. Huge Hen—Matthew 17:27 | 261 |
| 131. Two Thanksgivings—Colossians 3:15 | 263 |
| 132. Mellow Moods—John 14:27 | 265 |
| 133. Delightful Day—Psalms 118:24 | 267 |
| 134. Rejoice Reflections—Philippians 4:4 | 269 |
| 135. Climate Change—Psalms 68:9 | 271 |
| 136. Windy Wind—Psalms 55:8 | 273 |
| 137. Several Senses—Deuteronomy 4:28 | 275 |
| 138. Providential Provision—Matthew 17:27 | 277 |
| 139. Special "Ships"—Psalms 107:23 | 279 |
| 140. Deep" Disciples—Luke 5:4 | 281 |
| 141. Patient Pastor—1 Timothy 3:3 | 283 |
| 142. Productive Pools—Song of Solomon 7:4 | 285 |
| 143. "Fishers" Fraternity—Jeremiah 16:16 | 289 |
| 144. Sweet Species—Numbers 11:5 | 291 |
| 145. Picture Proof—Jonah 1:17 | 293 |
| 146. Dragonfly Distraction—Psalms 8:8 | 295 |
| 147. Shore Stroll—Psalms 147:18 | 297 |
| 148. Lucifer's Lures—Psalms 91:3 | 299 |
| 149. Beelzebub's Bait—Psalms 141:9 | 301 |
| 150. Fatal Flies—Psalms 119:110 | 303 |
| Postlude: Both Boats—Luke 5:6 | 305 |

# Acknowledgements

I would not have gotten this book project finished if not for the typing, editing and compiling by my friend and sister-in-Christ, Rosemary Campbell. I would like to thank her for the numerous hours and many days she spent typing, reading and correcting the errors in the original script. Thanks again Rosemary for all your work; may you share in the eternal rewards of this book.

# Prelude

## Angling Admonitions

Simon Peter saith unto them, I go a fishing.
—John 21:3

I am sitting beside one of my favorite fishing holes as I begin this series of "Angling Admonitions." I am once again at the Anchorage, a small cottage owned by my brother-in-law's family. This shore retreat on Big Lake in Downeast Maine has been a stopping off place for my dear wife Coleen and me for over ten years now. I fish for smallmouth bass, white perch, and chain pickerel in its shallow waters, but just ten miles up Route One is one of the finest landlocked salmon fisheries in North American, the fabled Grand Lake Stream. I have been "fishing" longer than I have been a "fisher-of-men," but I wasn't long into the ministry for the Lord Jesus Christ before the two began to merge in one area—the theology of admonitions and the practical applications of their teachings.

    I recall my first fishing admonition. I was on a trout fishing day-trip with my father, Wendell E. Blackstone, and his cousin, Hartson Blackstone, and my cousin and his son, Bob Blackstone. We were heading for our father's favorite fishing hole, Beaver Brook. Our goal was the elusive Eastern Brook Trout. Bob and I were excited because we had heard for years the legendary fish "tales" of the huge trout that could be caught in that Great North Wood's stream. After an hour and a half riding in Hartson's pickup, we still had a 45-minute hike down a winding woods road to the secret stream. Those were the days when Beaver Brook was only accessible by daring and determination. Eventually we arrived at the brook but instead of waiting patiently for our fathers to catch up and instruct us how to fish and where to fish, Bob and I immediately began fishing with our "chicken coup" worms. However, as soon as my dad made the bank of the brook I heard this admonition, "I hate to tell you this, boys, but you are standing in the middle of one of the best pools on the brook!" I learned then and there that excitement and enthusiasm aren't enough to be a successful fisherman, and neither are they sufficient to be a successful fisher-of-men.

Over the years I have fished for many species of fish in numerous fishing holes in the United States and Canada, even Alaska. I have also learned that you need the right equipment as well as the right techniques. It is important to study the fish you are fishing for as well as studying the fisherman who fish for those fish. One of the best lessons I learned was to listen to my fishing "guide." Over the years I have had the privilege to fish with some good and knowledgeable fisherman, including some of the finest Atlantic salmon guides in Canada. I was too proud early on to learn from them, but as the years passed and I humbled myself to be taught by those that had fished a particular pool before me, the more I witnessed and watched the unfolding tactics for fishing for fish. The more I fished and the more I studied the Bible, I saw the amazing parallels between fishing for fish and fishing for men.

In 1970 I began witnessing for the Lord. I had been saved since 1958, but had never taken part in the grand fishing expedition called "The Great Commission." (Matthew 28:19, 20) As with fishing experiences, I was slow to learn and observe. Instead, I just jumped in with both feet. Oh, I got my feet wet, but I saw few results like on Beaver Brook that first morning with Bob. Once I realized I needed a "guide" (Holy Spirit) and that I could learn from the great fishermen (soul winners) of the past, I soon was taught the techniques and tactics that work well in the ongoing ministry of fishing for the souls of men.

I also saw through my fishing experiences that many other Biblical principles could be more easily understood if applied to angling. So contained in this series of articles are some "Angling Admonitions" that I have learned from blending together Biblical precepts and fishing concepts. I tell people all the time that I take the greatest vacations in the world fishing for fish, (recently I finally took my first trip to Labrador) and that I have the greatest vocation in the world: fishing for men. Let's "go fishing" and see what we catch in the "pool" we call the Word of God!

# 1

# Wonderful Wings

too wonderful . . . the way of an eagle

—Proverbs 30:18, 19

Just as the sun was starting to set I heard the hollow cry of a bald-headed eagle drifting down out of the evening clouds to the east. In a 360-degree search of the horizon I soon spotted not one but two adult eagles in fresh, full plumage working their way slowly along the wooded shore just above the "narrows." These grand birds were winging their way towards our ice shack on Branch Pond.

Cutting gracefully through the cold air, the pair soon flew by our camp at about fifty feet above the ice. I watched them as they reached the main part of the lake and turned back. They must have spotted what remained of the three lake trout we had cleaned by our water hole. Within minutes they were back soaring easily in a giant spiral waiting patiently for us to leave so they could have supper. How did they remember that we always stopped fishing with the setting of the early afternoon January sun? They must have been watching our pattern all winter because they were just in time for dinner, that is, if the "lame" seagull didn't get the scraps before them. I have often wondered what a duel that would be, but I suspect a crippled seagull is too smart to tackle a pair of healthy eagles. To defy an eagle over a few togue parts wouldn't be wise or healthy.

But as I watched for our seacoast neighbor, he never arrived. He must have suspected that seagulls hadn't been invited for supper at the Braley,

Ingalls, Parker ice house and fish shack. The eagles had the sky to themselves as they hung lightly on a gentle breeze that had begun to blow up the lake. Finally, the two magnificent creatures settled down on the bare branches of an old pine just on shore. The heavy weights formed the classic eagle perch as they watched the four of us pull our traps for the last time. What an amazing, superb sight they were, my closest and most consistent view so far in my life. The pair had been coming to visit off and on all winter according to the "boys." They fished every good day, but I could only fish on the "odd" day. They said on rare occasions the pair were joined by a juvenile eagle still dressed in gray. The eagles were back to Branch Pond, and, like their cousins to the north, they only had a few miles to go to the crags and cliffs of Acadia National Park as the "eagle flies." The warmth of the ocean kept the eagles in Maine, and they only ventured inland when lake trout was on the menu.

Dusk was breathtaking that night because at sunset a full snow moon was coming up. As we made our way off the ice that afternoon, the eagles left their resting place and took to the air again. No doubt they ascended just long enough before they descended to eat their supper in private. God is right. "The way of an eagle in the air" is a wonderful sight, especially when the eagle is American and the air is Maine.

# 2

# Curving Creek

I press toward the mark for the prize of the high calling of God in Christ Jesus.
—Philippians 2:14

Having been raised in the brooks and streams of Aroostook County, Maine, I know of the lure of "beyond the bend." I have waded along many a winding stream, and the thrill is always around the next corner or around the next curve. It is the romance with anticipation.

Anticipation is the true spirit of "beyond the bend." What we know and have seen often becomes dull and drab. Our daily paths often lose their glamour and glitter as we repeat our wading. "Beyond the bend" with its uncertainty and unexpected sights draws us onward and forward as we search for that illusive catch. I have this problem every time I fish a trout stream. The best hole has to be just around the next bend. I will always fish around one more corner before I head back upstream, fish or no fish; this philosophy makes for some long days.

God has created our lives much like the curving creek. How terrible would be our lives if it were just one long straight streambed. I remember in 1972 traveling on the straightest railroad track, at that time, in the world. It was 300 long, dull miles of straight rail without a dip or a drop or a diversion. I was traveling across the Gibson Desert in Western Australia with my cousin Bob. It was the most boring part of our ten-week mission's trip to Australia. Double the boredom when we had to retrace it on our way home! So is life without its curves and corners. We might not be able to see down the brook, but that is what makes life the adventure that it is. We never know what is coming up, but we know "Who holds tomorrow, and we know Who holds our hand."

Vance Havner has written, "Indeed, that is what faith is: confidence in God's future. We know so little of life, of truth, of God and destiny. Business crashes, health fails, and friends depart, cherished dreams collapse—yet somehow. . .most carry on." Who of us hasn't thought to ourselves, "Well, next year will be better" or "tomorrow will hold the answer" or "I'll feel better next month?" All those thoughts are of "beyond the bend." So with our creel over our shoulder and our fishing rod in our hands, we press on, push forward, our goal being the fishing hole "beyond the bend." It may be a bend of pain, of loss, of disappointment, but we know once we get around it, there lays "beyond the bend" a glorious pool, a feeder stream, a golden catch.

For the Christian there remains the last curve, the final bend, the ultimate corner. The world calls it death, but the Bible calls it a "departure." (2 Timothy 4:6) A life "beyond the bend" where there will be no more corners and no more curves because we will be living with God. Our journey will be over. Our wandering will be done. Our wading along the winding stream beds of life will end "beyond the bend."

# 3

## Star-Studded

By the word of the Lord were the heavens made;
And all the host of them by the breath of his mouth.

—Psalm 33:6

I have come to believe that the sky and all it stars are brighter and more brilliant in the country than in the city. Take away manmade lights and manmade illumination, and the star- studded sky will inspire.

Deep in the woods of northern Maine is Alagash Lake. Part of the Alagash Wilderness Waterway, this huge body of water is only accessible by canoe. It is one of the last truly wilderness areas left even in the State of Maine. They won't even allow you to take soap into the area; my kind of place. I first went into this area with a group of young men from my church in the spring of 1992. We were after lake trout, but I remember best the star studded skies we had every night we were there. Added to the glory of the stars was a full spring moon, and I came home with a creation memory that must be recorded.

God in his infinite wisdom has chosen to communicate with his creatures through various means. His principles and his precepts are not just limited by certain manmade methods. I firmly believe that along with the Scriptures and the Spirit, the eternal Father can also speak to his children through a star-studded sky. David believed in this method of communication for he writes, "The heavens declare the glory of God; and the firmament sheweth his handiwork. Day unto day uttereth speech, night unto night sheweth knowledge. There is no speech nor language, where their voice is not heard." (Psalm 19:1–3) Standing on the lake shore at Sandy Point Campgrounds on Alagash Lake, I heard no voice, but I received a lot of knowledge about my Creator by looking up into His star-studded sky.

As the moonshine and the star shine engulfed me, I thought first of this truth, "He telleth the number of the stars; he calleth them all by their names." (Psalm 147:4) Even man in his thousands of years has yet to come up with a number or enough names. Every time man thinks he has a telescope big enough to see the end of the universe, somebody develops a bigger one only to discover more space and more stars. Then I thought of "The moon and stars to rule by night: for his mercy endureth for ever." (Psalm 136:9) There is no greater place then a lakeside to learn the lesson of the rule of moon and stars and the depth of God's mercy. Mercy is not just a daytime grace, but nights are the best time to see God's grace. Finally, I thought, "Praise him, all ye stars of light." (Psalm 148:3) One of the wonders of a star-studded sky is its grip on your emotion to give thanks and praise for a Creator that would create such a wonderful world for you to enjoy. Surrounded by fir, spruce, pine, and water, I rejoiced in heart for the privilege of seeing a star-studded sky over water.

# 4

# Hallelujah Heron

the harvest of the river is her revenue.

—ISAIAH 23:3

It was one of those sights you rarely forget if you love the vista of the river.

I was fishing for the Atlantic salmon in B-Pool on the Penobscot. It was a warm spring day with a very blue sky and a very gusty southern wind. I happened to be alone at the time so the sound of the water pouring over the Veazie Dam had totally silenced my world, silenced in the sense that no other sounds could be heard. I could hear nothing else but the roar and rush of thousands of tons of water driving the spring run-off over the dam boards and through the four giant turbines at the side of the dam. Often, however, when one sense is blocked another sense becomes that much more alert. So it happened as I cast my Pink Ent into the bubbling and boiling water of the B-Pool that my eye caught a visitor to my vista.

It was not the visitor I wanted because my eyes were looking for a leaping salmon to enter the pool from the rapids below. It was not a salmon that caught my eye by the small island fifty yards off shore. It was a heron. I am no expert on heron so I couldn't tell you what specific kind of heron she was, but with her long neck, long legs, and her long, tapered bill, I knew she was an heron, and she was there for the same purpose that I was—fishing, even though our prey was different. I was after the big Atlantic salmon that swam up the Penobscot on their annual trek, and she no doubt was after small bait fish or even a small bass that might venture near shore. She had probably been at the point of the grassy island for a long time before I saw her because I hadn't noticed her flying in. Wading about slowly, her head was down, and her eyes were focused upon the slightest movement in the still waters.

As my salmon fly drew little interests from the salmon swimming around B-Pool, my interest was drawn even more to this magnificent heron wading gracefully below me. My disappointment in not catching a fish was soon changed to joy when my fishing partner claimed her first fish of the morning. The bill dropped in the blink of an eye, and the retrieval of the head from the water was just as quick. From where I stood it looked like a four-inch bass had become breakfast for my feathered friend. It was as if I could hear a hearty hallelujah echo off the face of the dam. As the lanky heron enjoyed the success of her patience, I thought of how enjoying the success of others is missing from our society today. We are so selfish and self-centered; we have missed the simple pleasure of watching others win. We want so much to be on the platform and to hold the trophy over our head that we forget that there is joy in watching others succeed. We are so competitive that we have forgotten to "rejoice with them that do rejoice." (Romans 12:15)

# 5

# Stream Stones

Among the smoother stones of the stream is thy portion; they, they are thy lot.
—Isaiah 57:6

At the time of this devotional, I have recorded in my journal the names of 25 streams I have dipped my feet in. Add to those streams, 23 different brooks and 32 different rivers and you could say I have spent a fair amount of time walking on smooth stones.

One of the perils of brook fishing is the possibility of each step being a watery slip. I have been very fortunate over the years to only have taken a half dozen full falls (the worst was on the rocky shore of Long Beach Island inlet in New Jersey while fishing for mighty bluefish when I hit a slippery rock and tumbled into the bay in the Spring of 2017), but I see now that my God had a lesson for me to understand in my encounters with "smooth stones."

I must say at first that smooth stones can be very beautiful. Polished by water and sand, some of these smooth stones are very attractive. I have a few small smooth stones sitting on my shelf in my study (my favorite are the five stones that represent David's 'smooth stones'-I Samuel 17:40 I picked off a remote shore on Frenchboro Island off the coast of Maine) which are special treasures picked up or given to me through the years. Each is a tiny "history of hardship" as wave after wave of current from the stream washed their roughness away. Small smooth stones can't be shaped in a season or a year. A single pass of spring water can't create a smooth stone. It is only in the turbulence of the stream and the grinding of the gravel that the finished stone is complete. So it is with life and "the man of God," Paul says that God's plan for us is "to be conformed to the image of his Son." (Romans 9:29) That is our portion. Without life's grinding, polishing, and buffeting, we will never be that smooth stone God wants.

Smooth stones are the end product of a painful process that takes a lifetime. Though the lifetime of a stream stone is longer than our lifetime, the pattern is the same. Any smooth stone from any stream starts out a jagged piece of bedrock from the bottom of a brook. Maybe a heavier rock breaks it free during a spring runoff. Bruised and broken, the stone is battered against the larger stone in the stream bed. A rolling mill of current and sand attacks the ragged rock from every side. Not until it comes to rest in a protected area does it stop falling. At peace, it now is assaulted by the weight and power of the flowing currents. Scores of fishing seasons pass before the smooth surface face begins to emerge, and then years and years more to refine and polish until the stone are completely smooth without any blemishes or broken edges.

The human soul is like that. Bruised and broken by sin, the soul is attacked by a wicked, cruel world. Only when it finds a safe place in Christ does the falling stop. Even then the vile, sinful edges are clearly seen. We are forgiven within, but rugged and ragged without. It is then that the water of the Word begins to chip off the unwanted pieces, and as the years pass the soul and the spirit of the man is polished until the image of Christ shines on its surface.

# 6

# Riverside Reflections

*And I saw in a vision, and was by the river.*

—Daniel 6:2

What is it about "still waters" (Psalm 23:2) and the "still small voice?" (1 Kings 19:12)

I have spent a large percentage of my life near, in, or around water. I love streams, and I love the sea. After starting a devotional series titled "Sermonettes from the Seashore" (a book I got published in 2019 by Resource Publications) I realized I had just as many freshwater reflections as saltwater remembrances. Not only have the oceans in my life inspired me, but so have the rivers of my life. It was for this reason that I thought I ought to compile a companion set of devotionals for my "Sermonettes from the Seashore" under the title "Riverside Reflections." Instead of sea and surf, tides and terns, I would reflect on brooks, creeks, streams, and rivers, and the many spiritual lessons my Father in heaven has taught me by the riverside while fishing.

I was very young when I heard for the first time the sweet stillness by a stream. I certainly didn't understand it then, and I am still no expert, but this I know. There is something about a babbling brook and a calm creek that quiets the soul and calms the pulse. More times than not in my hurried world, I have to find "still water" to really relax. Recently, I discovered it by the seaside, but I first found it by the riverside. In trout fishing trips with my dad (Wendell E Blackstone) to Beaver Brook, and later during salmon fishing trips with my father-in-law (Stacy A. Meister) to the Penobscot River, whether rivers in Maine or rivers in Canada, each has fulfilled a vital place in my recovery from the ravages of modern living.

"Still waters" have never been places of stagnation for me. Quite the opposite, they have served as wonderful interludes with the "still small voice." Why is it I feel closer to God in riverside romps, I know not? Seaside strolls do the same even though I know He is everywhere, city or country. It seems that the pace and the practices of modern living don't allow for much reflection in the city. To daydream in the city could result in getting run over by a service truck. The only danger of daydreaming by a brook might be getting run over by a whitetail deer looking for a drink. City life seems so planned, but creek contemplation is so unplanned. Who can plan seeing a salmon jump clear out of the water? Who can plan seeing a family of ducks swim by? Who can plan watching an osprey dive for fish? Who can plan seeing an eagle fly by? Who can plan seeing a moose drinking from a stream? The instant delights are arranged not by man, but by my Father as precious momentary gifts from above that quicken the heart and excite the spirit. They are tiny treasures that forever stay in the mind and years later bring sweet reflections of just how wonderful our God is. My prayer is as you read this "riverside reflection" by the "still waters" that you too will hear that "still small voice" speaking quietly to your soul.

# 7

# Fishing Fog

The river is mine, and I have made it.

—Ezekiel 29:9

As we prepared to launch our boats into the Manicouagan River in Northern Quebec, Canada, a dense cloud of heavy, wet fog slowly moved up the valley before us. By the time we had our outboard motors roaring, the fog had engulfed the river in its thick, gray vapor. The sun that greeted us that morning at camp was gone, and so were the huge granite hills that lined the shores of this mighty river. The plan was for one boat to hug the east shore and other boat to troll the west bank. We were after the savage northern pike, but that morning all we got was fog!

I have pondered many times over the years about that morning on the Manicouagan. I was fishing with my brother-in-law (Larry Fox) and a cousin (Bob Blackstone). My father-in-law (Stacy Meister) and another cousin (Dale Blackstone) were in the other boat that foggy morning in July. I was at the motor, and it was my job to place my fishing companion in the way of a hungry pike. As I turned to my right for the far shore, I soon lost contact with the other boat as the fog simply swallowed them up. I had no fear for I had fished on this river before. Our plan was to meet at a spectacular waterfall a few miles downriver for lunch. I saw no problem as I boldly plowed into the "valley" fog. We had witnessed such morning fog before and were confident that within a few hours at best the fog would burn off by a hot summer sun.

As the morning wore on, the feisty fog seemed to get thicker. It was even getting difficult for me to see my cousin in the front of our 14-foot boat. Even the pike feared to surface as the fog surrounded everything. It became quite unsettling as a haunting silence settled over the fog-bound river. I was suddenly alerted to trouble when my cousin shouted, "Log barrier just ahead!" Because I was trolling so slowly, I was able to motor back and turn away. It was then I realized that I had made a terrible mistake. In my attempt to cross the river in the fog, I had gotten completely turned around, and instead of heading downriver, I was taking my comrades up river towards a huge power plant. The log barrier was a protection lest boats get too close. I had gotten lost in the fog.

Despite being the only time I ever got lost on a river, that experience has taught me that, as in boating so in life, it is easy to get turned around in the thick fog created by the sins of mankind. How many times have we headed down the road of life thinking we knew exactly where we were going only to discover a while later an obstacle in our path. When was the last time we thanked our heavenly Father for His barriers that don't allow us to go any farther? We motor on enjoying our company and our pleasures fog-bound in mind and soul. The river belongs to the Lord, and so does the road. As I should have followed my father-in-law that morning, so we need to follow our guide.

# 8

## Penobscot Prayer

And on the Sabbath we went out of the city by a riverside, where prayer was wont to be made.

—Acts 16:13

The young man waited patiently on the old log that had been deposited on shore by the ice flows earlier that spring. As the river flowed quietly in front of him, he gazed into the water looking for the slightest movement. High rolling clouds drifted slowly over head, and a light breeze blew gently through the fir trees behind him. The tranquility of the spot was highlighted by the roar of the rapids just below him on the bend of the river. The smell of spring was in the air, and the cool wind felt good against the warmth of the sun blazing high over his head.

He looked across the river and saw a fisherman wading deep into the waters of a salmon pool. He seemed to be keenly aware of a fly being cast directly into the rips that cut across the ledge at the base of the distant pool. Up river he noticed a few boats hugging the far shoreline while a number of men were wading, almost in slow motion, along the water's edge. Downriver he observed canoes anchored like a picket line straight in front of a series of rips formed by an underground pipeline that stretched across the width of the river. Also across from him, square stern canoes and boats were staked three deep as a multitude of salmon flies were cast to the lip of the drop off.

In front of the rookie salmon fisherman the river was also full of fishermen wading slowly over the jagged ledges that jutted out as great granite breakwaters. The resulting rock formations cut the flow of the river and fashioned its current into a perfect salmon run. The returning salmon could be seen lying three and four deep, maneuvering for the best flow of the waterway. Big salmon were known to haunt that salmon run from early spring to late fall.

Waiting his turn to fish brought opportunity for meditation. Rarely were his thoughts on anything other than the wonder of his God's beautiful creation. Over the years that followed that old log would become his easy chair as he waited his turn to catch the mighty Atlantic salmon. As the sun passed behind a white puffy cloud, he leaves to take his turn on the river. Entering the river, he prays his fisherman's prayer:

> My Father which art in heaven, hear this angler's prayer. Thy help I need, thy will be done in stream, as it is in river. Give me this day my daily limit. And forgive me my exaggerations as I forgive those who exaggerate to me. And deliver me not into unproductive waters, but save me from being shut out. For thine are the fish, and the fishing, And the fishermen forever. Amen.

# 9

# Penobscot Psalm

By the rivers . . . they . . . required of us a song.
—Psalm 137:1, 3

Most of the time, the shores of the Penobscot River hold more fishermen than the shoals hold salmon. It often takes an act of Congress just to find a place to fish let alone find a salmon. The sweet noises of the river are overshadowed by the chatter along the bank from storytelling salmon fishermen relating their latest exploit. And if you are one of the fortunate ones to hook a salmon, you will have more spectators watching you then the lowly Patriots on a sunny Sunday afternoon after an 0–15 season. Make one mistake in play and you will hear more criticism than either the Red Sox's after the 1976 playoff game or Bill Buckner following the 1986 World Series. I like the way Tom Hennessey put it in one of his articles years ago, "But you know it as well as I do there will come a time when, wading just a little deeper to get just a little closer to a showing salmon, you'll step into a hole that's just a bit lower than your waders are high. Be assured that your impromptu impersonation of 'Flipper' will be witnessed by more than a few yelling, cheering, hooting, and delighting disciples of Izaak Walton. Don't feel downcast or dejected. They'll see to it that your performance gets at least as much publicity as it would if it were plastered on page one in 48-point type." Such are the perils on the Penobscot when fishing with people, but there is a time when all those hazards are avoided.

Having fished the Penobscot every spring since 1979, it was not until 1984 that I fished it in the fall. Fall fishing on the Penobscot is void of long lines even at the best pools. It is a time to pick your spot, have time for quiet mediation, and to remember that moment I penned, THE FISHERMAN'S PSALM.

> The Lord is my Guide, I shall not boast.
> He maketh me fish in bountiful rivers.
> He leadeth me beside beautiful lakes.
> He restoreth my bait.
> He leadeth me in paths of yonder pond
> For fish unlimited.
> Yea, though I wade in brook or stream,
> I will always catch fish.
> For thou art with me.
> Thy rod and thy reel will produce for me.
> Thou prepareth a fish for me
> In the presence of my fishing partner.
> Thou anointeth my fly with attractiveness,
> My creel runneth over.
> Surely catch after catch shall follow me
> To every fishing hole,
> And I will come home with my limit every time.

# 10

# Salmon Search

In the morning, rising up a great while before day, he went out,
And departed into a solitary place.

—MARK 1:35

By nature I am a loner. Lindbergh and I would have gotten along well. So it is not therefore surprising that I enjoy fishing alone. Whether on a rippling brook or a pulp road pond, the silence and solitude is a haven for me. Walking along the banks of a river brings tranquility to my soul that few activities can, and to add the occasional spotting of a salmon, the heart slows to such a rate it is hard to even find a pulse.

The sky was a September blue, and the puffy white clouds were numerous overhead. The wind was light and cool, and the sun was hot, but refreshing. The river was low, very low. I breathed in deeply as I realized I was the only person immediately below the Veazie Dam on the Penobscot River. Even the noise of the traffic that passed close to the river on both sides was silent and still. It was as if I was standing on a lonely Labrador river all by myself. For that moment at least the river was mine and the fish in it. As far as I could see, the river was my own private domain, and it felt good. Only those who have experienced such an emotion can understand how I felt at that moment. Lewis and Clark must have felt it as they stood looking at parts of America no white man had ever seen before. Hillary must have felt it as he stood looking down on the world. Byrd must have breathed it in at the South Pole. Can anything compare with being absolutely and totally alone with nature and God? You get so caught up in the beauty of the changing fall foliage, the peaceful river, and the simple solitude that you forget the purpose for being there.

With the roar of the river behind me, the last sounds of civilization soon disappeared. Now I was really alone, both physically and mentally. Absolute solitude was mine at that moment. It seemed as if the casting and retrieving of my fly went on automatic as my arms, wrists, hands, and fingers went through the motions, but my memories and mind were a thousand miles away. I might as well have been on the River Spay in Scotland fishing for Atlantic salmon. The water flowing passed my legs could just as well have been from the River Wye in England. The Grimshaw River in Iceland or the Rangitikei River in New Zealand could just as well have been my fishing hole at that moment on the Penobscot as the river engulfed my "Butterfly." I could have just as well been casting for Big Rainbows on the Big Horn River in Montana, speckled trout in one of the streams of the Catskills in New York, or fishing for cutthroat in one of the creeks of Yellowstone. However, fifteen minutes into my lowly quest for a lonely salmon, my solitude was interrupted as a good sized swirl swallowed my "Butterfly." Praise the Lord for the solitude one gets in searching for a solitary salmon.

# 11

## Scott's Stones

*And chose him five smooth stones out of the brook.*

—1 SAMUEL 17:40

As my son Scott and I left the house that cool spring afternoon we headed for the stream only a two minute walk from the parsonage of the Calvary Baptist Church in Westfield, Maine. For this first fishing expedition I had dug out all my old fishing equipment from my boyhood. Over Scott's right shoulder I placed my old green fish bag where dried up grass and worms were still in the bottom. Over Scott's left shoulder went my old green handled trout net. The elastic line was too long for my son, but no matter, a fisherman needs a net. Then into his little hands I placed the pride and joy of my boyhood, an old fiberglass spinning rod. The old green closed-face reel had never been off the rod since my dad gave it to me. The cock handle was partly missing, and the reel handle had an odd sized nut holding it together. The reel set was bent, but despite its wreaked look, it still could catch fish. As I stood back to take a picture of my fisherman warrior, the only thing I could think of was David wearing King Saul's armor just before his battle with Goliath. Each piece looked big on the body of my thirty-month old son, but unlike David, Scott did not complain as we headed toward the stream.

When we got to the stream, I picked a nice spot to start fishing. It was on a bend where a gravel bar split the brook in half. The water was shallow so my boy couldn't drown if he happened to fall in. A trout pool was also within casting distance, and trout were known to reside there in the spring.

I took a fat squirming worm from my old green bait box and showed Scott how to thread it on a long shank hook. He wasn't too impressed. After the baiting was over, I showed him how to cast the worm into the pool. Telling him to stay and wait, I moved down just a bit so I could cast over the pool from below. We hadn't been there fifteen minutes when it happened. Paying attention to my fly casting, I hadn't noticed that my son had long since put down my old rod. Instead of fishing he had taken up rock collecting. After the first rock hit the water, I turned to discover my green fishing bag full of rocks. Scott's pockets were bulging with rocks, and his tiny arm was throwing rocks into the stream like a batting machine arm. Again, all I could think was I had brought David to the brook and five stones were not what he took. There was no Goliath around, but you couldn't tell it by the way my son was slinging stones. Before long instead of fishing I too was collecting rocks. Like David of old, Scott had won!

As we headed home after a few hours of throwing rocks, I can still hear my son say, "Thanks Dad for taking me fishing!" I could only smile as I emptied my pockets of skipping stones. David would have been proud!

# 12

# Heavenly Handywork

The heavens declare the glory of God; and the firmament sheweth his handy work. Day unto day uttereth speech, and night unto night sheweth knowledge.
—Psalms 19:1, 2

Despite being raised in the woods of northern Maine, it wasn't until I met Stacy Meister, my father-in-law that I learned of the great lessons one could find in those woods. When America began to modernize, she turned from the out-of-doors to the indoors. Stuffy office buildings and foul apartment complexes are where most people spend their time today. Even when they get outdoors, they are caught in traffic jams where the air is anything but clean. Ceilings have become a curse to our society because they have blocked out sky, star, and sun. Walls meant to shelter have become prison gates to most, blocking out the singing birds and the refreshing breezes. We have become narrow in our vision and intolerant in our attitude towards others. That is what the indoors creates, but once back to the great outdoors our sight broadens and tolerance becomes a way of life.

The average outdoor person can get a lot of information on nature through books and magazines, but nothing can be truly learned until one is taken into the woods. Until you see it, smell it, touch it, or taste it, it is but an artificial image in your mind. I learned very early just how artificial this mechanical age is that we are living in. We pay others to play our favorite sports, and we watch them from the comfort of our indoor arenas. As for me, I might be looked at with ridicule and suspicion, but I would rather be found on the banks of a Miramichi river than on the sidelines of a NFL football game. I would rather be sitting in a canoe on a northern Quebec lake then in the box seats at Fenway. I would much rather be watching trout rise on a small Maine pond then watching the score raise in the Boston Garden. Why? There is only one word for why—God! I have been to football games, and baseball games, and basketball games galore, but none has thrilled me more then to spend time in God's great creation learning more about Him.

Vance Havner once wrote in the late 1920s these inspiring words, "Yes, the woods were God's first temple, and we have lost much by not worshiping there more today. For all our radios and airplanes, I am not much impressed with the fever of modern progress. I am afraid what we have gained will not justify our loss of this one thing. We have exchanged the glory of the outdoors for a generation of provincial anemic. When I read of the suicides among out college youth who have found life uninteresting and wearisome, I cannot but wonder. If you have never sat in the woods 'knee-deep in June,' as James Whitcomb Riley says, or tramped across snow-blanketed hills, or watched the falling of autumn leaves, or danced in your soul with the daffodils, please don't shoot yourself until you have done that!"

# 13

## Eagle Excitement

Things which are too wonderful for me, yea, four which I know not: the way of an eagle in the air.

—Proverbs 30:18, 19

Once after a fruitless period of fishing on the Penobscot River with my father-in-law, we were returning to the boat landing at Greenbush when we saw one of the greatest spectacles in nature.

As we were chugging along in the middle of the river pushed by Stacy's five-horse Evinrude, a bald eagle suddenly appeared overhead. Its huge wings were outstretched and motionless as it soared high over the water. Its white head and tail were gleaming in the late morning sun as it wheeled left and glided silently up the river. Stacy and I stopped talking as we were entranced by this unexpected visitor. After a short flight up river, the eagle turned back towards us. Its flight path once again took it straight over us. As we both stared upward in amazement, we could see that his gliding pattern was steadily downward. Nearing the surface of the water, the powerful wings began to flap as the eagle gained altitude. "No fish that trip," said Stacy. "He's having as much trouble finding lunch as we are!" It was my first, but not my last encounter with an eagle in the wilds of Maine.

I have watched Aliaeetus Leucocephalus many times whether soaring majestically in the sky or sitting in a tall tree along a lake. The brownish black bird with the snowing white head, bright yellow bill, eyes, and feet, is the most impressive fowl in God's bird kingdom as far as I am concerned. I have seen them along Maine's rocky coast, far inland in the foothills, and along the rivers and lakes of the central plateau of Maine. Only at the MooseHorn Reserve outside of Calais in Downeast Maine have I seen a group of eagles: that is until I went to Alaska to visit my soldier-son and saw them numbers in Valdez. More often than not it is the single solitary eagle sitting motionless on its perch usually in the highest dead tree in the area. I have seen them feeding, but as of yet, I have not seen them at the moment of attack, a thrill I still expect to see one day.

Long before you spot an eagle, you will probably see its nest. Situated atop the dominate tree in the area, the nest is built of twigs and sticks, and is, as I am told, added to year after year until many can be measured between five and eight feet across and four feet in depth. Once lined with grass or other vegetation, one to three eggs are laid. Both parents, who mate for life, feed the young eaglets for about ten weeks. The family structure is a consistent part of God's great creation. It is too bad that his crowning creation, man, is so quick to disregard what the rest of nature sees as so basic to life and living.

I know of four things of the air that Stacy showed me to be wonderful: a flock of geese in an autumn sky, a sparrow's song, an osprey's dive, and "an eagle in the air."

# 14

## Satan's Snare

*And that they may recover themselves out of the snare of the devil, Who are taken captive by him . . . ?*

—2 Timothy 2:26

I came upon a section of the stream notorious for trout, some too wary to be caught, but I would try. From the far shore I could see them lying still in the pure clean water. Many were resting behind small rocks that helped cut the flow of the water, but these slicks gave the position of the fish away. If that wasn't enough, periodically these fish would rise to the surface of the stream to sip in tiny flies off the surface tension of the water. I stopped for a moment watching intently for the largest swirl hoping to make it my next target. I quietly tied on a number 16 Yellow Caddis because I felt it best represented the insects I saw flying about me. A couple of false catches latter, I placed the small fly into the middle of the rising trout. The dry fly had barely touched down when a large brook trout took.

The trout headed back to his place of rest as before, but this time he realized something had changed. He is hooked. He fights against the foreign body that has him by his lip. He runs, but he can't escape the steel buried deep in his mouth. He is strong at first, but within a few moments the line has taken all his strength. He struggles, but the man on the other end of the line is more powerful. He has lost the battle, or has he?

Once the trout is in my hand, I turn him upside down which disorients him temporarily relaxing his muscles. I ease the hook out of his mouth gently lowering him into the water facing upstream so his gills will fill with oxygen. I slowly move him back and forth in the oxygen-rich water until he swims off under his own power He heads back to deep water, tired and sore, but alive. The trout experiences something like death when he fights against the hook and line, and something like resurrection when he is released.

Who of us has not been caught by something greater than ourselves? It seemed so innocent at first that we didn't see the danger, only the pleasure. A taste and we are hooked. At first we fight and try to run, but we cannot outrun the hook planted deep in that pleasure. It is then we realize that we are at the mercy of the one that holds us.

I ponder today of the many still caught on the line of drink. The hook is buried deep, and there is no fight, struggle, or battle that can let them go. They only have one hope and that in the graciousness of the "Fisher-of-men," the Lord Jesus Christ. Only He can lift them from the troubled waters of their lives, gently remove the hook, and mercifully let them go. My advice to a struggling soul in the battle with sin is to yield. Let go. Trust in the great Fisherman, Jesus Christ, who believes in "catch and release." My father-in-law was caught by drink for nearly forty years, and then he was caught and released by Christ.

# 15

# Waiting Wader

Enclosed a great multitude of fish . . .

—LUKE 5:6

The fishing wasn't that great. I had walked two miles for two small trout. I had come to the bend in the brook where I usually turned around and headed for home, but today I would press on, exploring for a new fishing whole.

As I waded on down through the brook, I kept both eyes on the water ahead looking for good water. Exploring a new segment of a stream requires alertness. I screened everything—the water, the birds, and the surrounding trees, the insects in the air; listening and watching for anything that might indicate the presence of trout. I scanned the surface of the stream to discern its rhythmic patterns, my eyes looking for a sip, a splash, or a swirl, something to indicate the presence of feeding trout. If the signs were right, so would be the fishing!

Eventually, I came upon a deep, quiet swirling side water pool. The fishing hole was created because of the combining of a small wilderness brook merging with the main branch of the stream. The speed of the main current caused the glassy water to spin slowly. I knew that trout liked this kind of water so I moved carefully around the hole lest I cast my shadow on the small pool.

It was a typical lazy trout hole. Fish food sliding off the main current enters the spinning pool. The brook trout waits in the quieter water as the placid current of the pool brings the food to its hungry mouth. Without effort and without expending too much energy, the lazy trout gets his meals with no hunting required.

I cast my home-tied #16 Spruce Fly into the pool. My father-in-law, Stacy Meister, had tied it for me for such occasions when a Royal Coachman wasn't quite right. Again and again the tricky current of the whirlpool pulled the line and the Spruce Fly into the feeding land of the trout, but to no avail. The late afternoon sun was nearing the tree line when finally one cast placed just right tempted a big trout. The feathers and thread of my Meister original was too much as the bookie rose and sip it in. The fight was short and sweet, and the very next cast produced again as did the next and the next. My perseverance and patience finally paid off with a creel full of native Maine trout.

I have often thought of that experience on Beaver Brook as I cast again and again the same fly called the Gospel of Jesus Christ into the same pool called Emmanuel Baptist. It would be easy to press on, try something different, get discouraged and give up, but I know like the junction of Beaver and Bull Brook the fish are there. The place is right, the bait is right; all I have to do is wait. So it is with fishing for men. Peter and his friends had fished all night and had caught nothing, but at the word of the Lord they cast out again and caught two-boats full. Let's wait!

# 16

## Ghost Grieving

And grieve not the Holy Spirit of God . . .

—Ephesians 4:30

It was one of those clear September afternoons in Maine when the leaves had turned but not fallen. The air was cool, but the ground was warm, a good day for cleaning things and a good day for Atlantic salmon fishing. The Penobscot River was lined with colorful maples and high rocky slopes as I made my way down to one of the best wet fly fishing pools.

Standing on the shore of this mighty river, I recalled the days when the Penobscot was clean, cold, fertile, always moving forward, always cutting new banks, and provided constant nourishment for central Maine. Much like the freshness that comes when the Holy Spirit makes its home in the life of a believer. Jesus taught, "He that believeth on me, as the scripture hath said, out of his belly shall flow rivers of living water. But this spake he of the Spirit, which they that believe on him should receive." (John 7:38, 39)

However, a problem had developed on the Penobscot, and I was witnessing the affect. My memory of a river unpolluted and not damned had come from the remembrances of the old salmon fishermen I had met on the river over the years. By the time I was drawn to her pleasant banks, mankind had polluted her waters, damned her flow, and rerouted her course. Other men have tried to restore her to her former glory, but to no avail. The damage had been done, and the catch of a lone salmon does little to change the truth.

My eyes survey the river for a rising salmon, but my mind surveys the Spirit for a lesson. It was then a verse by the Apostle Paul flashes clearly in my mind, "Quench not the Spirit." (1 Thessalonians 5:19) Like mankind has done to the river, man can pollute the soul, dam the body, and reroute the spirit thereby quenching the Holy Spirit. If this process goes on over a period of time, the life of the believer becomes a useless instrument. Oh, it continues to flow, but instead of life, it only carries death. The power of the Spirit is held back much like when Jesus went to his home town of Nazareth desiring to work his wonders there, but instead this sad commentary was written. ". . .and he could there do no mighty work, save he laid his hands upon a few. . .And he marveled because of their unbelief." (Mark 6:5, 6)

The mighty Penobscot, like most river systems, is made up of "many rivers." Combined they create a wide, deep flow of water seemingly unstoppable in its unceasing march to the Atlantic Ocean. So it seems with the Holy Spirit. Who could even imagine that mankind could literally stop the flow of such a mighty body of water, yet they have. Who could dream that the very might of God could be stopped by the frail creature we call man, yet it has. Dammed with sins and iniquities, polluted with transgressions and wickedness, rerouted with self-will and pride, the mighty Spirit is quieted in the life that once welcomed it with open arms.

# 17

# Tier Truth

Before I formed you in the womb I knew you, before you were born I set you apart; I appointed you as a prophet to the nations.
—JEREMIAH 1:5

Stacy ties his own flies and a few for some special fishing friends of whom I have been one for 25 years now.

Stacy has taught me that real fishermen prefer to fish with flies from their own vise. The fly is the fisherman's personal extension. Stacy not only ties his own flies, but he creates most of them. Oh, he can tie from a book, but he is the most productive when he ties what he knows and feels about the attractiveness of a fly to a fish. Stacy has also taught me that custom flies, tied to the specifications of a specific pattern of aquatic insect, are the best possible bait for fishing. So if you are a fly tier, and you love to fish, putting yourself in your fly is the best way to catch a fish.

To tie a fly Stacy first squeezes a bare hook in a fly vise. According to the picture in his mind, Stacy winds thread around the hook to bind feathers and fur into place. The thread is pulled so tight the strands threaten to snap at every turn. How the hook must hate the pressure, but it knows to become a beautiful, attractive fly it must take the strain. A little head cement here and there finishes the process, and the bare hook has become a colorful creation. Some of Stacy's flies are so beautiful I have put them in picture frames instead of on the end of my line. My study walls are covered in Stacy's flies, some surrounding fishing pictures, and others simply appearing alone; they need nothing to enhance their beauty. Then there are others, those who have stood the test of battle and have come forth victorious, landing the prize catch of the year, whether trout or salmon. These are the most beautiful of all.

I have come to believe in my study of God's word that God is also a fly tier. Instead of hooks, God uses people to catch people. Jesus was a fisher-of-men, and he spent three years developing other fishers-of-men. Jeremiah was the bait, and he was cast into the nations to expose himself as God's representative to the people he came in contact with. His life was put in a vise numerous times, and the threads of affliction were wound tight around his life. The feathers and fur of persecution were wrapped even tighter around his body, but in the end he became God's man to the sea of humanity. He stood out, and he drew many to God.

As with the fly tier, God chooses carefully the ingredients he will put in his bait. Each species of human being requires a different kind of bait. That is why certain people lead certain people to the net of salvation. Whether you believe it or not, your life has been in God's vice, and He has created you for a purpose. That purpose is to lead others to a saving knowledge of Christ.

# 18

## Penobscot Praise

O Lord our Lord, how excellent is thy name in all the earth!
—Psalms 8:1

My father-in-law and I would drive all night and cover every inch of Route Two from Houlton to Bangor to get to our favorite stretch of the Penobscot River in time to fish salmon at sunrise.

In the early 1980s the Eddington shore of the Penobscot River was our constant haunt when we could get away from the "County." Its waters contained the finest Atlantic salmon fly fishing in America. Most fishermen drove past it figuring a river so near to big cities couldn't be any good. That didn't bother either Stacy or me; the fewer the better we always said; more chances to fish for us.

It was an exceptionally warm May morning as Stacy and I once again drove down the road leading to the Eddington Salmon Pool. This makeshift gravel road ended on a high bank overlooking the mighty Penobscot River. Stacy parked his pickup on the fifty foot bluff, and we walked the rest of the way to the water's edge. To our surprise we were alone. I sat on a huge boulder facing the river as I rigged my salmon rod for fishing. I prayed, as I always did, for another experience to catch the world's greatest game fish. As I prayed, I enjoyed the warmth of a bright spring sun as it made its way over the top of the tree line behind me. As I tried on a No. 2 Pink Ent, all I could think of was my favorite verse of praise printed above. If you think I was stretching the context just a bit on the banks of a river, I would have you scan your eyes to the end of the Psalm where it says, "Thou madest him to have dominion over the works of thy hands; thou hast put all things under his feet. . .and the fish of the sea, and whatsoever passeth through the paths of the sea. O Lord our Lord, how excellent is thy name in all the earth!" (Psalm 8:6, 8, 9)

Then thinking stopped, and talking stopped. The sun which by now had made its way completely above the trees embraced me, and a million small reflections sparked off the Penobscot. I took a deep breath as Stacy began to throw his Thunder and Lighting into the swift current next to shore. God's presence was there in its glory. The roar of water pouring over the Veazie dam to the side of me only made the scene more majestic as I stepped into the river behind Stacy. Time became irrelevant. Was I sixty seconds or sixty minutes from the head of the run to the bottom? I know it was minutes, but it felt like seconds.

So many people ask the question, "Where is God?" The answer, "Right here!" After a few hours of this pattern, I rose from the river and climbed the steep slope to Stacy's pickup with a deep spiritual experience. I didn't encounter any salmon on that particular trip to the Penobscot, but Stacy had taken me to a spot where we met our Lord again.

# 19

# Special Stringer

The prayer of the upright is his delight.

—Proverbs 15:8

One of the first calls I made as the new pastor of the Calvary Baptist Church of Westfield, Maine, was to the home of Hazel McCarty. The small broken down three room hut was a sad sight to behold. I thought to myself as I knocked on the battered door, what will I find in this poor cottage?

A middle aged woman greeted me at the door with a smile as wide as her backyard. She welcomed me in as a friend, not a stranger. She had heard a new preacher was in town and was thankful I had made the call. Only months before she had been told she had cancer. They didn't expect her to live through the year, and it was already February. She had decided to take what treatment they could give, and she was wondering when her daughter couldn't take her if I might have time to drive her to the hospital. I said, "Of course."

Over the months and years (yes, I said years) that followed, I got to know Hazel very well. The hours I spent with her were always positive despite the progression of her disease. Our trips to the hospital became more frequent as her blood supply became less and less, and often our trip for treatments was supplemented with a trip for a blood transfusion. She never liked to talk about her conditions, but her condition became her life. It wasn't long into our relationship that I discovered that one of the things Hazel loved the most was right-out-of-the-pond, pan-sized brook trout, and right across the road from her home was a private trout pond owned by a couple in the church. I remember the day I asked Herschel if I could catch some trout for Hazel. He simply told me that anytime Hazel wanted fresh trout I had permission to catch her some. Thereafter, instead of going to Hazel's home to pray for her, I went to Smith Pond and fished for her.

I still recall the day I stood on the bank of that small pond and prayed for a few fish for Hazel. My goal was five small trout, not many from a pond that had been over the years stocked with thousands. Yet on that day the trout didn't seem to be interested in being dinner for a dying widow who enjoyed trout for supper. I went to all my favorite spots and tried all my favorite techniques, but in three hours I only had two trout. I knew Hazel could eat five so I pressed on, and a couple hours later I had a stringer of five fat brook trout.

When I arrived at Hazel's, I didn't stop in and pray with her. I just walked to her sink and cleaned her five trout. Tears came to her eyes as we talked of how I had caught her favorite meal. That evening I know she fried them up in cornmeal and a little butter and ate every one. Over the years (I was her pastor for eight years) I took her many a feed of trout, and I learned that to serve some saints you have got to go fishing.

# 20

## Stacy's Sermon

And he gave some . . . pastors.

—EPHESIANS 4:11

David Hansen made this comment to end his book, *The Art of Pastoring*, "Job lacked one thing: he never had a pastor." If there is one thing I have learned during my years of fishing with my father-in-law, Stacy Meister, it is that even the best fishermen need guides. I have come to the conclusion that the best analogy to a pastor is a fishing guide, and the best Christian need a pastor.

Hansen further writes in his book, "It goes without saying that a fishing guide needs to know the skills of fly fishing and needs to know how to teach the skills of fly fishing. A client may know a lot about fly choice, casting, line mending and reading the water; the client may well be another fishing guide. In fact, I've learned that the best fishing guides allow themselves to be guided by another fishing guide on occasion to learn new skills and new water and to break out of ruts. Or the client may know almost nothing about fly fishing. In either case, all through the process of guiding, the fishing guide is teaching." In Paul's qualification for the pastor he lists, "apt to teach." (1 Timothy 3:2) Stacy was my teacher.

Hansen goes on to say, "The fishing guide needs to be able to focus simultaneously on two objects: the client and the water. Clients don't know where the fish are on the stream (or they wouldn't need a guide), and they almost always have a hard time seeing the fish, even if the trout are rising.

The fishing guide looks for the fish and points the fish out to the client, all the while giving close attention to the client's manner of fishing. The guide watches the client's casting, making comment here and there, reading the client as the client reads the water, the fight, the catch! Because of this, the cardinal rule of guiding is that the fishing guide does not fish during the trip. The guide gives absolute, undivided attention to the client and the water!" Paul wrote, "Obey them that have the rule over you, and submit yourselves: for they watch for your souls, as they that must give account. . ." (Hebrews 13:17) I always listened to Stacy.

I have fished with many guides over the years, and the best in my opinion was a man from Washburn, Maine, named Stacy Meister. Like any pastor guide, Stacy loved to watch me catch fish as much as he loved to catch fish himself. How often Jesus led his fishing disciples to a productive fishing hole, physically or spiritually, and allowed them the joy of the catch. The same is true today, and this pastor gets no greater joy then to see or hear that those he guides has led someone to the net of salvation. Some think I learned this valuable lesson at seminary, but I learned it on fishing trips with my pastor guide, Stacy Meister.

# 21

# Fishermen, Fishermen?

Follow me, and I will make you fishers of men.

—MATTHEW 4:19

I found this in *The Pastor's Church Growth Handbook* by Win Arm, and I must pass it on.

> Now it came to pass that a group existed who called themselves fishermen. And lo, there were many fish in the waters all around. In fact, the whole area was surrounded by streams and lakes filled with fish. And the fish were hungry. Week after week, month after month, and year after year, these who called themselves fishermen met in meetings and talked about their call to go about fishing. Continually they searched for new and better methods of fishing and for new and better definitions of fishing. They sponsored costly nationwide and world-wide congresses to discuss fishing and to promote fishing and hearing about all the ways of fishing, such as the new fishing equipment, fish calls, and whether any new bait was discovered. These fishermen built large, beautiful buildings called 'fishing headquarters.' The plea was that everyone should be a fisherman and every fisherman should fish. One thing they didn't do, however; they didn't fish! All the fishermen seem to agree that a board was needed which could challenge fisherman to be faithful in fishing. The board was formed by those who had the great vision and courage to speak about fishing, to define fishing, and to promote the idea

of fishing in faraway streams and lakes where any other fish of different color lived. Large, elaborate, and expensive training centers were built whose purpose was to teach fishermen how to fish. Those who taught had doctorates in fish ology. But the teachers did not fish. They only taught fishing. Some spent much study and travel to learn the history of fishing and to see faraway places where the founding fathers did great fishing in the centuries past. They lauded the faithful fishermen of years before who handed down the idea of fishing. Many who felt the call to be fishermen responded. They were commissioned and sent to fish. And they went off to foreign lands, to teach fishing. Now it is true that many of the fishermen sacrificed and put up with all kinds of difficulties. Some lived near the water and bore the smell of dead fish every day. They received the ridicule of some who made fun of their fishermen's clubs. They anguished over those who were not committed enough to attend the weekly meetings to talk about fishing. After all, were they not following the Master who said, 'Follow me, and I will make you fishers of men?' Imagine how hurt some were when one day a person suggested that those who don't catch fish were really not fishermen, no matter how much they claimed to be. Yet it did sound correct. Is a person a fisherman if year after year he or she never catches a fish? Is one following if he or she isn't fishing?

# 22

# Tide's Time

*To everything there is a season, and a time to every purpose under heaven.*
—Ecclesiastes 3:1

I remember the first time my good friend Calvin Greenlaw said, "We have got to wait for the tide." I was a new resident on Moose Island, and I knew nothing about the rising and falling of the tides in Passamaquoddy Bay. All I knew was that I wanted to go fishing, and that I had never had to wait before. It was then I got my first lesson in the timing of the tides.

Calvin was one of the deacons of the Washington Street Baptist Church (at the compiling of this series of 'angling admonitions' (2020) Calvin is a member of my current church, the Emmanuel Baptist Church of Ellsworth, Maine.) where I had come with my family to minister in the autumn of 1986. Until then, I had never, ever looked at a tide chart as there was very little need of one in the hills and hollows of central Aroostook County. The ocean was 200 miles away from Westfield, and only occasionally did it affect that small farming community. Now, however, I was living on an island off the coast of Maine, and the tides began to affect every aspect of my life, especially when I wanted to go fishing with Calvin and his friend Ted Atsalis for flounder off Campobello Island.

It was then I began to learn that the tide was critical, not only in the fishing, but our ability to get to Ted's fishing boat. The more I experienced the limitations the tides forced on the residents of Eastport, the more I began to understand why these people were so patient; the most laid back group of individuals I have ever met in my nearly 50 years. People who had learned by living, working, and resting by the seaside that one must adapt to the tides or be engulfed by them. Solomon's practical principle in Ecclesiastes was very applicable to life on an island off the coast of Maine.

How often I have resisted the tides of my life. I have tried to sail against an ebb tide only to find myself stuck in the mud of an empty cove. Instead of waiting for the flood tide of God's will, I tried and failed to make any progress in my timing. As I learned in life, so I saw demonstrated dramatically in the tides of Passamaquoddy Bay. If you wait for the tide and work with the tide, life actually becomes pleasurable and plenteous. I never once went to sea with Calvin Greenlaw on a right tide and came back empty of fish or fun. I learned to trust his understanding of the tides. Why is it I have so much trouble trusting my Guide's timing? Why is it I have so much trouble waiting on my Guide's time? Why is it I have so much trouble relying on my Guide's times? As He controls the ebb and flow of the coastal tides, so too does he control the ups and downs of my life, the stays and delays as well as the starts and stops.

He has given me His time chart in His Word, and He simply asks me to check it before I venture out on life's troubled sea. Patience and trust is all I need to believe.

# 23

# Downdraft Disaster

The fowl of the air, and the fish of the sea . . .

—Psalm 8:8

I walked up Casperson Beach in search of a fisherman. I couldn't imagine coming to such a body of water like the Gulf of Mexico and not do something in connection with fishing, even if it were just to watch. Surely in all this beach there was a fisherman or two trying their luck?

I didn't go far before up ahead was a man with two surfcasting rods in the sand. Despite the fact he was the only fisherman in sight, I thought at least one man isn't letting all this water go to waste. However, as I neared his fishing hole, my attention was drawn away to the many birds that were gathering on the rocks jutting out from the beach. At first I thought that they might be waiting for some scraps from the fisherman's success, but soon I realized that it was something more.

Next to fishing, I love to watch birds in flight. Because they live on the edge of the wind, I marvel at the God-given ability of birds to soar and glide and fly. During my days in Florida I watched the terns and seagulls, but I was fixed on my first up close and personal look at pelicans. What an ugly bird I first thought; nothing to be compared to our graceful Maine eagle. Not even in the same class as the osprey or the raven, I thought, as I came close to the fisherman and the pelicans sitting on the boulders. They seemed unconcerned that I was drawing near their perch. Ugly birds, I thought, as I pressed on to see if the fisherman had any success. They don't even like to fly, I thought, as I watched the seagulls and terns drifting effortlessly along the updrafts created by the ocean and the shore. Probably so heavy they can't even get off the ground, I thought, as I asked the man, "How's the fishing?" "Nothing," he replied.

With no action on the fishing front, my eyes turned back to my serious friends, the pelicans. It was then my Heavenly Father impressed on my heart this truth about these ugly birds. Wise is the bird that knows when to fly and when to adjust to the winds. Like the birds along the beach, mankind faces all kinds of winds. Humans insist on testing the winds of fortune and misfortune. Instead of sitting and waiting for a more favorable wind, like the pelicans, we test fate in our prideful and arrogant haughtiness only to encounter the cross winds of calamity. We try to soar against the downdrafts of disaster. We try to sail against the wind shear of worry. We set our flight and fly right into fret and fear. As I watched the pelicans on Casperson Beach, I began to realize that their strength was in knowing when to soar and when to set. Instead of bucking a contrary gale, they waited for a favorable breeze, and so too must I. When I become sensitive to the changing wind patterns of the Holy Spirit and move at His direction, I will be lifted to new heights far above the downdrafts of disaster.

# 24

## God's Gifts

In everything give thanks: for this is the will of God
in Christ Jesus concerning you.

—1 Thessalonians 5:18

O Lord, we thank you that in your marvelous design of creation, you included the creature we call fish. For salmon mighty and majestic, for trout grand and great, for pike wild and wonderful, for walleye savage and surprising, and for bass large and little, we thank you for all the interesting variations you have given us to explore.

We thank you Lord for the gift of senses that help us to hear the laughter of foothill brooks splashing through a hardwood forest as we stock the wily trout; to feel the pressure tug of the mighty river on our waders as we cast for ocean-wise salmon; to taste the fur and spruce-spiced air as we paddle slowly over our favorite pond in search of the one that got away; to smell the edge of salty breeze and fresh water joining as the tidal pools meet and the king of ocean and river flashes "silver in the sun;" to see a feeding moose on a quiet lake and baby loon with mother swimming gracefully by as we await the sparkling swirl that signals a trout has taken; to watch as sunlight fades over a distant river as a leaping pike dances merrily with spoon red and white; to wait patiently for the song of rod and reel as a streaking walleye dives deep with shining lure; to work the line back and forth to put life into a stately streamer as it slides quietly through a cold northern lake; and to witness the poetic grace of a jumping bass that paints pictures in the mind that will never be erased.

We thank you Lord for the gift of small insects and tiny fish, and for the animals and birds whose feathers and fur help us to re-create their likeness that has enriched our lives while fishing; for the inspiration to create the fly, wet and dry, the streamer, bright and beautiful, the nymph, dark and deceiving. We thank you Lord for the gifts of steel and wood and for the ability to make rod and reel, large and small; for graphite that bends at the slightest touch to warn us of nibbling fish; for steel spoons of red and white, iron lures of silver and gold, and brass spinners that assist us in catching that gift so elusive; for nets tiny for trout and huge for salmon; and for line, light but strong, giving but tense, and for the pressure it withstands especially when it should have broken but lasting long enough to land the fish of our dreams.

And Lord though you might smile at how we take our angling so seriously at times, we pray that you will help us to always keep fish and fishing in your perspective. We know you have given us these for joy and pleasure as well as opportunities to renew our bodies, souls, and minds. We accept these your gifts with thanksgiving and responsibility that when the fish story is told, we would not fail to give to you the ultimate glory.

# 25

## Patient Partner

Ye have heard of the patience of Job.

—JAMES 5:11

As Stacy continued to explain to me the fine points of salmon fishing, I watched intently the red/white bobbers that kept our smelt at preset depths moving lively around. As one bobber would slightly go down, I would make a lunge for the rod. I was quickly rebuked with a "Patience, Barry, patience. You will know when the salmon hits. That's just an active smelt trying to get away from the Eagle Claw."

The morning dragged on into midday, and I was getting bored. I had never had to wait this long to catch a trout at Beaver Brook. I couldn't see what all this excitement about salmon fishing was about. I had come to the conclusion that it had been blown way out of proportion. Soon we were changing our smelt regularly as they died. Morning came and went with no strikes or signs of any salmon, and all Stacy could say was "Patience, Barry, and patience." Of course, Stacy kept me on edge with a string of fish stories, each one painfully describing in vivid detail about the salmon he had caught in the past in that very spot. Nevertheless, each tale would end with Stacy's, "You got to have patience!"

At lunch time, a can of soda, a spam sandwich (how Stacy loves Spam!), and a few cookies took away the gnawing in my stomach, but not the yearning to catch a salmon. Then around 2:00 PM, after I had replaced one of my smelt for the countless time, I noticed my other bobber was missing.

I looked around carefully, but it was nowhere to be seen. I looked at Stacy and saw for the first time that big "salmon grin" on his face. I smiled back and made a desperate attempt to get to my rod. Stacy met me halfway with, "Patience, Barry, patience." I thought if I heard that one more time I would throw Stacy out of the boat! "What are you doing?" I demanded. "I have got a fish on my line! If I don't hook it, it will get away." To which Stacy calmly sat me down and tried to explain to his impatient fishing partner that might be okay with trout, but not with salmon. As the salmon continued to move away, Stacy kept using that "P" word. As the line from my reel unfolded, the next few minutes seemed like hours, but the excitement was indescribable. Was this what salmon fishing was all about? Was this where the thrill was? I must admit I liked it despite having to endure Stacy's patience.

When I finally set the hook, the salmon was firmly hooked. The tug of war only lasted a few minutes as I yielded no ground to my first landlocked salmon. As soon as it was near the boat, Stacy had the net ready. As the net engulfed the fish, I experienced my first salmon smile. Only those who catch salmon will know what that is like. As Stacy took the fish from the net and handed it to me, all I could think of was "patience" had paid off after all. It will pay off in life too!

# 26

# Experience, Experience

And patience, experience; and experience, hope . . .

—ROMANS 5:4

The best way to learn anything is to get involved with it. Stop studying and analyzing it and start dreaming and living it. Take what you have in your head and put it into your hand. Experience firsthand what you read about in your textbook. Only then will your skills in a certain field really come to light. I have known individuals who have gone to school for years studying a particular subject only to discover when they finally began to work in their chosen field that they had no deep seated desire to do it for the rest of their lives. Why are our community colleges full of people seeking training in a secondary field? Most are there because unlike me they never learned in a small country school that information is not education. I know of countless individuals that read fishing magazines and talk to other fisherman, but never get their line wet. Whether physics or fishing you have got to go to school to learn, and you have got to experience firsthand if you're really going to learn something. When Professor Meister is teaching, results is the name of the course. It was during a lake fishing trip with Stacy to northern Canada that I learned Paul's pattern stated above.

One of our favorite eating fish is the walleye. Despite the fact they don't grow as big as the pike, their meat is sweeter. Up until this trip we had only caught a few walleye each year, just enough for a walleye feed made with Stacy's secret recipe. However, Stacy had been studying walleye all that winter and had concluded that there was a way to catch walleye in large numbers. He had discovered that walleyes schooled. In the past we had caught one then moved which was our mistake because where there was one there was probably a few more. Stacy was determined to try out his new theory on the lake located near mile marker 68. At 2:10 in the afternoon Stacy caught the first walleye of the day while trolling. Stopping his motor, he anchored his boat over the spot of contact. Calling for the other boat to come over, we began to jig for walleye. This lesson on "walleye" was highlighted when within minutes we had boated nine big walleye including one three and a half pounder, the largest to date. Stacy, the teacher, had the upper hand landing five of the nine. By day's end we had landed 98 pike and 10 walleye, by far the best day in numbers we had ever experienced. Included in those numbers was the first triple play I was ever privileged to participate in. While trolling up through a thoroughfare between two lakes, Curt, Dale, and I hooked, played, and landed three good sized pike. The marshmallows tasted sweeter around the campfire that night, a reward for good fishing.

Patience was always one of Stacy's fundamental virtues of fishing, and experience teaches that with enough of it there will be hope for a good catch. So it is with life.

# 27

# Outfitter's Outings

Prepared unto every good work.

—2 Timothy 2:21

Not only has my father-in-law, Stacy Meister, been my number one guide for over twenty years, he has also been my outfitter. In the nearly forty fishing trips we have taken together, Stacy has planned every one of them. Every detail of the trip was organized long before we headed off to a favorite fishing hole. To say I have been spoiled over the years would be an understatement. Except for my personal effects, Stacy has provided all the needed materials for an enjoyable time fishing. Ever since our first trip to Canada in 1975, Stacy has filled his garage with the necessities of an outfitter. Tents, boats, canoes, motors, camping gear, cooking materials, and all the little things most people don't even think about taking on a trip to the north woods. Stacy has been a constant example of an organized outfitter. I remember the time, deep in the tundra country of northern Quebec, Canada, when my brother-in-law, Larry Fox, lost a screw out of his eye glasses. Larry is one of those people that if he doesn't have his glasses, he will get terrible headaches. Taping the glasses didn't seem to help much so Stacy began to dig around in the things he brought. Sure enough, he found a tiny screw that fit and fixed Larry's eye glasses. How often in our preparation we forget about the small things. Let us never forget this truth from the prophecy of Zechariah, "For who hath despised the day of the small things?" (Zechariah 4:10) Stacy never did.

Another time, just before we headed out on a trout fishing trip up the Manaquagan, I noticed Stacy putting a small hand pump in the back of his truck. I asked why, and he simply said, "We might need it." Sure enough, the only trip I ever remember having trouble with a slow leaking tire was that trip, and we had the pump to get us back home. You ask any of Stacy's fishing trip partners about him, and the first thing they will say is what an excellent outfitter because he is always prepared. You never have to fret or worry when Stacy is planning a fishing trip, out of town or out of the country. We too have been given the means to be a "man of God. . .thoroughly furnished unto all good work." (2 Timothy 3:17)

Jesus Christ is, of course, our great outfitter. He told his disciples just before He went to Calvary that he was going to "prepare." (John 14:2) Jesus is preparing a place right now for everyone who believes on him. (John 14:3) There will be no details overlooked in that place. How often I have stayed overnight in a hotel or friend's home and had to ask for something. My host wasn't totally prepared for my visit. In my father-in-law I discovered that if he could do it for a fishing trip, Jesus could do it for my trip to heaven and the eternity I will spend with him there. Is Jesus your Outfitter?

# 28

# Polished Pond

...the still waters...

—Psalm 23:2

I walk again through the seasons of my memory to recall the rhythms of my life. Mine has been more then sunrises and sunsets. I have had the privilege to watch the rising and setting of the tides, but I must admit the most beautiful of all is the steady stillness of a lake or pond or sea totally at rest.

Many a time in the brevity of my life, I have treasured precious moments watching water in a dead calm. What can there be learned from "still waters?" Rare is the day at Big Lake in Downeast Maine when the surface of that large body of water is smooth, yet I have seen such days. Rare are the days in my life when I too have been still. This world is not known for its peace, yet, like Big Lake, life does on occasion give us a refreshing stillness to enjoy. Like an oasis to the weary wanderer, a polished pewter pond is refreshment unequaled. Our Father in his infinite wisdom knows we need a calming and quieting if we are to continue the journey through this life of storms and sorrow.

I remember clearly the first such pond I happened to find. I was fishing with some friends of mine in Baxter State Park. Little Grassy Pond was located under the shadow of Mount Katahdin, the tallest mountain in the State of Maine. On this particular day my travelling companions decided to climb the hill instead of fishing. I was the only one in our party that decided to fish instead of hike. As they made their way up the steep slope, I made my way to the shore of this shallow pond. It was a beautiful June day with few clouds. When I reached the canoe on the near shore, the reflection of Mount Katahdin engulfed the small pond. The mirror image of the great mountain was without a ripple or a wave. The pond was completely smooth as polished pewter. As Phillip Keller once put it, "The beauty and serenity of these still waters is duplicated by the incredible reflections mirrored in its shining surface. Every tree, snag, rock, distant ridge, soaring mountain peak, and fluffy cloud suspended in the sky are reproduced as if by a miracle in the gleaming water."

Such was the case as I pushed the Game Warden's canoe into Little Grassy Pond. Only where the canoe cut the water and a jumping trout broke the surface was the reflection of nature changed. As I paddled from fishing spot to fishing spot, I began to realize just why God creates such mirrors. "He restoreth my soul." (Psalm 23:3) There in the stillness of that isolated pond in the Great Woods of Central Maine, I discovered that on the surface of my soul the great God can also reproduce His reflection of peace. "Peace! Peace! Wonderful peace, coming down from the Father above; sweep over my spirit forever, I pray, in fathomless billows of love."

## 29

# Restored, Refreshed

Restore unto me the joy of thy salvation . . .
—Psalm 51:12

The giant rocks of a Maine lake are places of enormous interest and beauty for me. There is a grandeur about them that makes any lake more impressive. People often talk about the rocky shores of coastal Maine, but few see for themselves the rockbound lakes and ponds of Maine. Some of these massive stones are larger than a house standing high above the water. Others begin deep in the water and soar above the surface of the lake. It has been to such bodies of waters I have returned again and again for refreshment of mind, body, and soul.

    Just a few days ago I returned to one such spot. Despite the fact it is February, I walked to this secluded spot. Branch Lake is a favorite ice fishing lake for some friends of mine. Over the last five years they have taken me along on some of their fishing expeditions. Two of these gentlemen are in their eighties and the other is rapidly approaching the fourscore mark. Ice fishing came late this year because of an unusually warm December. It wasn't until the end of January that serious ice on Branch Lake was formed. I was unable to join the "boys" until the first week in February. I was happy to hear that their ice shack was still located near "Mile Rock," my favorite fishing hole on the lake. It was near that landmark I first fished for togue through the ice. That day is still etched on my memory because before the sun set I had landed three huge lake trout. I wish I could say I always caught fish, but I haven't. There have been many, many days in which I haven't even had a "flag," yet I go back to Mile Rock every chance I get. Why?

I have discovered the restoration that comes from walking the ice. I have found refreshment in strolling from hole to hole. I have been revived by simply leaving my home in the city for a hut on an ice-bound lake. With "traps" in hand I march off to the holes Buster has drilled. With "ice scoop" in hand I walk to the holes Irving has suggested. With "bait can" in hand I creep across the ice to see if I can catch one more fish then Harold. With each carefully placed step, I feel my sanity returning and my body restored. Each deep breath revives my sense of life and purpose. The wind might be raw and frigid, but there is a warmth that comes from "Mile Rock" I can't explain. I have often sat on that mighty, granite stone waiting a flag and hopefully a fish for Doris Grant. The winter sun has warmed it a bit, and it feels good against the gathering cold of a late afternoon. It is there that I meet my Maker and Master, and we talk of the needs of my church and my family. Without exception He rejuvenates my calling and balances out my priorities. There on a frozen pond by a snow covered rock, I am restored, refreshed, and revived. (I also caught two lake trout and two landlocked salmon that particular day.)

# 30

# Billy Bass

Behold, happy is the man whom God correcteth . . .

—JOB 5:17

"Here is a little story I wrote, you might want to think of it note by note, 'Don't worry, be happy, don't worry, be happy, don't worry, be happy!'"

On a wall of the Anchorage hangs three fish. The first two are cutout images of a rainbow trout and a large mouth bass. For as long as I have been going to this cabin in the pines off Corliss Cove, the first two trophies have been there on the wall between the two bedrooms and the living room. Sometime between August 12–20, 2000, a third fish was put on the wall by the Franklin fireplace. "Big Mouth Billy Bass" had been bought for Garth Story, the owner of the Anchorage, for his birthday. "Billy" is a singing smallmouth bass with two songs in his repertoire. The first little number goes something like this, "I want to know can you help me. I need help. Take me to the river and place me in the water! Take me to the river and put me in the water!" The second song "Billy Bass" sings I have written above. It is a cute invention of man with the fish actually moving it tail as the song starts, but when it gets to "Don't worry, be happy," the fish literally bends in the middle and looks at you with its mouth mouthing the words. I have played "Big Mouth Billy Bass" a number of times on this late September fishing trip to the Anchorage, and I have gotten a bit of correction.

I stand in need of a bit of correction. My life's work, the Church of the Living God, isn't going very well at the moment. Apathy, affluence, and lack of commitment abounds where I am, not to mention that the laborers are few and the leaders even more rare. Yet out of the mouth of a mechanical fish I hear, "Don't worry, and be happy." Why? Because I have committed my way to the Lord, He will bring it to pass. I took a number of strolls this trip by the shores of Big Lake. It seems walks like that always refresh my work-weary soul. I said to myself many times this trip, "I am doing the best I can *under* the circumstances," when the Lord keeps telling me to rise *above* the circumstances and trust Him for the outcome because He has promised to see me and take me *through* all circumstances. He keeps telling me to be of a good cheer because He overcame the world, and I need not worry that I will too.

Faith is the opposite of fear and worry, and worry is nothing other than fuming over situations I cannot change, fussing over people I cannot alter, fretting over circumstances I cannot resolve, and fighting over policies I cannot modify. As I leave my hideaway on Corliss Cove, I will take with me a bit of advice I heard from a talking bass, but really learned through "the still small voice" of God. "Don't worry, be happy. I am still on the throne, I am still fully in control, and all things will work out for your good and My glory."

# 31

# Lingering Lunch

Ye have tasted that the Lord is gracious.

—1 Peter 2:3

I will never forget the first meal I had of onion hash and moose steak, and tonight I will have it again. I am no "cook," just ask my wife and others, but onion hash and moose steak aren't really a meal, but a memory.

    I am once again at my favorite cabin in Maine, the Anchorage. The air is cold and the seasons are definitely changing from warm to wintry. I have come to the cottage on Corliss Cove for a few days of rest, relaxation, and reflection. My wife, who normally comes with me, had to stay home because of other obligations. As I was packing to come she asked if she could do some grocery shopping for me to which I said, "I have all I need." I had packed two large packages of moose steaks and a few pounds of potatoes and a big, sweet onion. When I go camping and fishing, I love to eat onion hash with a piece of Maine moose meat. It was my wife's father who got me addicted to this savory combination. On a wet April day in the early 1980s Stacy first introduced me to this manly meal. He fixed this tasty treat under dripping cedar trees, and I have been hooked on its flavor and savor ever since.

    For years Stacy fixed this special meal as we took forty-three major fishing trips together. Exactly three years ago my wilderness cook passed away. Perhaps that is the real reason I had made this trip to the Anchorage. I must admit I thought of Stacy as I travelled up Route 9 through the

Washington County woods two nights ago now. It reminded me so much of the trips we took in the dark to be at the Miramichi or Penobscot rivers by first light to fish. There too he would fix his special hash for lunch at times or for supper at other times. Sometimes it would be moose meat and at other times deer meat. I remember one memorable meal it was elk meat, but it was always onion hash as the main dish. I never cooked for Stacy, but upon his departure I was determined to keep our tradition alive. My wife hates to cook wild meat so if I was to continue to eat my favorite camp meal, I had to do it myself, and though my wife still doesn't like the meat part, she too has fallen in love with Stacy's onion hash.

Last night I made a big plate of hash, and I fried up three pieces of moose meat. As I write these thoughts another package of moose steaks are ready on the sideboard with three potatoes and a half of an onion. As soon as I finish this article, I will start the process of making Meister's Meal. Cooked in plenty of butter with a liberal sprinkling of salt and pepper, it is a meal fit for a king. Why is it we can't feel the same way about a meal from the Word of God? Do you have a favorite portion of the Bible? When was the last time you sat down and tasted that savory Scripture which has sustained you all these years?

# 32

# Whirlwind Way

*The Lord hath his way in the whirlwind and in the storm and the clouds . . .*
—NAHUM 1:3

I was a stream fisherman until I met my future father-in-law, Stacy Meister. He took me lake fishing for the first time after landlocked salmon on Portage Lake in 1970. Over the years, until I married his oldest daughter Coleen, we returned to that body of water again and again. It became a favorite fishing hole for Stacy, special enough for him to build a small A-framed camp on its southern shore.

    I remember well one particular trip to Portage Lake with Mr. Meister. It was a perfect northern Maine day. As the afternoon wore on the water became very still and the air a dead calm. We hadn't caught much, and there were still a few good hours left in the day when Stacy suddenly said, "Let's head for camp. Now!" To be honest I couldn't believe what he said. The weather was nice, and the fish would start biting I was sure. "Are you sick?" I asked. "No," he replied, "but a storm is coming, and you remember what happened the last time we got caught on Portage in a storm." That was enough for me so we pulled the lines in, restarted the engine, and headed down the lake for Meister's camp looking over our shoulders for the coming storm.

    Stacy had lived long enough on Portage Lake to know the signs of an approaching storm, and sure enough by the time we made the dock the lake was covered in whitecaps, and the sky was an angry black. We made it to the cottage just before the air was saturated with a heavy downpour. The calm air had turned into gale force winds, but where had the storm come from? How can an area be calm one minute and the next be a whirlwind? I learned from Stacy over the years the meteorological whys of Portage Lake, and I also learned that life's storms are similar. They often come out of nowhere to blow you somewhere you don't really want to go. Such storms are always coming at the wrong time, changing our course, and disrupting our dreams, and panicking our plans. Some of these storms are literally life changing in nature, and we are never the same again.

Whether a natural storm or a manmade storm, all storms are "the Lord's" whether by plan or permission. Take the storms of Job, satanic in nature, but approved by the Almighty. (Job 1,2) Nahum the prophet tells us very clearly that storms come in a variety of sizes and shapes. There are firestorms, snowstorms, windstorms, rainstorms, hailstorms, but all are God's storms, unpredictable and unavoidable, so it is essential we put our trust in the God of the storm. Oh, how foolish it is for us to believe just because the storm has come that God has abandoned us. God didn't abandon Job, and Jesus didn't abandon his disciples in the whirlwind that nearly sunk their boat. God is in the "eye of the storm" because He is keeping an eye on you!

# 33

# Fishing Fathoms

Launch out into the deep . . .

—LUKE 5:4

I am by my very upbringing a freshwater fisherman, but I have ventured a time or two off shore to experience deep-sea fishing. From those few fishing trips I have learned something about fishing in the fathoms.

Peter knew that to catch fish during the day that the shore was the best place, yet Jesus insisted that he and Andrew launch out into "the deep" for "a draught!" What was it about fishing "deep" that the Lord wanted to teach us:

1. *You must be determined to fish in the deep.* I have gone as far as ten miles off shore. Many people go farther than that. It takes time, a good boat, and an expert guide to go into the depths in search of fish. We are also invited to go into the deep of society to fish for men. "Go out into the highways and hedges, and compel them to come in, that my house may be filled." (Luke 14:23) Are you so determined?

2. *You must be dressed to fish in the deep.* I have lived 16 years on the coast of Maine. Even in the hottest day if you move off shore just a few hundred yards, the temperature drops into the 50s and 40s. With a constant cool water temperature it is always cold in the Gulf of Maine. You must wear your best and warmest clothes to fish in the deep. So too we must be wearing our best when we witness for the Lord. ". . .for the fine linen is the righteousness of saints." (Revelation 19:8) How are you dressed?

3. *You must be directed to fish in the deep.* Go where the fish are, but what do you do when you don't know where the fish are? I could get a boat and fish for the rest of my life and probably never catch a fish in the ocean. I remember the first time I went deep-sea fishing. My wife and I were on our first trip to Prince Edward Island in Atlantic Canada, and I decided I wanted to try deep-sea fishing. Instead of trying on my own I went to a local fisherman and hired him for a morning's fishing. He took me and my wife eight miles out, and guess what? We caught fish! Jesus promises, "Howbeit, when he the Spirit of truth is come, he will guide you. . ." (John 16:13) Who guides you when you witness?

4. *You must be diligent to fish in the deep.* Deep water fishing takes patience and perseverance to be successful. With shifting tides and below surface currents the challenge is difficult. Yet with each "drop" in a productive place one's stick-to-it-of-ness will pay off with a catch, so too it is with dropping the Gospel line with the bait of love into the depths of humanity. I learned to jig on my deep-sea expeditions, and the dangling of the bait at the right depth in the right school eventually pays off. "Therefore my beloved brethren, be ye steadfast, unmovable. . ." (1 Corinthians 15:58) How diligent have you been witnessing?

I hope these deep-sea fishing suggestions will be useful the next time you "launch out into the deep."

# 34

## Fishers-of-Men Fishermen

*Follow me, and I will make you fishers of men.*
—MATTHEW 4:19

Fishermen aren't born, they are trained, and so are fishers-of-men.

If I am considered a successful fisherman today, it is all because of my dear father-in-law, Stacy Meister. In 1970 he asked me to join him for a day of fishing on a northern Maine lake called Portage Lake. Oh, that day my instruction in being a fisherman began! I would eventually follow him to the Canadian provinces of Quebec and New Brunswick and throughout most of the State of Maine. At each fishing pool and hole, he taught me the fine art of catching salmon and trout, northern pike and walleye, and just about every other American and Canadian fish. What we forget is that for the first three years of our Lord's ministry, he primarily re-taught fishermen how to be fishers-of-men.

I like what E.M. Bounds writes. "The training of the twelve was the great, difficult and enduring work of Christ. . .It is not great talents or great learning or great preachers that God needs, but men great in holiness, great in faith, great in love, great in fidelity, great for God: men always preaching by holy sermons in the pulpit, by holy lives out of it. These can move a generation for God." And that is exactly what the disciples of Christ did (Acts 17:6) because they were teachable, trainable, moldable to the great task of fishing for men.

Bounds goes on to say, "Men are God's method. The Church is looking for better methods, God is looking for better men...What the church needs today is not more machinery or better, not new organizations or more and novel methods, but men whom the Holy Ghost can use..." As Jesus walked the shores of Galilee He was looking for a "few good men" that would follow Him and learn from Him just how to fish for men. He found the rare talent He was looking for in two pairs of brothers who just happened to be fisherman. He would in time train them into some of the greatest soul winners in church history, but what did it take?

Another classic work in Christian literature, in my opinion, is Dr. and Mrs. Howard Taylor's (son and daughter-in-law of the great pioneer missionary to China Hudson Taylor) work, *Judson Taylor's Spiritual Secrets*. In that book Howard tells how Hudson became a great fisherman of the Chinese people. He says this. "Instead of going to Church twice on Sunday, he gave up the evening to visiting in the poorest part of town, distributing tracts, and holding cottage-meetings...All this led to more Bible study and prayer, for his soul found that there is one and one Alone who can make us 'fishers of men!'"

When will we realize it takes a great Fisher-of-men to train a good fisher-of-men? That Fisherman is Jesus Christ.

# 35

# Miramichi Messages

*For the invisible things of him from the creation of the world are clearly seen . . .*
—ROMANS 1:20

I am setting at Martin Vickers' desk in his private cabin on the banks of the Miramichi River in Howard, New Brunswick, Canada. This is my fifteenth visit to his salmon lodge complex on this picturesque provincial waterway. I don't know how many more trips I will get here so I thought it was time to start writing down some of my observations and opinions on this piece of God's creation. I have discovered over the years that flashes of revelation come more quickly to me by a riverside than even in a manmade sanctuary. A riverside is like a fireside.

Suddenly, swiftly, and spiritually "the still small voice" of God seems to be the loudest here. Illumination and inspiration abounds in such places as Vickers' Salmon Pool Lodge known locally as Squirrel Tail Cottage. As with Christ Himself I too get moments in the out-of-doors when spiritual perception into profound truth is so clear, and I wonder why I haven't seen it before. What is cloudy in the city is crystal clear in the country, especially the country of the Miramichi River Valley. Let us never forget that before we had the Bible to know about God, we had God's creation.

I have come to believe that the two realms, the Word and the World, are contiguous and complimentary. As Jesus spoke of soil and seed, birds and beasts, trees and lilies, He was telling us that truth can be found in them all. So too have I discovered that there are spiritual messages at the Miramichi.

Granted, I have come to this fisherman's heaven to fish the prize-worthy Atlantic salmon, but I have also come to listen, to observe, to learn, and to obey. As I left home for this rustic cabin, I was told by "the still small voice" to bring pen and paper; that there would be some "Miramichi Messages" on this trip. There had been others in the past that I will share later in this set of angling admonitions; this being my tenth year coming to this peaceful place, but each of those messages were only written after I returned home and not while I was here. This, you see, is only the second time I have come to this cottage on the cliff alone. Except for a short trip I took a few years ago in which I only lasted twelve hours because of a kidney stone attack, I have come all other times either with my father-in-law, Stacy Meister, or my good friend, Mike Hangge. It is hard to write when you have company, but alone the pen seems to jump across the page.

Having now spent a great part of my life in the outdoors, I see clearly the parables of the "pond," I understand the lessons of the "lake," and I reflect on the revelations of the "river." Christ has revealed Himself more to me in His creation than He ever did in college. He has given me a love of this river run because there are messages here that can only be taught here.

# 36

## Miramichi Migrant

...no certain dwelling place...

—1 Corinthians 4:11

Strolling over to my study at the Emmanuel Baptist Church for another Friday night at the computer brought to mind a memory I must record. Early this morning I returned from a three-day fishing trip to the Miramichi. The scene of spring on that majestic New Brunswick river is still vivid in my thoughts. Retreating from those tranquil waters, the mighty Atlantic salmon has started its long trek to its feeding grounds off Greenland. On this trip I figured out that like the salmon I am also a migrant. Its stay in any one place is only temporary at best, but in all the thousands of miles of travel, the salmon, like me, knows how to return home. The Miramichi with its countless rivers, brooks, and streams might seem to the unknowing as an unbeatable maze. Yet the salmon knows how to return to its place of birth. Likewise for me as I drive the roadways, byways, and highways, they all lead to my earthy home.

As I drove six hours in a car yesterday, I had time to think of just how much of my life has been a pilgrimage. I have been an exile from home for over fifty years. Despite the fine house I was returning to in Ellsworth, I realized that was all it was, a fine dwelling place. I had slept in three different beds in the past week. Like the salmon I make no ties to any temporary resting place. Like them my only attachment is to home because I too will soon move on. When my journey is over and my travelling is done, I like the salmon will overcome any obstacle, press on through any difficulty, and will do whatever it takes to get back to the place I call home. For like the salmon I too have a God-given scent of what feels and seems and acts like home.

On this last trip of mine, I travelled near my birth place. I came within seven miles of the homestead, and I felt the tremendous tug and the powerful pull that told me that I was nearing my first earthly home. It must be the same for a salmon as it gets near to the spot of its creation. Yet I did not travel those extra seven miles, though in my journey to that point I had already covered five hundred miles. Why, you ask? Because there would have been no one there to greet me. The old rambling farmhouse would have been empty. My parents were away on a trip to visit my brother who lives in Pennsylvania. So I travelled two hundred more miles alone through the depth of darkness that had engulfed my day to return to a place where there was someone to meet me, greet me, hug me, and say they love me. For as I have learned in my many travels, in my numerous wanderings, in my countless treks, home is not a place but a person, and the joys of heaven will also be in the person of Christ. This migrant is pleased that the Almighty has given him a travelling companion through the maze of migration that makes minor anything the Atlantic salmon has to face.

# 37

# Miramichi Moon

...lesser light that rules the night...
—GENESIS 1:16

I have just returned from my annual spring fishing trip to the Miramichi River in Upper Blackville, New Brunswick, Canada. It was a great trip with many black salmon fishing tales to tell. But on this first night back to my computer, it is not a "fish story" I wish to record, but an encounter with a full moon and the memories that heavenly body brought to my mind.

The full moon of which I speak was the full moon for the month of April. It shone brightest on the twenty-fourth of that month. I drove to my father-in-law's home in its glare through a foggy northern Maine Sunday night. When I saw it again the next night, I was sitting on the porch of Vickers' Camp on the banks of the mighty Miramichi River. Both encounters with this "lesser light" sparked remembrances from my childhood when the full moon would rise over my beloved homestead in Perham, Maine.

I recalled the evenings that same moon would shine down on my winter wonderland. Peeking out from behind a cloud bank, its rays would turn the whole countryside around my folk's house into a ghostly gray. As the clouds parted and the moonshine was unobstructed, the light reflecting off the white snow turned heavenly. I can still see it in my mind's eye as I look out my second story bedroom window at the scene before me. Despite the cold chill in the room, I felt warm in the glow of that brilliant moon created by God.

I recalled the evenings that same moon would shine down on a summer evening setting on the porch. Rover, my dog, would be relaxing in his favorite corner as the moon made its way up from behind the eastern hills toward Caribou. Dad would come out for a moment of fresh air before heading off to bed as the moon shone through the hardwood ridge that overshadowed our old farmhouse. Sylvia, my sister, would be reading as the moon crested the tops of the trees. Mum would come out and say it was time for bed just as the full moon took command of the night sky. I am fifty years old and how many full moons I have seen I know not, but last week I stood and stared again as if it were the first time, just as I did the first night I watched one of God's great creations make a curtain call over my homestead.

I recalled the evenings that same moon would shine down in a full harvest moon. Fall is my favorite season, and a full harvest moon is one of its highlights. Usually that special moon came out sometime during the annual potato harvest. It always brought with it a risk of frost, but its brilliance was worth the threat. Besides, we couldn't do much about it anyway! I remember as we brought in the last of the potato barrels for the day that white ball rose slowly in the dark autumn sky. As we drove the truck into the potato house, God's moon seemed to say, "Good job."

# 38

## Morning Moonset

Abundance of peace so long as the moon endureth.

—Psalms 72:7

The moon has been a highlight in my life these last few weeks. After experiencing a full spring moon on the banks of Miramichi River in New Brunswick, Canada, last month, I watched just a few days ago the only annular eclipse I will ever witness in the skies over Ellsworth, Maine, where I now live. Not since 1875 in the northeast had the moon passed before the sun as it did Tuesday, the full moon surrounded by a blazing ring in mid-afternoon.

It was one of those clear, chilly nights. A full moon aglow in milky white rose steadily into a star-studded spring sky. A typical country day on the homestead was coming to a close. The barnyard was settling down to a much needed rest. Hour by hour the moon rose higher and higher from the eastern horizon. Soon every hill and hollow, field and forest on the farm was shining with a bright mantle of light. A lonely moo could be heard from the pasture behind my father's huge cow barn. A dark ghostly shadow could be seen crossing the road as Rover made his way home from an afternoon excursion to somewhere. The final cock-a-doodle doos could be heard from the chicken coup as the round ball of white escaped the tree line. The evening breeze subsided as I got into bed, but I knew I would be up before the moon set because this was planting season.

W. Phillip Keller once wrote, "All the world waited for morning, but before dawn came, the moon must set." I hear Dad up first as I sleepily got out of bed. My job was to get the barn chores done before I headed for the potato house to cut seed. As I made my way out through the pantry, I noticed the moon through the window slowly, steadily, and surely sinking behind the low hills to the west of Perham. The white light of night had turned into a golden glow reflecting the morning sun to the east. Stepping into the barnyard, the setting moon spread its final glow over the landscape. Rover barked with joy at its fading splendor as we made our way across the narrow gap between house and barn. Just before I walked through the broad doors of the barn, I took one last glance at the morning moonset. Its final few moments of glory captured my attention and, as I think now, my imagination and inspiration as well. Only those who have witnessed the ending of the dark and the beginning of the dawn know of the breathless beauty of a moonset, "the mystery and the majesty of the moment."

How can such a moment last these many years? Buried keep in my homestead memory that moonset has survived while countless other events have become lost in time. Could the answer be in the simplicity of the occasion? Majestic in its movements, the moon is only as brilliant as the sun that reflects its brilliance off from it. A morning moonset is only as good, glorious, and grand as a Miramichi spring sunrise on another fishing day.

# 39

## Eastern Eagle

Who satisfieth thy mouth with good things; so that thy youth is renewed like the eagles.

—Psalm 103:5

On a recent trip to the Miramichi River, I again saw one of God's greatest wonders in nature, "the way of an eagle in the air." (Proverbs 30:19) As a matter of fact, I saw this spectacle sight twice, and both times the eagle flew in from the east.

Have you ever watched an eagle in flight? At first you are drawn by the power of the wings as they slowly flap. You wonder what is keeping that huge bird in the air, and then you realize that it is the air as this wise fowl is able to find the warm air currents rising around him. These thermal currents allow him to ride almost without flapping his wings. The change of a wing here and they propelled the royal eagle down the river in search of lunch. The occasional updraft would take him higher and higher until he was nearly out of sight, but then he would slowly drift downward as his patrol down the river continued. On that particular day I never saw that eagle from the east catch anything, but neither did I.

The next day the show was repeated. We had motored up river to see if we could find an interested salmon when from out of the east the eagle returned. With broad wings and a snowy white head the eagle appeared to be the same one as the one the day before. I asked my guide if that was the same bird, and his reply was that there had been a few eagles flying the river all spring. So whether it was the same one or not I will never know, but what I do know is that we can learn a lot from an eagle. It amazes me to see how often the Bible draws our attention to the eagle. Shortly after I returned from that fishing trip, I was reading W. Phillip Keller. He wrote about an eagle with this exhortation: "Have you ever watched an eagle get ready for flight? At first, almost imperceptibly, but growing ever stronger, he feels the warm air currents rising around him, lifting gently from the valley floor past his perch. Presently the regal bird spreads his wings and launches himself confidently into space. At once the thermal currents are bearing up beneath his wings, and he rides them splendidly. By deliberate effort the eagle keeps himself in the center of the updrafts, rising higher and higher, borne aloft, mounting ever upward until he is lost to sight. What a sublime etching this is of the Christian in his relationship to God. On the outstretched wings of prayer and praise he launches himself out upon the promises of God, depending on the great updrafts of His faithfulness to bear him up. It takes courage to do this. A daring act of faith is required for us to let go of the limb to which we have clung for so long and launch ourselves fearless into the great open space before us!"

# 40

## Meister's Mazda

Can two walk together, except they be agreed?

—Amos 3:3

I am at the Anchorage alone thinking of my dear father-in-law. I am just a few days from the third anniversary of his home going. Recently, my mother-in-law visited my wife and I, and during her stay my wife finally shared with her a painful event that took place after Stacy's death. Coleen's dad had promised her that after his departure she was to get his truck. The problem arose when Stacy failed to tell Opal of the arrangement. Opal sold the pickup not knowing of Stacy's desire. It wasn't until last weekend that Opal heard about the deal. Coleen and her mother have worked out the misunderstanding, but the whole affair has brought this memory in focus.

    I never drove Meister's Mazda very much, but I still rode thousands and thousands of miles in it. On our numerous fishing trips together Stacy was the driver, and I was copilot. What happy times we had over the last seven years, especially on our fishing trips to the Miramichi River in Canada. We loved that waterway like no other. The trips back and forth were just as special as the trips up and down the river. That old truck contained a pickup body full of sentimental remembrances when it was sold. Stacy kept it spotless and lavished on it attention and care that few trucks have ever had. It was one of his joys because it was a brand new pickup bought with money left to him by his father at his departure. He also bought his wife a brand new car at the same time, and they both were white.

There were so many tender memories carried around by that Mazda that it had taken on Stacy's personality. And to lose it as Coleen did, I guess I too haven't been able to see the situation as a simple business deal because another sweet chapter in Stacy's and my relationship was forever closed when it was sold. A treasured 5 by 7 snapshot hanging on my study wall is of my dear fishing partner sitting on the tailgate of his prized pick up next to Vickers' Camp on the shores of the Miramichi. Stacy is resting between two knap sacks he had made for each of us to carry our stuff back and forth from home to camp. Only I know what blessed recollections that old picture stirs up. The coffee stops at Fort Fairfield and the roadside stops shortly afterward; the potato doughnut treats along the Renuos Highway; the hours of conversation as we talked through the night to get to our favorite fishing hole before sunrise; the annual stops at the Renuos River bridge to see if any salmon were in the river; the time we drove through a mid-May blizzard just to go black salmon fishing one more time that spring. That new pickup that became an old truck before it was sold was as faithful to us as Stacy was to it. The memories go on and on, all provoked by a photograph of a pickup and the importance of fishermen being agreed to ride together.

# 41

# Meaningful Moon

...is a chosen generation, a royal priesthood, an holy nation,
A peculiar people; that ye should shew forth the praise of him
Who hath called you out of darkness into his marvelous light.

—1 Peter 2:9

I don't know how many times it has been now that I have fished the Miramichi River in Howard, New Brunswick, Canada, on a full moon, but each time has been memorable.

The Bible simply calls the moon, "the lesser light to rule the night," (Genesis 1:16) and though sunlight is more powerful than moonlight, I like it best. In the oasis I call Vickers' Camps, the moon is but the topping on the cake on a day spent on the Miramichi. To set back on the observation deck and watch the full moon rise over the small hills across the river is a pleasure worth spiritualizing. "The moon and stars to rule the night. . ." (Psalm 136:9)

The sun has but one phase when it comes up each morning—complete. Its power might be greater or less depending on the time of the year, but when it is seen on a clear day, it is round, bright, and distinct. The moon on the other hand goes through phases that changes its appearance throughout the month. I feel that is why Christ is seen in Scripture as the "Sun" (Matthew 5:14) or we the "moon." As the natural moon gets its power from the reflected light of the sun, so do we get our spiritual power from the life Christ lives in us through His Holy Spirit. (Galatians 2:20) Depending on our relationship with Christ, we too are reflecting that example. When the sun and moon are at extreme angles, then the moon is dark, barely seen in the night sky. As the sun and moon get into better alignment, then the full reflective light completely covers the moon, and a full moon is the results—the best the moon can do.

So too with our angles on the Spirit. Despite the appeal from Paul to be "filled with the Spirit," (Ephesians 5:18) most of us look like a quarter moon or a half moon. Others appear invisible and the odd Christian at three quarters. There is a discipline of the soul, a setting of one's will, a determination of spirit that is required to be a full moon in a dark world. To shine against the gathering blackness of wickedness and to reflect the absent Christ at midnight is what we were placed in our sky to do. That is why we must rendezvous with Christ on a daily basis so that there are no obstructions and no unwanted angles in our life that would not allow the full reflective example of Christ to be seen in our lives. As a night sky watcher, I enjoy the full moon best because its light allows me to see other things in the night I would miss without its light. So too in the mirroring light of the Christian example; if we don't show forth, how will the blind ever see Christ? (2 Corinthians 4:3, 4)

# 42

## Miramichi Mud

He brought me up also out of an horrible pit, out of the miry clay, and set my feet upon a rock . . .

—Psalm 40:2

Day after day the snow fell steadily. Its depth was soon measured in feet, not inches. The landscape was a wonderful white. The heaven-sent carpet of snow soon covered everything including the river and the three cabins on one of its corners. One look at the snow pack and Irving, my Miramichi guide, knew that spring would be late this year.

Irving did his best to keep the road to Vickers' Camps clear of snow. He was the caretaker, and he still had to finish the third cabin, Green Machine, before fishing season. The last of the three cabins would be the best of all. Its angle on the river allowed anyone sitting in the living room to view the mighty Miramichi for nearly a mile up river. As Irving travelled down from his home daily, he watched the snow banks grow and the drifts enlarge with each passing day, yet he knew that when the Good Lord was ready, He would melt the snow. Through the long winter his work kept him busy, but his heart rejoiced in the promise of spring. Then one day it happened—the beauty of Miramichi snow turned into Miramichi mud.

The first time I opened my eyes on the Miramichi River, it was while walking on that mud. My father-in-law had brought me on my first black salmon fishing trip. It was on that first trip I met Irving Vickers, and he was standing in Miramichi mud. As I walked down the hill into the camp yard, I noticed a set of very big boot prints. "Someone has beaten us to the camp," I said. "That will be Irv," replied Stacy. Sure enough. Waiting for us by a small cabin was this winter woodsman who turned into a salmon guide in the spring. The cottage was stacked with fire wood, and the curtains were pulled back exposing a breathtaking view of the river. Miramichi mud was all over his boots, but as I learned on that first trip, Miramichi mud is nothing more than delicate snowflakes mixed with a bit of Canadian soil.

Tracks in the snow had become tracks in the mud. As I thought of Irving's faithfulness in keeping the cabin ready for our arrival, I thought of how the Lord Jesus Christ left the beauty of heaven (spotless and pure as snow) to walk in the mud of the depraved, disobedient and damned. The footprints of Christ are best seen now in the lives of those He has saved. Tracks of truth now define who we are and where we are heading. As I took my first step in Miramichi mud, I wasn't upset. I was heading for a clean, comfortable camp. So it is with heaven as we step from the "miry clay" onto a solid Rock. It wasn't long before Irving showed me how to walk around camp without walking in the mud. There was a high ground and a hard ground for me to take. So too has Jesus showed me the safe and dry path that leads to my home by the river. (Revelation 22:1)

# 43

# Osprey Order

... the fowls of the air, and they shall tell thee ...

—JOB 12:7

Despite what Moses wrote about the osprey ("And these are they which ye shall have in abomination among the fowls; they shall not be eaten, they are an abomination. . .and the osprey" (Leviticus 11:13), next to the eagle, which is also considered in the Mosaic Law as unclean, the osprey has been an inspiration since my first sighting on the Godbout River.

The osprey is a fish hawk which spends most of its time by water in search of fish. Ospreys have very large feet with extra-long toes, the surface of which is covered with sharp spicule which is helpful in holding onto slippery fish. Their feathers are dense and compact which helps when the bird goes into the water after its prey. If you have never seen an osprey in full dive, you have missed one of nature's greatest sights. Because their feathers do not get waterlogged, the osprey is able to take off directly after coming up out of the water. Once again God created special characteristics for the specific need of one of his species. So with us, God has created each of us with the ability to accomplish the task he made us to perform.

When in flight looking for lunch, the osprey flies between fifty and one hundred feet above the surface of a body of water. When a fish is spotted, the osprey stops soaring and for a moment hovers over the spot. Its tail is spread, and its wings fan rapidly. In a flash, its wings arch back above its back, and the osprey dives straight into the water with the feet and head going first. The bird may completely disappear under water or barely touch the surface of the river, depending how deep the fish is. Scientists have estimated that the osprey is so adept that they are successful in catching a fish on as many as 90% of their dives. Many a time fishing I have seen an osprey flying off with its catch, and I haven't even had a nibble. Even when I do get a bite, 10% is about my record most times. Just ask Russ Coffin. A careful look at God's creation will reveal that man isn't as proficient as he thinks he is. We still have much to learn from the fowls of the air.

Although found near any body of water, the osprey is best seen along the sea coast. Their nests are usually built in rock crags or solitary trees with the same nest being used year after year. Usually seen in pairs, the female osprey usually lays three eggs and always incubates alone. What is curious is that only the American osprey is like this. Elsewhere the male and female share the responsibility for incubation. When I learned this fact about American ospreys, I thought how typically American. American couples aren't noted for their sharing of the responsibilities of child rearing. We would do well to learn that God created them male and female, and he expected them to be a partnership in whatever endeavors they get involved in.

# 44

# Penobscot Perseverance

... watching thereunto with all perseverance ...
—Ephesians 6:18

Perseverance is a quality an Atlantic salmon fisherman must have in order to keep fishing for the greatest game fish in the world. It is also a virtue needed in the Christian's armor. I was taught this characteristic one day on the Penobscot River by my father-in-law, Stacy Meister.

As I studied the water of the Guerin Pool, I saw what I thought was a salmon just behind the flat boulder that highlighted the center of the pool during dropping water. Wading into the river for a closer look revealed a lone salmon. Turning to Stacy, I told him of my discovery. Then I began to cast for the fish. My fishing partner moved up river so his big bomber could float over the salmon.

The two-pronged attack went on for a couple of hours with no success. He did give us a thrill or two slashing after a bomber or rolling after a wet fly, but with each new fly he seemed only to be recording its size, shape, and color—probably thinking to himself how many times he had seen each pattern before during the long days of summer.

Over the next few hours we fished Wringer Pool, Eddington Pool, and Dixon Pool, but we saw nothing. Returning to the Veazie Salmon Club lodge a little after noon, we had a wonderful shore lunch of onion hash and elk steak. After lunch I walked down the hill to check the salmon. Sure enough, he was still there proposing and flashing his dorsal fin and wide tail in the high noon sun. I began to work over him again. My desire to catch that salmon was beginning to verge on the fringes of an obsession. I wished I had kept track of the number of salmon flies I used that day on that finicky fish. From four ought's to #16s I tried all sizes. From classics like the Jock Scott to the traditional Mar Lodge I tried all kinds. From feather wings to hair wings I tried all types. From skinny low water flies to big fat bombers I tried all shapes. I even switched lines, sinking tip, full sink, to floating. I tried them all. I fished beside him and below him. I fished from shore and waded out and stood on the flat rock above him, but nothing worked.

The day wore on into early evening. Leaving Guerin for the second time, we fished B Station Pool, Second Pool, and the Beach Pool until nearly dark. We saw no other salmon that day. As we once again passed Guerin Pool on our way back to the truck, I noticed Stacy undoing his line. "One more try?" I questioned. "Sure. I'll get him up with big brown bomber, and you attack him with another fly," Stacy suggested. Within minutes I was casting a fly toward the last fall resident of Guerin. On the third cast the fly sank deep into the water behind the rock. A slight tug surprised me. Perseverance landed me that salmon, and perseverance has landed me many a "soul" for Christ.

# 45

## Creek Carving

My river is mine own, and I made it for myself.
—Ezekiel 29:3

Whether you are talking about the Colorado River and the Grand Canyon or the creek that runs through my hometown of Perham, Maine, there is a mystic in the craving of a river bed. Its path, turns, and depth are all governed by the flow and volume of water.

I first walked to Salmon Brook when I was just a lad. It crossed under the High Meadow Road where I lived just a half a mile below my home. It was not a mighty stream by any stretch of the imagination, but to a young boy it was big. The impulse of the water flowing through the valley drew me to its banks. I liked to listen to its sounds and watch the water bubble through the gaps under the road. The creek was a small stream that came from Salmon Lake in the deep woods north of my homestead. In the winter it froze. In the spring it was a rushing torrent. In the summer it became a trickle, and in the autumn it was highlighted by a rainbow of colors along its shores. As I watched its transformation season after season, I failed to see the silent changes in its course. The abrasive action of the water was subjecting the creek bed to new shapes.

Little did I realize it then, but my life is a living parallel to that creek. As the creek changed with the seasons, so did my life. I didn't notice the changes, but now that I have nearly seventy years to ponder, I see that my character has been carved by "the rivers" (John 7:38,39) that have been flowing through my life for over sixty years now. The Holy Spirit is not a still resident, but like the creek, a constantly flowing house guest, always moving and working on the course of my life. It has only been in recent years that I have become sensitive to His subtle flow. Recently, four events have happened in my life that has reconfirmed to me the divine principle written above. I am but God's river bed, and it is His river that flows through me. My life is not for me, but for Him.

Sometimes, like the spring runoff in Salmon Brook, the Holy Spirit flows mightily through my life sweeping all before it. Magnificent things are accomplished. However, like the quiet flow of the summer stream, the Holy Spirit seems to flow meagerly through my soul. It is the same Spirit, same stream bed, yet different flows. Is it me? Am I resisting? Could there be obstructions that "quench" (1 Thessalonians 5:19) or "grieve" (Ephesians 4:30) the Spirit? Yes, there can be, but when there aren't any dams or bottlenecks, what is happening? I have come to believe that the craving of the character of the soul as with the stream can take place equally in both extremes as well as the silence in between. The shaping Spirit of God craves in magnificence and meagerness: whether the solid stone of a besetting sin or the soft soil of a selfish wish, the patient Spirit craves our character into Christ-likeness. (Romans 8:29)

# 46

## White Water

If I wash myself with snow water, and make my hands never so clean.
—JOB 9:30

Despite it being the middle of May, the snow was falling. I was travelling with my father-in-law, Stacy Meister, to the Miramichi River in New Brunswick, Canada, for our second salmon fishing trip of the season. We had travelled the Renuos Highway three weeks before in beautiful spring weather, but now it looked like winter had returned. Thousands unto thousands of snowflakes drifted peacefully down upon us in big, bulky flakes that stuck to the first object hit. Soon the shrubs and newly grown grass on the roadside were covered. The cold ground was also soon blanketed by the heavy snow. Even the warmer road was beginning the yield to the constant bombardment from above. As Stacy and I drove carefully through the deep New Brunswick woods I thought to myself, "Snow and fishing don't mix!"

It was a quiet snow that fell that day; no gusty winds accompanied the storm. Despite the innocent snowfall, the storm was totally irresistible. It was also imperceptible that this storm had come at this time. I had driven up the night before we headed for the River, and the snow had then begun to fall. The annual potato planting had begun in Aroostook County, and it was strange to see the tractors and potato planters covered in snow. Snowflake after snowflake fell until the entire countryside was covered in white. Nothing escaped this massive snow. Within a few hours the entire landscape was covered in a white mantle. Stones and stumps, fur and ferns, homes and hovels alike were crowned by the engulfing whiteness. As Stacy and I drove on towards our beloved Miramichi, nothing stirred except a group of white tail deer feeding beside the road. As we came around a corner and saw them, they too looked puzzled by the unexpected snow storm in May.

Coming out of the foothills of central New Brunswick, the land had been transformed into a magnificent mirror. The snow finally let up, and the sun began to reappear. The freshly fallen snow had erased every dirty blemish of a muddy spring. The land had been cleansed, and the devastation of winter had been covered from above. Right to the river's edge the carpet of snow had rolled it loveliness until white met blue. As I stood by the riverside upon a mantle of snowflakes, I reflected on the attraction that had drawn Stacy and me to this far off river and to the drive that didn't allow a mid-spring snowstorm to distract us from our destination. To Stacy and me a trip to the Miramichi was like that canopy of white that covered the ground. It was a place of freshness and cleanness, a place to wash one's hands in snowy water and to enrich the soul and strengthen the spirit. The dazzling dawn had revealed a new day, a day in which white by water refreshed the soul.

# 47

## Stream Song

I will sing a new song unto three, O God . . .
—Psalm 144:9

It was my first overnight camping trip, and our plans were to sleep on the banks of Beaver Brook. My cousins and I had been fishing the stream since we were small boys. Our fathers had introduced us, but our imagination for adventure had brought us to this campsite.

We had fished downstream to where Beaver Brook merged with Burp Brook. One corner up from where these two small streams joined was a fairly open area. As we made our campsite, the song of the stream was blocked out by the numerous forest creatures that understood our intent and were voicing their objections to our invasion of their home land. Between the squirrels and the black birds the air was filled with haunting sound, but nothing would stop us from fulfilling a boyhood dream. We ignored their cries and calls and established our home base. The weather report had called for no rain so we didn't even bring a tent. A little food in case we didn't catch any fish was the only provisions we had brought. We were there to fish and have fun in the deep north woods and to sleep under the stars.

As darkness began to engulf the forest, my cousins and I were back from a very productive evening of fishing. Trout sandwiches cooked over an open fire was the menu. We laughed and joked well into the night as a starry host exploded above us. The slight breeze that had blown all afternoon died down and the cooler night air began to settle into our campsite. The night animals began to speak, and softly the stream beside us began to sing. As the forest creatures slipped off to sleep one by one, the sound of the stream got louder and louder. I had made my bed on a level spot just a few feet from the streamside. The tall grass that had been growing there all spring and into the summer made a comfortable mattress. A light sleeping bag on the spot was more than enough as I laid back and gazed into the brilliant sky. I could hear my cousins beginning to breathe heavily as the long day on the brook took its toll. The twinkling stars and the bubbling brook were soon all mine.

It was then the Eternal Composer played one of His stream songs. The section of the brook where we camped cascaded over a series of rocky bars. Water against stone added to the rippling sound of the stream above. The soft and loud blended together to form an aria that can only be heard when the conditions are just right, and that night the Beaver Brook balladeer was playing quite a song. I drifted off to sleep with that melody playing softly in my ear. There were no words to the song, just a simple instrumental played on God's natural instruments. That natural number has been heard again and again each time I have laid my head down beside a riverside or a streamside. For me it is the number one song on God's Top Ten Hit List.

# 48

## Sparkling Stream

... the streams whereof shall made glad ...
—Psalm 46:4

It was finally spring. The sun was warm on my face as I made my way down the lane that led to my favorite salmon pool on the Penobscot River. I had taken this walk every year for twenty years, ever since my father-in-law had introduced me to this mighty stream in the late 1970s. It was time again to revisit old fishing companions and welcome in the season of renewal and restoration.

As I caught my first glimpse of the huge river, I was struck with the reflection of the rising sun off the water. The light sparkled in the stream like a myriad of diamonds bounding off the surface of the stream. The bright bits of light seemed to bounce off everything along the bank of the river. The trees and shrubs glowed in the reflected light. The high walls of the brick front power station bled red as the top of the sun peeked over the tree line on the opposite shore. Everything the sun touched along the river and in the river was transformed by the brilliant power of the sun. The very sight turned my heart glad. It was as if the Creator Himself was joining me beside the river. In a loud, clear voice I could hear Him say, "This morning is for you."

The sparkling water continued to flow past me as I cast my salmon fly into the troubled water of B-Pool. The four powerful turbines to my left kept the small salmon hole bubbling and boiling. This only caused the uneven surface of the river to sparkle even more. The source, strength, and surge of light was the sun, but the draw was the water. With each passing wave and wavelet a new pattern of light could be seen. Because of the added dimension of water tiny colorful rainbows were added to the sparkle. The spray of water off the top of the dam also added to the array of colors produced as the sun slowly rose in the east.

Added to the sparkle was the sound of falling water from both my right and left. Every second the spilling tons of water going over the boards at the top of the dam face was combined with the singing of the falls at the bottom of B-Pool. The combination of a sparkling stream and a singing stream only highlighted the wonderful sense of rebirth that was taking place in the woodland surrounding the river. The vigor and vitality of budding trees and blooming bushes can't help but bring such emotions to the human soul. As I stood on the riverside that morning and drank in the creation of a new day, my soul was also renewed. For that I am deeply glad.

In a society where instant gratification and immediate revival is desired, I find no remedy better than a walk to a streamside, a place alone where the "Son" can reflect His gold light off your soul. A place where being still and quiet doesn't mean "still waters" or a "quiet spot." It simply means a place where the "Son" can sparkle.

# 49

## Stream Solitude

And in the morning, rising up a great while before day, he went out,
> and departed into a solitary place ...

—Mark 1:35

My father-in-law was an early riser. Rarely did the sun ever beat him up. I on the other hand am a late riser. The only times I beat the sun up is when I am heading for the riverside and a favorite fishing hole.

I learned very early in my fishing adventures with Stacy Meister that sometimes along the river's edge there can be a wonderful solitude. As Phillip Keller once wrote, "There is a sense of stillness great and more majestic than mere silence." To fish the Penobscot River during the height of the Atlantic salmon run isn't a good time to find solitude. I have been at the better pools at 3:30 AM and still been tenth in line. The conversation along the banks of the river silence even the Veazie Dam. Stacy taught me to pick my times, and I soon learned that there were seasons that you could stroll the shore of that mighty stream alone, yet not alone. For no one goes to such solitary spots to be completely alone. The early rising and silent journey is made, like with Jesus, to meet someone.

If there is one thing I have learned about the Almighty in scripture is that He loves privacy with his saints. Don't get me wrong. I am not saying that God can't talk to you in a crowded mall or a packed sanctuary. All I am saying is that He seems to prefer a solitary stream. In my quest for the "silver-sided" salmon I have discovered this fundamental fact. God loves one on one. Our God covets Him and me—alone with Him where our thoughts are His and our mind is under His control. Granted, the beauty of the banks and the splendor of the stream might distract momentarily, but quietly and quickly the Almighty Presence is staring you in the face again. His "still small voice" is speaking to you again from His "still waters."

Alone with the Almighty by the riverside is what the modern individual needs to soothe the stress in his or her life. There is too much turmoil in the average life; there is too much tension in the average life; there is too much trauma in the average life. The fragile foundations of modern society can't handle for long these heavy weights. Stripped and exposed by suffering and sorrow, the human spirit is soon at a breaking point. Instead of seeking solitude, the world system insists that the struggling soul simply press onward. Even Jesus found in His early form the need of coming aside and finding a solitary spot to commune with His Father. If Jesus needed the solitary lakeside of Galilee, don't we? If Jesus needed the solitary riverside of Jordan, don't we? If Jesus needed the solitary seaside of the Mediterranean, don't we? The solution to most stress is in finding a solitary solitude where you can get alone with your Saviour and talk it out.

# 50

## Stream Sunrise

...in the wilderness...toward the sunrising...

—NUMBERS 21:11

For water lovers sunrise is a wonderful time of the day. The unique splendor and stillness is unmatched in any other hour of the morning. I must admit that it was only the lure of fishing that got me up originally, but eventually the highlight was the sunrise over the Penobscot River.

For twenty years I have fished the central Maine river called the Penobscot. Named after a tribe of Indians by the same name, this massive watershed drains most of central Maine. I have fished its branches, but the bulk of my time on that river has been spent between Veazie and Eddington and Bangor and Brewer. I still remember the first time my father-in-law, Stacy Meister, took me to the Penobscot to fish for the Atlantic salmon. As an additional bonus, I watched my first Penobscot sunrise.

There are those moments when the wind is down and the water is calm that you stand in awe as the early morning sun casts its first reflection on the river. I remember the multitude of fishermen at the Eddington Pool waiting their turn to fish, but I remember more the quietness that came over that group of men as the sun hit the stream. Peace for a moment pervaded the shore line; the long, bright fingers of sunlight reflected off the misty water pouring over the dam just a few hundred yards up river. The whole river seemed to be caught up in the golden glow and the brilliant light show dancing across and over the water. Small rainbows added to the array as the spray from the dam caught the sunrise and then captured the eyes of everyone there. Even the jumping salmon mirrored the rising sun from their sides as they leaped joyfully near the shore. As a local wilderness artist once called a painting *Silver in the Sun*, I still have those images in my mind today.

There is a peculiar hue in a sunrise by a stream. Yellow and crimson are the dominate colors, but under careful observation other tones also emerge. There is a prevailing hush in a sunrise by a stream. Birds seem to stop their singing, and the wind stops blowing momentarily. All of nature appears to love a sunrise. Everything stops to watch this marvelous morning masterpiece. There is a pervading holiness in a sunrise by a stream. One feels as if they are witnessing the birth of the very first morning when the Creator spoke and the sun broke through those first overcast clouds. The rest of the day is but a postscript to the zenith of a sunrise.

Quickly, the sun breaks clear of the tree line overlooking the Penobscot, and fish and fisherman go back to their cat and mouse game. The wind picks up and the birds begin again their unending noise. If it only happened once, we of all men would be most miserable, but the good news is the Lord will repeat the miracle in twenty-four hours, more or less.

# 51

## Stream Sunset

From the rising of the sun unto the going down of the same the Lord's name is to be praised.

—PSALM 113:3

My favorite sunset stream is the Miramichi River in New Brunswick, Canada. How I enjoy sitting on the deck of Vickers' Camp and watch the sunset behind the tree line behind the camp. It is time for the sun's afterglow to reflect off the river, and it is time for me to reflect on the God-given day just passed.

Eventide is a pondering time for me. A time to run through my mental checklist to see if I have accomplished those things I had planned to get done. It is also a time to meditate on those events that were not in my plans, but were found in God's daily planner for me. I learned years ago to be very careful in allowing God to interject his projects between those of my own. A sunset is a great place to seriously evaluate where you are on life's road and where you ought to be. In our work in progress called "living," a riverside sunset can help put everything into perspective.

An evening on a river bank is an interlude with one's Heavenly Father like those talks with an early father of one's childhood. It is a time to stop and listen and hear that "still small voice" speak at the close of the day. It is also a time to amen Robert Browning's famous phrase, *"God's in His heaven and all's right with the world!"* There is never a time, day or night, that I don't sense His presence more near than walking the banks of the Miramichi as the sun sets or sitting on its shore as the sun sets. There seems to be no barriers and no barricades on the Miramichi riverside at sunset. It is a time I have captured often with my movie camera, especially when the sun is setting through gathering clouds. The white of the clouds turns crimson which only adds to the celestial scene. The tragedy of the pictures is that they never really ever fully capture the real glory of the event. You just have to be there to fully drink in the wonder of those riverside reflections and Miramichi meditations.

Slowly the fiery globe settles into the hillside behind the cabin. Even when the sun sets the sunset is not over. One of the best parts of a sunset is the afterglow. The scarlet hue that painted the clouds now paints the trees and the landscape. The last time I stood on Vickers' deck with movie camera in hand, I filmed those few minutes of that rosy red color splashed across the tops of the trees. The river had quieted for the first time in days; the wind had died for the first time in days; the sky had cleared for the first time in days. The crimson banner held me spellbound as I thought of the verse above and praised the name of the Lord. The moment was fleeting, but the memory is not. Each day on a river is like that final few moments of a sunset, quickly gone, but worthy of praise because every day is a special gift from God.

# 52

## Snow Salmon

Hast thou entered into the treasure of the snow?

—JOB 38:22

On my "to do" book list is a series of snow stories I am going to title "White Rain." Being raised in northern Maine, I have plenty of snow talks to share. I have written many already in other writing projects so the first few will only have to be compiled. One that will be included will be this "riverside reflection." One of many treasures I have discovered in the snow is salmon fishing.

It was the last day of a black salmon fishing trip to the Miramichi River. The first two days had been difficult at best. Heavy, gusty winds combined with on and off showers had made it one of the hardest fishing trips I had ever taken. Added to the fact that it was still the last week in April, the collection of wind, water, and cold made the casting of a fly almost impossible. My fishing partner, Mike Hangge, eventually had to put on gloves. The wind created whitecaps on the river so we were restricted where we could fish. In two days we had only landed one small salmon though we had on a number of others. We thought that the third day could only bring a change for the better!

I woke at 3:00 A.M. to discover the yard around the fishing camp was covered with a fresh layer of snow. I went back to sleep thinking I was only dreaming. I woke again at 5:00 A.M when I heard Mike up. Once again I looked out the ceiling-to-floor window and sure enough—snow! The wind was still howling and the camp felt like winter had returned. As Mike and I got ready for our morning trip up the Miramichi, it started to snow again, a big flake snow, if you know what I mean? Irving Vickers, our guide, arrived about 7:00 A.M., and he didn't say a word except, "They'd said it would snow. This will be a first!" And a first for Mike and I as well as we walked down to the riverside.

The ride up to Washburn Pool was cold. I had on every layer of clothing I had brought for the trip. The snow was not only cold, but wet. As Irving motored back to drop the anchor, I thought to myself, "Salmon in the snow?" We hadn't been there half an hour when I hooked into a huge salmon. We knew he was large because he jumped immediately. I had hooked him a hundred feet behind the boat in very swift water. It was difficult to reel him in. When I got him within twenty feet of the boat, he leaped again, but this time he threw the hook. I will never forget the "treasure" of seeing that salmon jumping in the snow.

Within the hour Mike also hooked into a huge salmon. Mike managed to keep his on longer than I did, at least long enough for us to go to shore so I could film the action on my movie camera. As Mike played the big fish along the shore, I recorded the fight. The fish was eventually lost when a knot came loose, but another "treasure" in the snow had been deposited in our memory vault.

# 53

# Stream Springs

... like a spring of water, whose waters fall not.

—Isaiah 58:11

Recently, I had the privilege to attend my Grandmother Blackstone's 96th birthday making her the oldest living Blackstone in our family on record (she would eventually live into her 100th year). While home Grammy asked my father and I if we could get her a feed of her favorite fish—brook trout. My dad and I hardly need an excuse to go brook trout fishing, but this was an honor. We decided to go to a stream that we have fished together for forty years and my dad has fished over sixty years. Needless to say, we know this brook pretty well, but because of a road that now crosses the creek, many other fishermen also fish there. Instead of going to the easiest place to enter, my dad and I drove a little further downstream and then took a ten minute walk in. The whole time I couldn't wait to get to a little section of the stream where a spring comes into the brook.

    Clear, cold water pouring out of a nature spring makes this special place just below Bull Brook that feeds Beaver Brook, a trout fisherman's paradise. It is one of the last places on the stream you can really fish before the brook opens up and the water gets still. I will never forget the first time I walked that far down stream and found this spring hole. It has never failed to provide me with a number of nice brook trout each time, and this trip with my dad was no exception as I added to the collection of trout in dad's creel and Grammy's supper.

As I ponder on this special spring on this superb stream in Aroostook County, Maine, I am reminded of what Jesus said about the Holy Spirit. (John 7:37-39) Speaking to the woman at the well, Jesus also said that the water He would give her if she believed would be like "a well of water springing up into everlasting life." (John 4:14) Like a spring in a stream, it is a constant source of water for the stream of our lives. Despite the miles and miles of water along Beaver Brook, it was only in those special places we found the trout laying. As the summer heat increased, the trout in the mouth of that spring will increase as they seek cool water. I have concluded that springs are not only for thirst, but also for cooling. As with the trout of Beaver Brook, we too get hot in this very difficult world. As sin warms the society we live in, we also need a place to gather to cool down. Our spring, the Holy Spirit, can calm and cool in every trial and tribulation.

The final application I thought of as I visited the spring on the stream was the fact of the difference of the waters. The stream was a bit cloudy from the many sources that would darken it. The water from the spring was pure and clear without any pollutants. Why? Because the source of the spring water, the granite ground from which it came, had already been purified. Our testimony ought to be the same as we live our lives out on the Rock. (1 Corinthians 10:4)

# 54

# Holy Hardness

Thou therefore endure hardness, as a good soldier of Jesus Christ.
—2 Timothy 2:3

What is true of a soldier is also true of a fisherman.

I have learned over the years that a fisherman who delights in trout fishing must endure all kinds of difficulties when he is heading for his favorite trout hole. First, there is the exhausting hike just to get to the brook. Second, there is the discomfort when you step into a mud hole or a branch hits you in the face or your line gets caught up in the trees. Third, there are the annoyances at the brook itself. A good trout stream is a cold trout stream. I can still hear my cousin's yell echoing off the valley walls as he planted his feet into Beaver Brook at first light. It is a blood chilling cry that can awaken the dead. Then after a bit there are the millions of mosquitoes, horseflies, and blackflies that attack constantly and continually. Fishing isn't easy, but when you're fishing a productive section of stream, all the above and more don't seem to matter, or do they?

Once on the stream and once focused on the task at hand, there comes over your being a calm endurance unmatched. At home, these same annoyances would result in a strong protest or impatience, but on the brook, no such problem! Complaints galore would be the result if one fly invades your space at home, but not fishing. I grumble at a walk through a mall, but ten times the distance over slippery rocks doesn't even stir up a grunt. What is it about fishing that causes one to "endure hardness?"

The secret to me is in this simple poem: "Bear not a single care thyself, one is too much for thee; The work is mine, and mine alone; they work to rest in me!" I learned very early that unless God "giveth the increase" (1 Corinthians 3:7), I fish in vain. The same is true when fishing for men. I started fishing for men in 1970. Interestingly, the same year I started fishing for men seriously in the boarding homes and jails of Athens, Georgia. I came back frustrated more often than not because I thought I was doing something wrong. It wasn't long before I realized that my best resulted in little, but my worst resulted in much. The difference was I was trying to do it all myself. When I let God do his work and I did my work, then there were results. (1 Corinthians 3:6) My endurance depended on just trusting the Lord and doing what I must do—cast the line, throw the bait, and drop the hook.

Also in "holy hardness" you must have such a desire to fish that you overlook the difficulties. I have taken many people fishing over the years, but few are fishermen today. The same has been true with taking people fishing for men. Unless there is a drive and a desire to go fishing, you won't go fishing, and you won't go fishing for men either.

# 55

## Canoe Catch

And Jesus said unto Simon, Fear not; from henceforth thou shalt catch men.
—LUKE 5:10

Mike Hangge and I had been at Matthew's Pond many times before, but never had we had such success fishing at this secluded pond as we did one evening late in May, 2001.

Matthew's Pond is known for its large bookies, and we knew they were there because we had caught a few over the years, but usually only one at a time, one per trip. That special night the weather was ideal for Matthew's, no wind and warm air, just ideal conditions for a late day hatch (the reason we love Matthew's). Mike and I are fly fishermen. We were early enough in the season to escape the invasion of blackflies and mosquitoes though there were a few horseflies that evening if I remember correctly, but not enough to distract us from the numerous large trout beginning to rise around our borrowed canoe.

Trout were taking something just under the surface or was it they were just sipping something just above the water. Fly fishing is a delicate business with slight circumstances that change your approach moment by moment. The trout were not coming out of the water, but they were leaving huge swirls after feeding. After trying several patterns, Mike finally tied on a #20 Mosquito, one of the smallest flies in his fly box. He had picked up a few tiny flies for such an evening as this. I had none myself. Yet within a few minutes

Mike had on a 14-inch trout, and I couldn't believe it. After landing that beautiful fish, it happened again. Mike was into another big trout.

The feeding trout would make a bump in the water, then another bump would form a few feet away. By casting the tiny fly near the ring that was formed and simply letting the fly sit still on the surface of the pond would result in a strike. Before the evening was over I had hooked six nice trout and so had Mike all ranging in size from 12 to 15 inches. The trout fought strong below the surface. For nearly three hours we had the time of our lives catching these trout on tiny Mosquitoes and March Browns. Just before dark I landed my best fish of the evening, a 14-inch beauty. We proved it was no accident when on the next evening we came back and despite the weather conditions being worse, we landed six more big trout, more than we had ever caught before.

Such is the way when fishing for men. I have gone out time after time. I have preached message after message. I have witnessed again and again with very little results, maybe one heart here and one soul there. Then on those Spirit-filled nights or one of those chance encounters when the heart is open, the Spirit moves and many are "won." I will always remember one night at Hampton Bible Camp when after such a sermon I was able to lead an entire cabin of eight girls to the Savior. You don't forget such nights!

# 56

# Peter's Prize

Notwithstanding lest we should offend them, go thou to the sea and cast an hook, and take up the fish that first cometh up; and when thou hast opened his mouth thou shalt find a piece of money; then take, and give unto them for me and thee.

—MATTHEW 17:27

The rooster woke Peter early that morning, the morning of the greatest fishing trip of his life. Oh, he had been fishing before because he was by profession a fisherman, but this was the first morning he was going fishing for the "big one," just one fish that would contain tribute money for both him and his friend Jesus. (Matthew 17:24)

Peter threw off the covers, kissed his wife goodbye, and grabbed his fishing clothes putting them on hurriedly. He quickly worked his way through the streets of Capernaum. Usually he would stop at Andrew's house, but today he would be fishing alone. As he arrived at his fishing boat, the ducks were dancing near shore and the loons were calling offshore. The morning fog was just lifting as Peter rubbed his tired eyes. Once he got the old wooden boat at the water's edge, he rehearsed again in his mind the specific instructions of his Master. (Matthew 17:27)

Pushing off carefully with the oars, Peter rowed his way to a lagoon just up the shoreline from the landing. He knew of a hidden bar that gradually stretched from the shoreline to a deep pool a hundred yards out into the lake. Once he got to the right spot he carefully lowered his anchor, making no unnecessary noise so not to announce his presence any earlier to the school of fish he knew called that bar home. To catch the "big" one he had to do exactly what the Lord had told him to do. Instead of a net, his preferred way of catching fish, he would hand line for this special fish his Lord said would be there. How did he know it was there? How did he know the money was there and in the first fish?

Baiting the hook Peter dropped his line over the side of the boat into the deep pool. How far it went down Peter couldn't tell because within seconds he felt a tug on the end of the line. With the quick reflex of a veteran fisherman Peter set the hook and started pulling the first and only fish of the day to the boat. The prize fish put up a fight as it neared the surface of the lake. It ran deeper the minute it saw the boat, but the hook was set deep in its upper lip, and there would be no getting away from the powerful hands pulling it in.

Within minutes the fish was flopping at the bottom of the boat. A broad smile came to Peter's face as the early morning sun reflected off a silver coin in the fish's mouth. Peter picked the coin up and squeezed it tightly in his big hand. With the other hand he placed the tired fish back into the water as he was just after the money. As he rowed back to shore, he knew he was following "the Son of God."

# 57

## Studying Stillness

...study to be quiet...

—1 Thessalonians 4:11

If there is one bit of advice I would give to those who are travelling down the road of life after me, it would be to find a quiet place by the water. It doesn't have to be an elaborate place, but it must be a silent place, a place where there are no distractions of this world which can detract you from the purpose of "still waters." I learned this bit of advice from my father-in-law, Stacy Meister.

As the world grows more noisy, we need to withdraw to a solitary sanctuary where we can "study to be quiet" (1 Thessalonians 4:11) on a regular basis. This can only take place if we have a place where the crowd is replaced by the closet; where the world is replaced by the womb; where the rush is replaced by reverence; and clatter is replaced by calm. We need a place for moments of meditation as well as a chance to communicate with our Father. I remember from my earliest days as a dad I tried to teach my children that they could always talk with me. I made time for them to be with me, whether it was a quiet walk to school, or a quiet drive to school, or a quiet time around the supper table, or a quiet hour on a Sunday afternoon. My daughter and her brother are old now, and I have long since stopped forcing them into a quiet place, but I hope the time will come when they will reminisce and recall how precious those quiet places were when they were young.

Over the years, I have found my quiet places in the strangest places. Oh, yes, as time passes so do places. Rare is the man or woman who can keep a quiet place very long. If you discover it, so will others, and then when others have found your quiet place, it will no longer be a quiet place. Always remember that one of the ingredients of a quiet place is that it is a private place. Just you and God because any more and the peace and privacy are gone. I remember well a little fishing hole, Smith Pond, I discovered while ministering in a northern Maine town. At first it was an ideal quiet place by the "still waters" until I made the mistake of telling others that I was catching fish there. Soon there were more than one in the boat and no longer a quiet place. No, you can't be selfish if you find a quiet place.

What you do in your quiet place can vary. Sometimes I just sit and think quietly. At other times I reminisce quietly. You can read quietly, pray quietly, or just sit and relish the moment quietly. I have listened to music in my quiet place. Of course, only certain music will do. Don't I get upset when others bring loud music into my quiet place. How quickly a quiet place can be turned into a noisy place. I have napped in my quiet place. A good rest in a quiet place is better than a night's sleep in a noisy place. What you do in your quiet place is up to you, but what you do will determine how long you keep your "still waters." (Psalm 23:2)

# 58

# Window Works

*When I consider thy heavens, the works of thy fingers, the moon and the stars, which thou hast ordained . . .*

—Psalms 8:3

I have lived too long in the State of Maine not to have appreciated: a robin searching for the early morning worm in the back yard, a squirrel looking like a kid with mumps gathering its winter stores, a chorus of birds lustily singing in the wee hours of a summer's day, or a full harvest moon coming up from behind a ridge decorated in its autumn best. These and a hundred more sights have held me spellbound for years as I have travelled the State of my birth. Some of these sights and sounds I have seen and heard as I walked the various lanes that have become my favorite hiking paths. Others I have witnessed as I have simply gazed out the windows of my life. It was through my bedroom window on the old family homestead in northern Maine I was first put in a trance by the world God created for me to enjoy. I still smile as I see in my mind's eye a proud crow being chased by a group of barn sparrows. The brash bird thought he could taunt the smaller sparrows, but found himself harassed as he tried to make a speedy escape. Like a swarm of German fighters attacking an American bomber over Europe, the brave sparrows dive, setting the crow to a hasty flight.

    It was through a cabin window overlooking a great Quebec waterway that I came to love the combination of water and hills. Nestled in a virgin forest under the shadow of a hardwood ridge, the lodge (interestingly called

"Grog Island") captured my heart. For three years I was allowed to visit this restful point, and each time I came back thinking I had taken a trip to the shores of paradise. I thought after my last trip I would never discover a similar place again, yet I have, but only because nature has the God-given ability to renew itself periodically. So whether The Anchorage on Big Lake, Vickers' Cottage on the Miramichi River, or a favorite fishing hole, the view from the window of water and sky, hills and stars, is God's best.

For me each camp has been a gigantic prophet's chamber where I have been able to go and unwind. Away from phone and office work, I have been able to recharge my spiritual batteries at the outlet of God's creation. From the deck in the front of these cabins I have, with the psalmist, feasted on the breath-taking sights and the soul-stirring sounds of "my Father's world." I have watched the sunrise turning the water into a gray-blue mirror. Combined with a little breeze, the light and the wind turned the water drops into shimmering gems. When this sight is in conjunction with fall and the colorful foliage that lines the banks and covers the hills, then your eyes are in for the best treat of all—brilliant orange and fiery red maples scattered among the towering green of spruce and pine mixed with the luscious yellows of birth. Truly, "What is man?" (Psalm 8:4)

# 59

# Five Facilities

...who by reason of use have their senses exercised to discern...
—Hebrews 5:15

I have been blessed all my life with the same five physical senses I was born with. While others are born with a weakness or defect to one or more of their senses, I have had all of mine functioning properly from the beginning. I wish I could say that I have utilized them to their capacity, but I haven't. It seems as I get older and I sense that my senses are not as sharp as they once were, I am realizing what I miss from God when I don't allow my five fabulous faculties to focus on their Creator. My father-in-law helped me develop my out-of-door senses.

Over the years I have discovered that my five senses function better out-of-doors. Inside I seem to quickly get distracted by manmade technology that dominates my senses. Man has realized that to control man the senses of his body must be controlled. Away from such instruments man has a better opportunity to focus these God-given senses toward Him. I recall the first place this unique transfer from man's world to God's world took place.

I had just begun dating a young lady from the next town whose family owned a cabin by a lake. Tucked in the woods of northern Maine is a horseshoe-shaped lake called Portage Lake. Trips up to that lakeside were part of the early benefits of dating my future wife. It was there I first used my eyes to see God's wonderful hand in nature. Despite the fact I lived on a farm, my life was so filled with chores that I paid no attention to the beauty of the barnyard. In the still quiet moments around Portage I began to realize my eyes rejoiced seeing the glory of a sunset over water. It was at Meister's camp on Portage Lake that my ears first heard the pleasant sounds of wind and wave. To this day nothing relaxes me more than wind and waves. I revel in their calming grace. My sense of smell was also strengthened by Portage Lake. The strong smells of the farm were replaced by the fragrance of flowers, the perfume of pine, and the scent of a shower. Lakeside odors gave me a new appreciation of my sense of smell. Then there was the sense of taste. I learned very early in my relationship with my wife that her family knew how to cook. My taste buds began to experience tastes I had never experienced before, delicious foods that are still some of my all-time favorites. Finally at Portage Lake my sense of touch was realized. Whether the softness of my date's hand or the smoothness of her face; whether the warmth of sand between my toes or the warm sun on my face; whether a slippery salmon or the comfort of laying on a bed of pine needles, the special sensations these senses brought to me were all gifts from above.

Part of our Creator's blessing is the ability He gave us to enjoy His creation with these five faculties.

# 60

## Silence Sound

*There was silence, and I heard a voice, saying...*
—Job 4:16

One of the things I love so much about the Anchorage on Big Lake in Princeton, Maine, is "the sound of silence."

I can hear already those who ask, "Can silence have a sound?" Everything has sound except silence, but for those of us who have had the privilege of spending some time at The Anchorage that isn't true because we have discovered that in that tranquil place even silence has a very distinct sound.

First, there is "the sound of silence" when a storm passes by. The wind stops blowing through the high pines overhead, the waves of the lake stop lapping on shore, and the cabin grows still. It is then one hears "the sound of silence." I recall the first time I heard it. I was laying on the couch in the living room reading a favorite historical biography when I sensed the sound. You don't really hear this "sound of silence" with your ear, but with your soul. I looked up and the eyes of my wife Coleen met mine. Her smile told me that she too had heard it. It was as sweet as any music ever played, as calming as any lullaby ever sung, and as comforting as any hug ever given. It brought such deep soul relief that for quite a few moments Coleen and I just listened to the still silence of our God.

Second, there is "the sound of silence" when the sun sets behind Corliss Point. Often on a cooling August evening my wife and I sit out on the lawn overlooking the lake watching the heavenly pink clouds created by the dying sun. Because of Coleen's grandmother's paintings, pink clouds remind my wife of that special lady in her childhood. Just as the sun dips behind the tree line to the west, a silence engulfs Corliss Cove. Even the noise from the cabins and cottages surrounding the cove go silent. The kids stop yelling, the dogs stop barking, and everything that can make sound stops. Even the loons seem to respect this time of the day when silence can be heard. Eyes fixed above and ears deaf to any earthly noise, "the sound of silence" plays its glorious music of quietness. It has always been a highlight of our day and though short lived, it is worth the wait when conditions create "that still small voice."

Thirdly there is "the sound of silence" when the fire in the Franklin stove burns out. If there is one sound I love and one sight I am transfixed by, it has to be a campfire by a favorite fishing hole. I can watch and listen for hours a crackling, glowing wood fire. No matter how pleasant it might be, it can't compare to a fire that stops crackling and stops burning. Often in the evening of a cold night I will built a roaring fire, place the old rocking chair near it, and rock and watch the flames through the screen front. Then as the blackness deepens and the flames fade, a sound can be heard. It is the sound between slumber and sleep when the Good Lord says, "Good night!"

# 61

## Stream Solace

I will open rivers in high places . . .

—Isaiah 41:18

We disembarked from our boats along a rugged shore. According to our maps, the stream that flowed into this particular lake in northern Quebec was fed from an even larger lake on the other side of the ridge. A path followed the simple stream on its wet bank. As I left my companions behind I walked through virgin timber to reach that distant body of water. My quest was brook trout, but what I learned has far outlived my original goal.

It had been a frustrating fishing expedition to Canada. The weather was terrible, and the fishing was even worse. At that stage in my life I was an avid sportsman. The catch was everything, and the scenery was secondary. I didn't realize at that time that I needed the environment of the fish as much as I needed to catch fish. Now I am not ashamed to say "I caught nothing," but in those days it was an embarrassment to return to my fishing buddies empty-handed until I returned from my walk along that high ridge creek in Quebec.

The more I climbed the more I heard from this upper stream. The closer I got to its source, the louder its music. For the first time in my life I heard the unique blending of stream and stone. Combined with a gentle breeze blowing through the stunted spruce that lined its shore, the connecting river was nature's orchestra at play. It was when I stopped to bury my face in the sweet water that I began to sense the solace of soul the stream was giving me. The pristine purity of the clean flowing water was pleasant to my taste buds, and the quiet laughter of water tumbling over the ridge was calming to my ears. I drank deeply of the cool liquid, and my spirit drank even deeper of the sounds that surrounded my soul by that wilderness stream.

I discovered that day the music of a mountain stream. Beside my bed I have a tape of "mountain sounds," a nature tape that includes the sound of a high country stream rolling over boulders and rocks and stones. When I play that tape, I am transported back to that isolated trail off Lynn Lake, and I recall what happened to a frustrated fisherman the day he stopped seeking the next fishing hole and started listening to the music of God. There was such an uplift of my spirit I can't describe it. There was such a rejuvenation of my soul I can't explain it. There was such a refreshment of my mind I can't to this day fully understand it. Perhaps Philip Keller said it best: "There is deep and profound therapy in the flow of water, in the songs of a stream."

As the fog settled even lower over the ridge, I started my return to my friends. I found the lake, but I caught no fish. What I did catch on that late afternoon stroll was a love of the solace that comes from a high-place stream and the music of the mountains.

# 62

## Stunted Spruce

For when for the time ye ought to be teachers, ye have need that one teach you again.

—HEBREWS 5:12

I have travelled into the great north woods of Canada many times in search of a productive fishing hole. I have travelled in those fishing expeditions through hundreds of miles of virgin forest. By Maine standards theses woodlands aren't very impressive. The size of the stands might take your breath away, but the size of the spruce won't. I call them stunted spruce, some barely four inches through and stand barely thirty feet tall. Even the big ones aren't more than eight inches through and fifty feet high. They tell me that a tree might get plenty of light, but if that light doesn't produce a temperature of more than forty degrees there will be no growth. The trees of northern Quebec get plenty of sunlight I am sure. Their problem is that they grow in a climate where the growing season is very short. In short they are stunted by the cold. The long seasons of cold temperature put their growth on hold even by the river.

    In contrast take the spruce of Maine, my home state. I have seen spruce on my dad's farm two and three feet through. The difference is that the trees of Maine have the benefit of a warmer climate for greater periods of time. They enjoy a longer growing season during which the weather is sunny with plenty of water. The spruce of Maine experience a season of cold, but it is far shorter then in northern Canada. A combination of sun and rain will stimulate a healthy spruce to grow rapidly during the summer season. I have watched a hedge of spruce I helped my father plant when I was a young boy mature amazingly during my lifetime. When we planted them they were barely three feet tall, but now this group of spruce tower over the front lawn where they were planted. Climate and water conditions play a big part in the growth process of that stand of spruce and will determine whether they will be stunted or stately.

Isn't it interesting that people are like spruce. I am not speaking physically. Some people have stunted personalities. Some people are dwarfs in their character. Despite the fact that they have been exposed to tremendous amounts of water (Bible) in their lives they show no growth at all. They have virtually stood still in the development of their spiritual skills. Unmoving and unchanging, they are content to stay childish all their lives; they are willing to stay seedlings and saplings for the rest of their life. Then there are others that spread their branches and expose their leaves to every moment with the Son. Every twig and needle of their being draws in the love and care around them. They reach rapidly for the Son and benefit from every minute in the Bible (Ephesians 5:26). The instant response to these periods of learning year after year reflect the secret of their spiritual stature.

# 63

# River Run

Are ye steadfast, unmovable, and always abounding in the work of the Lord.
—1 Corinthian 15:58

I stand beside my favorite river in Canada pondering again. I ask myself this question, "What is the business of a river?" Answer, to flow!

A river's banks may be covered in snow or lush green; its current might be white and raging or sluggish and slow; the sky above it might be blue or gray; its waters may mirror spring flowers or fall's colorful leaves; its bowels might be full of salmon or full of ice flows, but no matter what appears above, beside, or inside, it must keep on running.

It starts as a babbling brook in some distant glade, but even there it flows. It grows to a gentle creek, but its motion is still onward and forward. It flows. Soon it becomes a noisy stream behind your house, but its movement is to keep on running. Eventually, it flows with others until it becomes a noble river with direction toward the sea. It is deep and wide, but still it flows. It may in its quest for the open ocean be checked momentarily by a manmade obstacle, but it is born to flow, and somehow, somewhere it finds a place to escape and continues its run. It can be checked at times by a resisting arm of land that might seemingly cause it to retreat in an eddy, but its advance is only stopped for a short time until it regains its bearing and once again surges forward towards its destiny. Nothing can stop its flow to the sea!

Is not this the "steadfast, unmovable" intent of Paul in our key verse above? Is it not our God's will and wish that we press on? (Philippians 3:14) Is it not that our Lord wants us to steadily flow in obedience no matter the obstacle, the detours, or the interference? If we are flowing in the channel of His will, neither sunshine or shadow or pleasure or pain can stop us from "always abounding in the work of the Lord." Ours is to gladly and joyously flow onward and sing with the song writer, "I'm pressing on the upward way, new heights I'm gaining every day!" Our heights are the overspreading of every peril and plight before us. It is in our nature to pause and ponder at times, but with a refreshing surge of the Spirit within, we can move on or over or around anything that blocks our way to the sea that surrounds the throne of God.

Remember then, amid the changes in our course, because God sometimes redirects the current of His will, we must not take our eye off the ultimate goal, the ocean of God's eternity. Steadfastly, we face our Lord and flow forward on the strong and peaceful tide of this Almighty love. This love flows deeper than any difficulty, and if we stay in the middle current of this Godly stream, the water that first bubbled from that Godly spring will reach its heavenly home.

# 64

## Water Walk

Fear not; from henceforth thou shalt catch men.

—Luke 5:10

On a recent trip to Grand Lake Stream, I once again waded a section of that stream bed that reinforces each time I walk it that I am a walker not a rider when it comes to fishing. I have spent many a day in a boat over the years, but my most pleasant travels through water have been wading, not motoring.

My first experience with a stream was wading. My father is a wader, not a boater. He has never owned a boat, and I dare say he never will (and he didn't dying at the grand age of 93). There is something about wading into a gently flowing stream with a fly rod in your hand and a hope in your heart; of feeling the current against your legs and the cold flow against your skin. Water walking is unmatched in making you one with the brook and one with the fish in it. On Grand Lake Stream the water is so clear you can see the fish before you hook the fish. Holding firmly to a spot near a rock or a log, the salmon awaits your presentation. What a thrill it is to see fish swimming about as you walk about. It makes the anticipation of a hookup thrilling, and the expectation fulfilling.

I guess what it is for me is wading represents the unhurried life. Bass boats with 175 horses behind speeding off to this fishing hole and that fishing hole isn't for me. Wading Grand Lake Stream brings me back to the reality that life was intended to be at a "garden" pace, not a "city" pace. Our society that includes the American Church has forgotten how to wade in its lifestyle. Instead of taking time with each catch (convert) we rush them through a ten-week course, if that, and in the end pronounce them fit and able to face all of life's battles. With the new fishing gear fishermen are able to get there more quickly, cast more quickly, land their catch more quickly, and move off to the next catch more quickly. They no longer savor the thrill of the catch. So it is with the mass evangelism of the present age. Fly fishing in a stream is still one by one, and Won By One is still the Bible way of leading someone to the Savior's side.

It is time we get off our fancy boats (buildings), step again into the stream bed of humanity, and start wading into the world of sinners. It is time we spot our "man" and carefully and prayerfully lay the gospel before him. And when we get a bite, we need to play him wisely and calmly until he is landed in the church where he must be trained deliberately and doctrinally before being released back into the world. We need to take the time to rejoice over one sinner that comes to repentance (Luke 15:7, 10) and treat each one as the special treasure the Good Lord sees them. It is time the Church of the Living God gets "wet" again. It is time the Christian "fishers-of-men" start wading again, forget about modern methods, and start fishing one on one with the hook of love and the fly of grace.

# 65

## Stream Statute

All things work together for good . . .
—ROMANS 8:28

I came to the Washington County waterway of Grand Lake Stream to catch a landlocked salmon, but instead I caught a fresh sighting of my Lord and Savior Jesus Christ.

 I sit once more beside my favorite salmon stream and ponder, "Swift to its close ebbs out life's little day." Just a short four months ago I was fishing well after nine o'clock, but tonight I can't see much, and it isn't even seven o'clock yet. That evening in June I landed twelve feisty fish, but today I have had only one faint hookup. Two quick head shakes and my lone salmon of the evening threw my Black Ghost and left me with an empty net, but a valuable lesson. If one compares these two days one might think that God blessed in one and withdrew his blessing in the other, but I discovered as I meditated on this day on Grand Lake Stream that God was with me on both these days.

 I have come to believe that no matter what, God makes no mistakes, ever! I have been recently reminded that the same God that delivered Peter from Herod's dungeon let John the Baptist be beheaded in that same dungeon? Successful escape versus sensual execution doesn't seem compatible or connectable to the same God, yet they are. A salmon-filled day versus a salmon-less day likewise seems to speak of two different blessings, yet I learned from the Lord that they both come from the same loving heart. One day Moses dies, and the next day God tells Joshua to move on. No mourning, no memorial, no monument to the great man? "That was yesterday and this is today, and I am the Lord of both," says the Eternal God. Daily outcomes might dramatically change, but my God, never!

We have for too long judged our God by successful results rather than God simply being God. We ask to be productive and when we are we rejoice, but when we aren't, we set our jaw and with tear-dimmed eyes think our Lord has abandoned us. What my salmon-less day produced was a redirection from fishing to writing, to face why I had really come on this late season fly fishing trip to Grand Lake Stream. I hadn't come for the thrill of catching a landlocked salmon, but to settle some personal things with the Lord. I felt the church I was pastoring had changed from being fruitful to being fruitless, and that somehow God was withholding His blessing. It was this statement by Vance Havner that made me think straight again. "Whosoever thinks he has the way of God conveniently tabulated, analyzed, and correlated with confidence, and has glib answers to ease every question from an aching heart has not been far in this maze of mystery we call life."

We may have difficulty reconciling Peter's dilemma and John's death, but, as with all divine sovereignty issues, God and God alone will harmonize for the good.

# 66

## Corner Concept

*They shall not be ashamed that wait for me . . .*

—Isaiah 49:23

My time is up and darkness came over three hours ago. My day of writing is over with these final thoughts from The Anchorage. The cabin is cozy now that I have gotten a wood fire going, and my heart is happy in the afterglow of God's revelation on the verge of inspiration. I don't know if my admonitions from The Anchorage have helped you, but they have recharged this old heart, restarted this old preacher, and rekindled the old fire that once burned within me. It is this saying by Vance Havner that I take back with me to the frustration that is now for me Ellsworth, *"I cannot trace His hand but I will trust His heart."*

None of my questions and inquiries has been answered by the Lord. I still don't know if I am going or staying. I still am confused over the mixed signals from Eastport and Dyer Brook and my visions for them. I still flip-flop over the issue of whether I'm a writer first and a pastor second or a pastor first and a writer second. But this I know, and Charles Haddon Spurgeon was also right, when he said, *"God is too good to be unkind, too wise to be mistaken, and when you cannot trace His hands, you can trust His heart."* Spurgeon's philosophy and Havner's phrase will be my blueprint for my coming days.

God's plans and my plans are now our plans, come what may. At times I only get glimpses of Him just like the salmon in Grand Lake stream, but I know they are there, and I know He is there. James Russell Lowell said it best when he penned, *"Standeth God within the shadow keeping watch above His own!"* I saw Him a lot in the shadows on this trip. His shadow fell across my path as I walked Anchorage Avenue praying. I saw His face in the flames as I built a wood fire in the Franklin stove to ward off a late September freeze. I waded with Him in the still flowing waters of the Corner Pool on Grand Lake Stream. I now see to only stay in touch with His heart, instead of His hand. Sometimes I can't feel His hand, but I can always know that His heart of love is within me. His heart of goodness is working all things out for His glory, not my goals. I believe that I have reached to some degree the soul rest I sought as I travelled to this cabin on Corliss Cove. There remains much more to understand about the heart of God because I don't count myself as one that has attained, but I am now at least on the right road, travelling the right pathway.

I dare not dream what is ahead for me or just how the Heavenly Father will deal with me concerning my church, my career, and my choices, but as Vance Havner ended his article on tracing God versus trusting God, so do I. *"If I trust the Heart, I need never question the Hand!"* There it is. So simple yet so inspiring. I wonder why I haven't thought of it before.

# 67

# Stream Storms

... but Satan hindered us.

—1 Thessalonians 2:18

I write this in the stillness of an autumn sundown in a lovely lodge we call the Anchorage. The back porch opens up to a matchless view overlooking Big Lake in Princeton, Maine. The early fall sun is just sinking behind the low hills on the other side of the lake. A loon sings just around the corner in Corliss Cove, and a gentle breeze is blowing through the surrounding pines that tower over the small cabin in which I am writing. It is my second day alone at the Anchorage and my first day writing. Grand Lake Stream isn't producing much in the way of salmon so I will write.

    I came alone to the Anchorage in the spring, but the fishing was tremendous. I hardly left Grand Lake Stream for three days, but this trip is different, and I prefer fishing for memories to fishing for fish. What I found was a resting place for a very weary mind. Things are getting complicated at the church I pastor, and I don't know what to do next. I needed this trip to just refocus on where and what. The trip started in the black of night, and I awoke the first morning to a cold, damp autumn rain. It rained most of the day until about 5:00 P.M. when a cold front settled in from Canada. The sun came out as I fished in front of Grand Lake Stream dam. The sun felt good after the chilling rains, but once the sun had set in the western horizon the frost also settled in. The few clouds that remained turned a heavenly pink, and it was then my mind began to realize that God who controls the weather is in control of my situation at the church. God's storms hadn't stopped me from fishing, and Satan's storms in life can't stop me from fishing for men either. I have fished Grand Lake Stream in boisterous winds and boiling waters so why do I allow boisterous believers and boiling babies to distract me from my calling?

If I learned anything from my stays at the Anchorage, it must be that the fury of a storm is always followed by a clearing, and the fury of a saint will be followed by calm as well. Vance Havner once said that *"the sun has outlasted all the clouds of all the centuries,"* and I believe this saint will outlast all the criticism of all the Christians, too. The storms that have lashed against my soul over the last year have been very personal. There have been many that have abandoned the ship in the midst of the storm thinking only of self, but, come what may, I am not the captain of this ship because that is in the worthy hands of Jesus Christ. I am a first mate at best, and I shall stay until he calls out loud and clear, "Abandon ship!"

I watch as a fall sun dips out of sight. In only 48 hours I am already renewed and ready for the difficult months that are before me because I am recharged and rejuvenated in body and in soul. Come what may, I shall keep on fishing!

# 68

## Water Worries

...when thou passeth through the waters I will be with thee.

—Isaiah 43:2

I am writing these thoughts from the neighbor's boat dock located next to the Anchorage. The fancy dock extends about fifteen feet into Big Lake, and I am sitting on a new green plastic chair at the end of it. I am also trying to warm up from a very cold start to the day and a raw northern gale that continues to erase a warming September sun. Despite the fact that it is a cool day at the Anchorage, my mind has been heated by a memory from that old classic by John Bunyan, Pilgrim's Progress. Remember Mr. Fearing who all his life feared the crossing of the River of Death only to find when he finally arrived at it banks "the water at a record low, and not much above wetshod!"

    I too often fear the worst in my life. An ache in my back is cancer, and a pain in my chest is a heart attack. A setback is permanent, and a rejection is the end of one's ministry. I have come to the "still waters" of Big Lake and Grand Lake Stream for such inspiration as this old thought has given. Even when the waters aren't still and the sea is high God has prepared "dry ground" ahead. It was James Russell Lowell that once said, *"Truth forever on the scaffold and worry forever on the throne."* At times I almost believe him. Especially when after ten years work I see the labor of my current church slowly dying in apathy, affluence, and anger. I am lost to what I have done or haven't done. I stand shocked and surprised by those who are leading the way to see a "good" work ruined, yet as I sit quietly surrounded by the gentle lapping of waves on a granite shore, I hear clearly that "still small voice" saying, "the end is not yet and, Barry, you do know how it will turn out." (15 years later as I compile these 'angling admonitions' I am so glad I stayed-29 years now, for in the end I have concluded that the God Lord gave me in this troubled church-'a church of a lifetime'!)

Yesterday I waded and walked Grand Lake stream. Places I couldn't hope to tread in June I easily trod yesterday. I don't know if the stream was at a record low, but I hardly needed my waders at places. So it will be if I but allow time to pass. My God has it all figured out, and by the time I get to my Red Sea or Jordan River dry land versus a tempestuous tide will be along my path. As with life, so will the end of the days. It was the great devotional writer Vance Havner that once recorded for me and others like me, *"Thank God for a Book that disposes of the devil."* As with the Bible, there will be no devil on the last page of my history. I live today in the calming chorus of water surrounding me that the correct path will end with a stroll through low water "and not much above wetshod!"

I will leave the Anchorage with a new confidence that my future is much brighter then the devil's, and that whether sunshine or shadow, my path is plotted and prepared by a loving Guide that knows exactly how much water I can tread.

# 69

## Creek Cleaning

Blessed are the pure in heart; for they shall see God.
—Matthew 5:8

I am standing next to Big Lake watching for loons and other interesting sightings on a chilly September day in Maine. I should be fishing, but instead I am writing. Friday is writing day for me. I can't say I have written every Friday since November, 1988, when I first began to put my thoughts down with ink, but now rare is the Friday that I don't write or think about something in which to put pen to paper. What makes this Friday so unique is that I am writing on vacation. I have taken three days off from a busy fall church schedule to fish for landlocked salmon on Grand Lake Stream. I have been spending my nights at the Anchorage on Big Lake. Yesterday I discovered that the salmon have already ended their biting season so I decided to end my fishing season and do some writing. One of the things I would like to write about is clear water. One of the reasons I love Grand Lake Stream is its clear water. From where I am standing on the banks of Grand Lake Stream I can make out every rock on the bottom.

In a day known for pollution it is nice to come to a place where the air is clear and the water is clean, a place where on a "clear day you can see forever." I have fished in dirty lakes and muddy streams when I had to pay more attention to my footing than my fishing. Hidden reefs and covered rocks are ready to land me high and dry or down and wet on some liquid bottom. I have been "baptized" a few times over the years. I remember one day on East Grand Lake actually driving my father-in-law's 14-foot boat directly onto a flat submerged rock while trolling for landlocked salmon. I never saw the reef because the water was so dark. I remember stumbling and falling over a stone in the Penobscot River while playing an Atlantic salmon because the water was so murky. So it is with this world's polluted minds and polluted media and polluted mankind; they have made a walk through this planet a dangerous journey. You have to spend so much time nowadays watching for hidden snares and sins, you can't enjoy the view of life itself. Maybe that is why I like to come to the Anchorage where I don't have to spend my time feeling my way along. I don't have to shut my eyes to the immorality around me. I can just walk along enjoying the scenery.

Pure hearts are like a clean stream. Everything can be seen crystal clear. If there are any obstacles, they can be avoided soon enough so that no damage is done. Praise God for feelings, but feelings can't replace sight as an affective watchman of the soul. In this world of murky, muddied convictions it is nice every once in a while to walk with someone that is as clear in their convictions and lifestyle as the water that flows in Grand Lake Stream.

# 70

## Creek Companion

... the Father hath not left me alone ...

—JOHN 8:29

I am within days of the third anniversary of the death of my beloved father-in-law and best fishing companion, Stacy Meister. I can't help but think of him each time I sit beside a body of water as I am now. Grand Lake Stream has been my companion as I finish a late September sabbatical to her shores. It still amazes me that I mourn over his unexpected departure. Stacy was only in his 60s when he finally yielded to lung and liver cancer after a quick fourteen-month struggle. When he left, I was left alone by the stream. I have yet to find someone quite like him (I would in a man named Hangge). I have found substitutes at best, but on an "alone" trip like this one, I realize just how much left when Stacy left.

    Don't get me wrong. Stacy is not lost because I know where to find him, and one day in glory I'll find him fishing near the rose bushes by the river of God that flows from under the throne of the Almighty. Even though he is not lost a lot of what we had together is gone. Gone with him are the many precious things that make a trip to a body of water delightful. Gone is the anticipation of hearing his praise when I land the largest salmon I have ever hooked on the Miramichi River. Gone is the greeting that always awaited me when I entered his fly tying shop in Washburn. Gone is the thrill in his voice when he would show me a new fly pattern he had created. Gone are the potato doughnuts he used to fry for our special fishing trips together.

I must admit my mother-in-law has conquered his recipe, but gone is the smile on his face when he would watch me eat his doughnuts with such pleasure. Gone is the shake of his dear hand after a day's fishing when I would "best" him. Gone is his rugged face at the other end of the table after a supper of onion hash and moose steak. Gone are the games we played to see who could catch the best, the biggest, and the better!

My only joy of this late trip and the anniversary of my dear companion's death is that Stacy's God is not gone. As I rode through the night to fish Grand Lake Stream the next day, Stacy was missing, but God wasn't. He was in the seat next to me talking through the gathering night. As I stepped into the fishermen-empty Grand Lake Stream, God was my only companion and fly counselor. It was William Jennings Bryan that said, *"Christ has made of death a narrow starlight strip between the companionship of yesterday and the reunion of tomorrow!"* As I leave another fishing hole without Stacy I am reminded that he is not really gone, but just gone on ahead. He is just around the bend, and God has stayed to take his place as companion and friend. What better fishing buddy could I have then Him. The day has passed, and the fishing has been very, very poor. Three small fish in six hours, but those six hours have been well spent in the company of the greatest Companion any man could want.

# 71

## River Reflection

When thou saidst, Seek ye my face;
my heart said unto thee, thy face, Lord, will I seek.
—Psalm 27:8

I sit alone by the riverside waiting the setting sun, my last setting sun over Grand Lake Stream for this year. Tomorrow I return home before the sun sets again. I have been alone on this trip. I came alone of my own free will, but I must admit as I sat with my back to the river a couple of times I imagined my dear wife coming up from behind and touching me. It was an imaginary touch, but I felt it because Coleen is everywhere here. How she would love the scene I am watching as a blazing orange ball dips into the hills beyond. I have sat for four hours listening to "the still small voice" of God whispering in my ear. How He has encouraged me in this matter of ministry and men, yet he knows that I still can't do either without companionship.

  I have travelled often alone on church business and fishing business, and I am by my very nature a "loner," but this trip has been different. I have found myself instinctively and subconsciously looking around seeking for my dear wife. I have not found her yet, but I smell her cooking from the kitchen, her perfume from the bedroom, and her presence in the living room. It seems that Coleen ought to be somewhere near whether reading a romance novel, sewing on a quilt, or wanting me to play a game of scrabble. How I have realized on this trip that no man is poor that has such a faithful, friendly, loving wife; that tomorrow I will find her where I left her and she will say, "How was the trip?" and I will simply say, "Fine," and nothing more.

    I have walked Grand Lake Stream and have seen a few men and even a woman fishing for landlocked salmon, but I didn't see one familiar or friendly face in the crowd of fishermen. I am spoiled I guess when you consider I only need one face really to set my world aright. It seems to be the same with my faith. In this world when people want a change because they aren't entertained enough, or given enough, or challenged enough that "*Jesus Is All I Need*." (As the old Church hymn goes, "Jesus is all the world to me!") If Jesus is there, and He promised that where two or three were gathered in His name He would be there, who cares who else is there or isn't there? That one familiar face in the congregation ought to be enough to keep us there and keep us coming. I care not where the Good Lord will lead me next because I know that as I look over the congregation that two familiar faces will always be in the crowd. I care not the order of service or the form of music because those two familiar faces will be enough for me. I care not whether in Northern Maine or Downeast Maine because in either place those two familiar faces will be smiling back at me. And those two familiar faces will be the radiant, glowing face of my dear Lord and Savior Jesus Christ and the lovely, caring face of my beloved wife Coleen!

# 72

## Saucer Sipping

My cup runneth over!

—PSALMS 23:5

Recently, at an opening to the Sunday School at the Emmanuel Baptist Church where I pastor, our Superintendent Danny Clark played a tape by Dennis Swanberg entitled *Drinking' From the Saucer*. It brought back a memory from my father-in-law when I use to watch Stacy drink his tea or coffee from a saucer on many a fishing trip. The reading went like this: "There is no place like home is there? Remember the old home place? When you would be out there on a Sunday afternoon and you'd had a good meal, but you'd always have a good desert and some coffee. And sometime later on in the day, when Mum would fix up another cup, another pot full and we'd drink it, but sometimes it was so hot we would just 'saucer it.'" Do you remember that we would 'saucer it' back then? Probably we'd get in trouble for it now! I have thought about that, and now that I have come down the trail a ways there is a lesson to be learned in that old saucer cup. Let me put it this way to you.

> I am drinking from the saucer because my cup has overflowed.
> Oh, I will never make a fortune, and it is probably too late now.
> But it doesn't matter all that much because I'm happy anyhow.
> As I go along life's journey I'm receiving better than I sowed.
> I'm drinking from the saucer 'cause my cup has overflowed.

I haven't any riches and sometimes the going is rough,
but I've got five kids and wife who love me, and that's rich enough.
I thank God for all his mercies and blessings he's bestowed.
I'm drinking, my friend, from the saucer 'cause my cup has overflowed.

Oh, I remember when times were rough and my faith got a little bit thin.
But all at once the clouds broke and that old sun peaked through again.
So, Lord, help me not to gripe about the rough rows that I hoed.
I'm drinking from the saucer 'cause my cup has overflowed.

And as God gives me the strength and courage when the way is steep and rough.
I'll not ask for other blessings, I'm already blessed enough.
And may I never be too busy to help another carry his load.
I think I will keep on drinking from the saucer because my cup has overflowed.

I too can see through my mind's eye as my father-in-law would pour his hot coffee or tea into the saucer. I can see his two hard working hands take each side and slowly swirl the liquid around. The steam would quickly evaporate, and Stacy would put the saucer to his lips and sip the cooled refreshment. The process was repeated until the drink was finished. I often thought Stacy did it because he was in a hurry to return to the boat or bank for fishing. Now I know for a certainty that he was drinking from the saucer because his cup had overflowed. I wish in the privilege of watching him drink from the saucer on many a fishing trip I had learned how he lived as David did in the philosophy of "My cup runneth over." (Psalm 23:5)

# 73

## Soaring Statute

...mount up with wings as eagles...

—Isaiah 40:31

I was fishing quietly along a shore on Big Lake when I came across an eagle in a tall spruce tree. The fish were not participating in my afternoon plans so I took to watching my new found friend. Immediately, these words of one of my favorite Old Testament verses came to mind, *"And they shall mount up with wings as eagles!"* Ever since I memorized Isaiah 40:31 in college, it has flashed back with every eagle sighting, especially if my father-in-law was there to teach me. As I pondered the words in light of the eagle, I realized that Isaiah also must have been the observer of eagles. As I recalled each eagle I had seen, I remembered that more often than not I saw them waiting, not soaring, just sitting and resting in high trees. What were they doing? They were *"renewing their strength."* My trouble is that when the Lord gives me some down time, I rarely rest, but instead waste my strength reserves on unprofitable activity. Not so the eagle! When darkness comes, he rests patiently renewing his strength. I party through most of the night. When will I learn, like the eagle, that I need renewal if I am to be the best for God I can be.

On this afternoon I also observed that this eagle waited for the late afternoon breeze before he attempted to fly. Not only was he renewing his strength, but he was waiting on the wind. He knew when the thermal currents over the lake would be just right. He knew when the updrafts would be strong enough to lift his heavy body. He had taught what I still struggle to learn, and that is *"waiting patience."* That eagle sat quietly unaffected by the calm. How often I have fretted and worried instead of waiting. My eagle friend didn't seem to worry that there might not be sufficient wind to fly. He just waited because he knew the breeze would come. What a lesson for me to learn as I wait on God's moving. I need not panic when the downdrafts of life assail me, but wait patiently for the updrafts of God's grace. Waiting and resting will in time bring renewal.

I sat in my brother-in-law's canoe and watched as the wind picked up. Then it happened! Lifting his mighty wings outward the eagle caught the first gust and lifted off. Entranced with the grace and beauty of its flight, I watched the great bird soar upward on the warm air currents off the lake. Soon the eagle was a speck against the bright blue sky. I last saw him heading for the upper lake, no doubt in search of supper. He had left me to return to my fishing, but I will never forget the sermon he preached to me that afternoon. He told me that I too can wait on God. He showed me the strength that comes when I wait upon the Lord. He demonstrated how profitable it is to be patient when soaring is the goal. He proclaimed the results of such renewal as he flew easily on his way.

# 74

## Riverside Renewal

...and be renewed in the spirit of your mind.

—Ephesians 4:23

I too have been caught in the trap of busyness. Preoccupied with the pressures of life and living, I have often become too hurried to get alone with my Master and Maker. It has taken me many a year to realize that I need renewal more than once a year or, if I am pushed, twice annually. Now I seek secluded spots in my busy schedule to get away on a regular basis. If I stay, I work or am forced to work by the "people" job I have. I have learned to revive rustic renewal by going to a pond or lake or another isolated body of water for serenity and stillness. This lesson I learned from my father-in-law.

In the quiet of a lake front cottage in Maine I sigh and pray, *"Speak; for thy servant heareth."* (1 Samuel 3:10) Samuel learned this prayer from Eli, but I learned it on my own through experimentation. I first went to fish or be alone with my wife. It was only after many a trip to this rustic cabin that I learned the Lord was calling. Like Samuel I questioned the voice many times before I realized that it was the Spirit of God calling me to renewal. We cannot find such restoration in the mayhem and madness of the gate. I, like Samuel, work at the door of a sanctuary. Many think what a great place to meet God. Yet I have discovered in my nearly fifty years of being a doorkeeper in the house of the Lord that it has more to do with the Lord's people than the Lord. The phone rings or a knock comes to the door, and my mind is on a hundred details I must remember to do. There is very little time for the Lord. Despite what others might think, the modern church has become a commercial-like complex for the pastor. Technology has given the pastor instant contact with his flock, but it has also given the flock instant contact with the shepherd.

To find renewal one must run away to the isolation of a lakeside. Instead of looking around one must look up to the sky edge and see the hand of God painting a pink sunset. One must watch a flight of geese as they journey across the lake heading south realizing the guidance of God on all life, including yours; to see the reflection of a family of ducks in a late afternoon swimming by reminds one of the unity that must be in the church of God; to listen to the song birds singing in the pine trees surrounding the camp bringing the melody of music that revives the soul. It is as one sits on the porch pondering the eternal values that one sees the contrast between renewal and just rest. The body needs rest, but the soul needs renewal.

In our innermost being we need to realize that it is only as we get alone with God will we be renewed. It is only as we set aside time to be still will our spirit be restored. Seeking renewal takes a commitment of choice and a good teacher like Stacy.

# 75

## Updrafts Upheavals

But they that wait upon the Lord shall renew their strength,
they shall mount up on wings as eagles;
They shall run, and not be weary, they shall walk and not faint.

—Isaiah 40:31

One of the great pleasures of a lakeside is the occasional sighting of an eagle. Watching these great birds has helped me understand Isaiah's purpose for using the eagle in the verse above.

Despite the eagle's great strength and flying ability, I have noticed that the eagle isn't always flying. There are those that teach that God would always have us soaring; we are never to be sad or down; life in Christ is always perfect with never a storm or shower. Yet in the reality of living the Christian life for over sixty years now, I have discovered that God does send rainy days of tears and stormy days with every wind of doctrine (Ephesians 4:14) that would threaten to blow us off our spiritual perch. We are destined for trials and testing against air currents that will alarm us and annoy us. What do we do when these contrary winds begin to blow? Do we see them as enemies or are they sent from God to uplift us and set us soaring?

I have come to believe that in these blustery times that the Spirit of God is in the wind. (John 3:8) He is at work in the environment of our experiences. It is in times like these he expects us to follow the example of the eagle. We are to open our heart and soul to the updraft of the Spirit. We are to place our full weight in the wind of His grace. Ours is not to beat our souls against the gales that blow, but to simply allow those gales to lift us up and above the storm. We are not to fight the fury, but we are to stand up against it. In that standing we will feel the gentle updraft of God's faithfulness carrying us aloft. Ours is to wait for the change, the uplifting hand of God. So often we wrestle against the wrong element. How foolish the eagle would be to start walking into the wind instead of opening his wings and allowing the wind to lift him on high. Yet so often that is what I do. I battle my way through the storm only to realize later that God was at work changing the weather and altering my way. I can only soar when I wait on the Lord. I can only fly as I wait for that updraft. I can only escape the storm when my strength is renewed.

Over the years I have witnessed the majestic flight of many an eagle, and more often than not Stacy was there, but so were other friends like Buster, Harold, and Irving. Each has been special and unique in itself. So too is the flight of the believer. My path will be different than yours. Your course will be different than mine. What we need to do is not watch each other, but set our eyes on the Lord ('turn your eyes upon Jesus, look full into His wonderful face, and the things of earth will grow strangely dim in the light of His glory and grace") if we are to run and not be weary, walk and not faint. Then we must wait for that fresh breeze before we take off. The uplifting Spirit of God will come. The updraft of God's grace will arrive on time.

# 76

## Scraggly Shrub

...ye are God's husbandry...

—1 Corinthians 3:9

The scraggly shrub took root after Martin Vickers planted it near his main camp many years ago. The owner of Vickers' Salmon Pools Camps is a "Mainer" that loves to beautify his cabins which are located on the shores of the Miramichi River in Howard, Canada. Every year (the number is ten now) when I visit the camps I take a look around to see what Martin has planted since I last visited his salmon pools. The scraggly shrub had taken root close against the concrete foundation wall of the first cottage built on the property by Martin's Dad. It is still the only building with a permanent foundation, and its next door neighbor is a work in progress to say the least!

One thing is certain. The straggly shrub is trying to grow in a really tough spot. Because it is so close to the building it gets very little water because the eaves of the camp overhang it. Little rain can get to it except that which is blown in by the wind. It is also situated in the south end of the building where the full sun radiates off the side of the camp making the shrub too hot most of the time. Then there is the soil the short shrub is in. Martin likes to plant things, but I have noticed over the years he doesn't like to tend things. Once they are planted they are on their own. Despite its unpromising location and misshapen appearance, the shoreline shrub is still alive, if not well! (Actually, I came to visit the salmon in the river, but on a beautiful evening like this, and after a successful day on the water I had time to go by and say "hi" to my little shrubby friend.)

Before I left for the Miramichi I got a call from a lady I have yet to meet face to face. She called because of a family that attends the church I pastor in Ellsworth, Maine. From the fifteen-minute conversation we had she sounds much like the shrub by Vickers' Camp. Life has planted her in a family that doesn't care much for her condition, and her condition isn't well. She calls it "Job-like." (Job 1–2) Many years of harshness has eventually made her a shut-in. Physically and spiritually she is a wreck in search of a few answers to her many "whys." The pastor of her church hasn't visited in over a year, and when she sought another pastor from a local church, he said he couldn't get involved. She is beaten and bruised like my little Miramichi bush, but not destroyed, not dying, just a bit discouraged. If I can like a sorry shrub, I can love a sad saint. Despite the fact we have nothing in common, including our "religion," I will visit this lady when I return to my "post" and try to restore her faith in Christians, Christianity, and Christ. If I can visit a shrub in the cool of a Miramichi evening, I can visit a shut-in saint in the heat of an Ellsworth summer.

# 77

## Spotless Snow

...they shall be as white as snow...
—Isaiah 1:18

Believe it or not as I drove into Martin's camp yard on the shores of the Miramichi River yesterday, there were still three feet of snow in places in the woods. This was the first day of May, but for those of us who live in the northern regions of the Americas, this isn't really unusual. What was unusual to me was that most of the snow I saw was still spotless. Granted, the snow near the camp road had been blackened by the cars and trucks that had travelled over the road, but the snow in the deeper parts of the woods protected by trees and shrubs still maintained its whitish color. In a forest that still hadn't changed into its spring green, the white of snow could be seen as spotless.

As I travelled up and down the river on my first full day of fishing, rare was the time I didn't look into the woods along the banks and not see a patch of white snow, snow that had been deposited by an arctic frost many months before, snow that had been piled up storm after storm weeks ago. Despite the nice days like today (that reached into the 60s), the snow is melting very slowly because of the angle of the sun and the cooler night temperatures.

Sometimes it seems that the principalities and powers of evil (Ephesians 6:13), the prince of the power of this world (Ephesians 2:2), can surround us with a drift of sin. Yet in the bleak colors of this world a saint can still keep himself or herself unspotted in this world (James 1:27), just like the patches of Miramichi snow. Locked in the shelter of God's Spirit, the evil powers that would melt us can't penetrate our shield. Instead of being discouraged we need to take a page out of the book of this spring snow pile. Despite the warming temperatures of the age and the hot winds of adversity, let us stay behind the wonderful armor that God has given to us. (Ephesians 6:14–18) As I witnessed the dogged determination of a few piles of snow resisting the forces to melt them, I thought I also can resist. (James 4:7) I can refuse to allow my spotless life to be blackened by the wickedness and muddiness of this world.

Like the patches of white in the forests along the shores of the Miramichi, we too need to be a bright spot in an otherwise bleak world. We need to hang on until the great Spotless One returns and covers this old black world with a glistening group of snow-white saints. You might be the only patch of white at your job site, or at your school, or in your family. Don't be discouraged over those who have already melted ("fallen away," 2 Thessalonians 3:2) and run off ("departed," 1 Timothy 4:1). Others might, but we don't have to. Granted, you will stand out, but spotless righteousness is still needed today. Remember that "pure religion" (James 1:27) transcends everything else in the Christian life. To be white as snow is more than a metaphor of an ancient sage.

# 78

## Twin Trees

Bear ye one another's burdens . . .

—GALATIANS 6:2

It is about seven o'clock, and I am looking out the back window of Martin's cabin watching a beautiful Miramichi morning developing. Immediately before me are two fir trees that have rooted themselves on the edge of the bank that drops quickly about twenty feet below to the river. When the land was cleared in the 1940s to create the first of what is now three camps, these twin trees were left to grow and mature. Their friends were removed so that an unobstructed view up the Miramichi could be created.

Tucked between the twin trees is an observation deck. It, like the trees, is anchored in the bank of the river. Sometimes, according to Irving Vickers, the caretaker of the camps, the water actually engulfs these trees. During the spring runoff the river can be backed up by an ice jam, and the Miramichi actually flows around the "clump" of trees. In order for the deck to survive it has to be chained to the trees. Yet from this shelter one can look both up and down the mighty Miramichi and in those cherished moments witness the rising or rolling of a salmon. I have sat and watched the boats cruising up and down the waterway from here. From between those two trees I have smelled that sweet smell of water and wind in my face, and added to the savor of the river is the pleasant aroma of the firs.

From the first time I laid my eyes on this set of trees they have become one of my favorite meditating spots, a sanctuary of peace and solitude unmatched anywhere. Oh, don't get me wrong. I have other spots as precious, but none so desirable than the tiny sanctuary overlooking the Miramichi River. Over the years I have played with deer and groundhogs from that spot. (I even have the movies and pictures to prove it!) I have read favorite books and just dreamed of the salmon I would catch on the next trip up the river and "around the bend." It has also been an inspirational spot for me as it is this morning. As the rays of a new day's sun filter through the branches to strike the front lawn just in front of my cabin, I see robins gathering for breakfast. As I observe this scene I think this is how creation must have been when the sun first cast its light on God's newly created trees. (Genesis 1:11–14) Unlike these twin trees God's first trees were created in an instant, born in maturity and fully developed.

Often as I visit Vickers' Camps I stand beside the trees coveting their company and finding in them a wonderful spot to meet my Savior. It is in such places I ask myself and my Master, "Are you as well pleased with my progress as you are with these twin trees? Do I give others as much inspiration and illumination as this clump of trees?" Then I pray, "Dear Lord, make me as pleasant to others. Allow me to shelter others and cast a helpful shadow."

# 79

## Barked Birches

Set your affection on things above . . .

—Colossians 3:2

In my region of the world, white-barked birch trees are a native species. Personally, I believe they are the prettiest trees in the forest. These elegant trees thrive in the cold and cool climate of Maine, my home state, and as I look out the camp window of Vickers' cabin I see two small birch trees thriving in a Canadian province.

Many people use the white birch tree in their landscaping which is fine, but I love the looks of a God-planted birch. These two stately trees on a bank overlooking the Miramichi River are two such examples. In my four days at Vickers' Salmon Pools, I have walked past them to and fro every time I have gone fishing with Jason, my guide. The two soaring spires of faded white sway gracefully in the breeze each time a wind blows up or down the river. They are sheltered from the upriver wind by two giant furs (giants compared to my two favorite birches!). They have become two friends seeing I have visited them fifteen times in ten years. I leave tomorrow for home, but I will take with me their barked beauty, their stately strength, and their enduring energy in this devotional.

They live in a threatening world. Where they are located a good sized ice jam could take them out. How they have survived up to this point is only by the grace of God. As darkness settles over the Miramichi River Valley, I see them still in the gathering dusk. Still bare-limbed, their slender length seems so fragile. Their buds are not yet open, and they seem so thin and vulnerable to the elements. Yet I know their strength, stability, and stamina comes from above, and so too should mine and yours.

There are no twin spires of a cathedral that are any more impressive to me. Stretching skyward, these two barked birches are a living testimony of where we ought to focus our eyes. They have been a constant reminder to me that I must focus my attention, fasten my eyes, and turn my heart towards God. Today I sought another blessing from God. Yesterday, it came in the form of a special salmon, but today I caught no salmon, no hits, no taps, and no landings. The closest I got was to watch as a fully grown male jumped completely out of the water just twenty feet in front of me. I tried to catch him, but I will only take that mental snapshot home with me. So my blessing today has been my two white birches. Whether in a wintry gale or a summer down pour; whether in a gentle spring breeze or a windy autumn, they stand clean and white always pointing heavenward and God-ward.

I too can stand white as snow washed in the blood of the Lamb (1 John 1:7). I too can stand where my God has planted me, pointing others upward. It is my prayer that by staying put and standing tall I might inspire others as my "friends" have inspired me.

# 80

# Bonus Blessings

... who has blessed us ...

—Ephesians 1:3

The morning was overcast as Jason and I waited for the sun to break over the eastern ridge. There was that muted promise in the air that the day would be the best a spring day could be in Canada. Jason and I were black salmon fishing upriver from Vickers' Camps. The wind was light, but the warming night temperatures had melted more snow and ice from the forests of central New Brunswick, and the river was rising which is a poor fishing sign. With the rising of the water came the dry grasses and dead twigs from along the shores of the Miramichi River which was turning the water a brownish color. Rising water and a dirty river usually means "no fish," but Jason and I were in for a special miracle from God on this "the day the Lord hath made."

Slowly, we fished a sheltered stretch of the river known locally as Washburn's Pool. Located on a narrow section of the river, this favorite hole of my father-in-law's has been a stopping off place for me for ten years now. This was my first time with Jason, my old guide's son-in-law. Irving had matched Jason and me up because he knew that I knew the river so this was a case of a "guide" trusting a "sport" instead of a sport trusting a guide. As I worked my way down through the run, I could see that Jason was getting a bit discouraged. The conditions on the river were getting worse with each "drop." Yesterday, we had seen fifteen salmon, but it appeared that this day would be a "fishless" day.

But I had committed my day to the Lord, and I had simply asked for "a blessing." Recently at church a young lady had read a story with the punch line being, *"God has many blessings for us, but we simple don't ask for them."* Jesus taught that our Father will give good gifts to them that ask. (Matthew 7:7–9) A few weeks before this trip my wife and I coveted together to simply ask and watch for God's blessings. Sure enough, within an hour when nobody else in the lodge was catching fish, I had caught two salmon.

I am writing this devotional as the sun sets over the Miramichi. I can look back on my day now and *"count my blessings"* and *"name them one by one,"* as the old Church hymn goes. Numbered among them could be the wonderful deer steak supper I just finished. I could also thank the Lord for the warmest day of the year—summer-like! But for the fisherman in me, the blessings of this day happened on my last "drop" before lunch and my last "cast" before supper. Catching an Atlantic salmon is hard enough so to catch not one but two on the last cast is amazing. Before lunch I landed a 25 inch salmon, but on the last cast of the day I hooked into a 33 incher. With each fish I laughed, and Jason rejoiced as the Good Lord blessed us with a four-fish day when everybody else went fishless. Next time you ask the Lord for a blessing, be careful to watch for the "bonus" blessings as well.

# 81

# Canadian Call

As cold waters to a thirsty soul, so is good news from a far country.

—Proverbs 25:25

Each time I visit Vickers' Camps on the shores of the Miramichi River, I am haunted by old memories. I am once again watching the last rays of a sunset on these beloved banks as I end another wonderful salmon fishing trip. I have had worse trips numbers-wise, and I have had better, but I can't stay in Martin's cabin without remembering my father-in-law and how each trip would start.

Between April 15 and May 15 for six years I waited by my telephone in anticipation of a call from Stacy. I knew that he in turn was waiting a call from Canada. Stacy Meister and Irving Vickers had a system in place which resulted in when best to make the annual trek to the Miramichi for spring salmon fishing. Irving would watch the river and say, "The salmon are biting!" Stacy in turn would call me and say, "Irving called. We leave in the morning!" I in turn knew that I must within hours be packed and on the road to Stacy's home in northern Maine. The call might come day or night so about the beginning of April I got ready.

Stacy left for his heavenly home nearly four years ago so now it is me that makes the calls to see if the fishing is good and if there is an opening at the lodge. Like Stacy my old friend and guide is sick, and I fear that I soon will not be getting any Canadian calls. What those old unexpected, expected calls use to teach me was the importance of being ready *"at a moment's notice."* Is not that what Jesus taught? "Watch therefore: for ye know not what hour your Lord doth come." (Matthew 24:42) As I finish up the final hours at Squirrel Tail Camp (Martin's new name for his cabin), I am reminded that there is still one more "far country call" that Stacy and I will participate in. "For the Lord Himself shall descend from heaven with a shout. . .and with the trumpet of God: and the dead in Christ shall rise first: then we which are alive and remain shall be caught up together with them in the clouds, to meet the Lord in the air. . ." (1 Thessalonians 4:16, 17)

When the Lord calls us home for the final time, Stacy will be united with his new body as I will be changed. (1 Corinthians 15:50,51) Like on our trips to the Miramichi, we shall meet at a chosen place (the skies) and will then travel on together until we reach our cabin on the shore of the river that flows from the throne of God. (Revelation 22:1) My prayer is that our guide will be with us on this final trip. I am still a thirsty soul waiting that good news from a far country that will unite me again with my favorite fishing buddy. My bags are packed, my fishing reel is greased, and my rods are ready for my next Canadian call, and so too am I ready for the celestial call.

# 82

## Frozen Flow

...showers of blessings...

—Ezekiel 34:26

In nine springs on the Miramichi I have had only one guide, Irving Vickers, the doctor's cousin, the owner of the camps. But when I arrived at Vickers' Salmon Pools this year, I found that Irving was sick. He had lost fifty pounds in a few weeks and was a shell of his former robust self. The iron man of the river who could pull up a heavy anchor rope with a few graceful jerks could hardly get out of his chair. The verdict isn't in yet, and I fear for him, but the truth was clear. There was no way Irving could guide me on this my tenth anniversary to the "river." So who would?

I am back after my first day fishing the mighty Miramichi without Irving Vickers as my guide. It has been a good day. I have had worse, and I have had better. I hooked five salmon and landed four including a 32 incher which jumped six times and just before being netted broke my rod. Besides the five salmon hooked six others came close with three taps and three rolls. My new guide was Irving Vickers' son-in-law, Jason Luce. Interestingly, on my first day on the Miramichi ten years ago I also hooked five fish with Irving as my guide. The difference between the two men was that ten years ago Irving was in his twentieth year of guiding whereas this was Jason's first spring guiding.

As we got to know each other our conversation worked its way to the Miramichi and the winter that had just passed. The normally free flowing

Miramichi gets ice bound in the cold of a Canadian winter. It is chilled by frosty winds and frozen by dropping temperatures until its banks are hard as stone, and its surface is locked with ice. Jason talked of the deadness of this sweet singing river which I found hard to believe because I had never seen the river covered in ice. Even in the deadness of winter I see only the graceful watershed as it flows unrestricted to the sea. Then it hit me. This is exactly how the Lord Jesus Christ sees us, not as a heart turned to ice because of the snows of sin; not as a life dead (Ephesians 2:1) because of the ice jams of transgressions; not as a soul covered in the drifts of iniquity, but as a life that only needs the spring thaw of God's love (Romans 5:8) and the cold, frigid frost of shortcomings forgiven and flowing again.

What God's spring rains and warm temperatures does for the Miramichi, God's sweet forgiveness and "showers of blessings" does for the frozen soul. Springtime changes things on the Miramichi, and so does God's amazing grace on the human heart. Despite the deadness, there is under that snow and ice a flow still rushing to the ocean, and as long as we live in the age of mercy and grace there is in each life a chance that the warm wind of God's Spirit can blow across the layers of sin and self until the day of "ice out" or in our case "sin-out."

# 83

## Home Hills

*I will lift up mine eyes unto the hills...*
—PSALMS 121:1

I am home again after another pleasant trip to the Miramichi River and Vickers' camps. The wonderful spot is only five hours from home, but each time I return I think about how I use to travel to and from my favorite salmon fishing hole.

In the early days I use to travel north to meet my father-in-law at his home in northern Maine. Before we headed east I would travel three and a half hours north. Then it was another three and a half hours to Vickers' Salmon Pools. Why I did this I really don't know. I knew of a shorter route, but I guess I wanted to be with my favorite fishing buddy. So I would travel late in the day to get to Stacy's so we could get up early and travel over the Renuos Highway. The winding country road runs from Plaster Rock to Upper Blackville for nearly one hundred miles. It is one of the most tranquil and delightful drives I know of anywhere—that is if you love salmon fishing. It is only two lanes wide cut out of virgin forest and rocky hills that reach deep into central New Brunswick. For most of its length the highway runs along the ridge of a range of hills. Throughout its entire length there are no homes or buildings of any kind. The only exception is that at the halfway mark there is a small gas station and motel. The roadway is lined with fir, spruce, poplar, and maple trees.

From Plaster Rock the road starts a gentle rise to the central hills. I have driven that road with Stacy in fine weather and in stormy weather, yet without exception, once over the summit a new world appears. On the backside of the range is the wonderful world of the Miramichi River Valley. It was to that world Stacy first took me in 1992. Each time we went we traveled back and forth across the Renuos Highway. More often than not we would return with a cooler full of fish and many a "fish story" to tell. As we started our climb back over the hills at a certain peak we could see the distant hazy hills of home—our first glimpse of America after a few days in a foreign land. Despite the desire to stay a bit longer there is something about the sight of home, even if it is only a distant hill.

I too come from the hills and hollows of northern Maine, and though I now live on the coast of Maine, I still see the hills of home as a welcome sign. It is sad, but there are many people that see God only as some distant hazy "being" sitting on some throne in deep space. The difference between the two is that I have climbed those hills and explored those valleys just like I have spent time with God and found Him to be personal, not distant. Even from afar I say with the psalmist above, when you know the Lord even a distant glimpse is like being by His side.

# 84

## Reverend Robin

Behold the fowls of the air . . .

—MATTHEW 6:26

I have been taking literally Christ's admonition to "look at the fowls of the air." Sometimes, however, His birds aren't in the air, but on the ground, like the camp robin. On this morning at Vickers' Camps with not so ideal conditions the neighborhood robin is still "bob, bob, bobbing along" carefree and careful not to miss his Heavenly Father's breakfast. He was so watching for Mr. Worm and Mrs. Grub that he didn't see the fisherman on his trail and tail. Just before I stepped on him I paused to view again the vista formed by the Miramichi River. I must admit I wasn't paying attention to the lone robin on the riverbank. As I stood there silent and still I noticed the dancing feet of the robin skipping from worm hole to worm hole. I took my eyes off the river to see the robin busy at his work. He or she was fat and plump. My first thought was, "Boy, your Heavenly Father has been feeding you well!" As my eyes saw the robin at my feet my eyes also saw my belly, and I thought, "Yes, your Heavenly Father has been feeding you just as well!"

As soon as Mr. Robin realized that he had been spotted, he raced up the lawn towards the big camp. I followed. The closer I got the robin took to wing and swiftly and surely flew away to the safety of a tree branch in the woods beyond. In an instant I forgot about the river and the salmon swimming down it, and my mind began to focus on our Father—Mr. Robin's and mine. We have the same one according to the Bible. Yes, the same one.

Despite our minds and imaginations and abilities to reason with emotion, will, and sensitive spirit, we are no better off than the robin when it comes to our Father's care. Granted, the Bible says we are more valuable than many birds, (Matthew 10:31), but in the category of supply and demand, God cares for us both.

We live in a world that "struts its stuff" thinking it doesn't need anyone's help including God's. We hear the scientists say that "mother earth" cares for the birds. The proud professors tell their students to "trust in themselves," yet as my robin friend headed for the woods I could only hear this little rhyme I learned as a kid.

Said the Robin to the Sparrow,

> "I should really like to know,
> Why these anxious human beings
> Rush about and worry so?"
> Said the Sparrow to the Robin,
> "Friend, I think that it must be,
> That they have no Heavenly Father
> Such as cares for you and me."

My feathered friend reminded me again that God wants "fat" robins and He wants "fat" Barry's filled to the brim with God's provisions, carefree and Christ-like. (Matthew 6:24–31)

# 85

# Special Salmon

I have fought a good fight.

2 Timothy 4:7

The rough, rugged shoreline winds its way through stands of fir and spruce. When I am at Vickers' Camps on the Miramichi River, I like to walk the waterside of this watershed. I go alone to find quiet company with my Heavenly Father. The great river dominates the wild terrain on either side. Its broad sweeping flow fills the valley area of central New Brunswick, Canada. This is the kind of walking path of which the artist dreams and the author writes.

Two days ago and for the fifteenth time overall, I stood alone again in the presence of the old river. Its whole world however is buried beneath a quiet surface of ice and snow fed runoff. More than ever its banks are full, and its runs are brimming with escaping Atlantic salmon. It is for that I have come to this mighty river. Strong, superb, and silvery, these great travelers are about to travel again. After resting and spawning in the gravel bars of home, the Atlantic salmon is off with the ice flows to their great feeding grounds off Greenland. It will be a tough trip with thousands of miles of obstacles and predators, but they shall overcome until they return to this same river a few years from now. As they go my Copper Renuos (a bright spring salmon fly created by my father-in-law, Stacy Meister) will bid them a fond farewell.

In three days I hope to catch and release as many of these salmon as possible. I hope to record their images on film, both still and moving. I have quite a collection of pictures now, but a fisherman never has enough. With my guide Jason Luce we had a good start yesterday as we saw and recorded fifteen sightings. We got four of them to the boat, but each close encounter was a treasure. Slipping my camera from its waterproof case, Jason captured a picture of the first monarch I took from the river about an hour after we started fishing. Against an overcast sky the glittering sides and size of the "big black" stood out against my bright blue jacket and hat. The picture turned out to be a grand old veteran that had fought the good fight. It had been many years since a spring-run salmon had put up such a struggle. At least six times the submariner came airborne. Jason got every jump on my movie camera. After fifteen minutes I nearly had the heavy weight to the boat when it made its final attempt to escape by snapping my rod in two. But the old warrior was hooked well, and I hand-lined the special salmon the rest of the way to Jason's net.

My years have been long, and I too have travelled and battled many a foe. I remember well the day I was caught by the fly of love cast to me by the Lord Himself. I thought when I was hooked it was all over, but the Lord caught me and then released me back into my world.

# 86

## Silent Sun

... the Sun of Righteousness ...

—MALACHI 4:2

We all know that the sun is at the epicenter of our solar system. I also believe it was created on the fourth day of time as we know it, and that it has faithfully fulfilled the function for which it was created. Because of its size its strength pulls everything towards it, but this gravitational pull isn't its only power.

I am ending my second day on the Miramichi River for this trip. I came 48 hours ago to fish for spring-run salmon. I am staying at Vickers' Camps located in Howard, New Brunswick, Canada. For as long as I have been coming to this place I have brought every piece of warm clothing I own. More often than not the temperature rarely reaches fifty. The 40s are a normal temperature for this time of the year with the teens being the normal night lows. The cabin I stay in normally becomes a "moose yard," what my father-in-law would call a cold night in camp. We always had to build a fire in the Franklin stove to ward off "frostbite." Rare has been the night that Jack Frost's footprints haven't been seen on the front lawn and the cottage roof. Yet when I arrived on Tuesday, it was in the 60s. Yesterday it was in the 70s, and this afternoon it hit 80. (I have the sunburn to prove it. Winter skin isn't use to the 80s!) The sun showed off its second greatest power today—a hot heat.

In the last 48 hours the sun has created rivulets of running streams from every snow bank still in the woods in the Miramichi River Valley. From every frozen ice chunk has come more liquid, and with every passing moment since I arrived the Miramichi River has been rising. It is my custom upon arriving at the camps to put a marking stick on the shoreline. Because the salmon fishing depends so much on the dropping of the river it is important to watch its progress. I have seen the river rise four feet in a day, but always because of a heavy rain. I had never witnessed the river rise under sunny skies until now. The power of the sun had turned a fishable river on Tuesday to a fishless river on Thursday. The Lord had been good to me and my guide Jason Luce despite the worsening conditions. We caught nine fish in two days. Nevertheless, the Lord was reminding me of the strength of the silent sun.

Malachi tells us that Jesus is "the Sun of Righteousness." Sometimes we don't see Him as He works in our lives until we place some marker on our soul to visibly see the change. A case in point has been the tremendous spiritual progress my dear wife has been making over the last few months. She doesn't see it herself, but I do because like my Miramichi marker, I see where she began and to where she has risen. The Lord is melting away banks of old feelings and frozen situations that will bring new life.

# 87

# Theological Thaw

We love him, because He first loved us.
—1 John 4:19

As I wait the promise of spring I thought often about the unusual winter we were having. It wasn't that it was not typical of the old fashioned Maine winters of the past, but this was my fifteenth winter on the coast of Maine, and I had been spoiled along with the rest of my neighbors. Snow, ice, and bitter winds hadn't lasted long on the previous winters of memory so when this season lasted well into spring it became a cruel contest of wills. Many people got dismayed and discouraged, but I kept saying, "Fishing is just around the corner." I too was disappointed when I made my annual call to the Miramichi guide Irving Vickers to learn that unlike last year the ice was still in the river. That meant there would be no salmon fishing on opening day (April 15) this year. I would have to wait a bit longer.

And then it happened! A stiff southern wind arrived and with it milder temperatures. The high snow banks began to disappear rapidly. The entire coast of Maine began to stir from its wintery slumber. It was as if someone had flipped a switch, and winter simply melted away. From every high place I began to hear the "drip, drip, drip" of water. These soft drops were like the opening notes to a new song. With the drips came the small singing streams that trickled down the streets and lanes of the city. Within days I had taken off my long johns, my heavy coat, and my winter boots. Day by day and hour by hour the snow and ice disappeared and the call for which I had been waiting. "The ice is out of the Miramichi. Come next week. It ought to be perfect fishing." I am writing these thoughts from Vickers' Camps on the shores of that river. I have just finished my first day with five salmon hooked, and I have the "thaw" to thank.

As I ponder this blessing I am acutely aware of another thaw taking place in my family. After nearly thirty years of struggling with her relationship with her Heavenly Father, my dear wife is coming out of a theological frost that has stunted her spiritual growth. After years of frosty relationships I see a beautiful thawing taking place. What used to be winter weather in her soul has burst forth into a spiritual spring, a warming up that is wonderful. It is a gradual and gentle thaw at best, but as with the Miramichi River, they are the best. If the temperatures rise too quickly, the snow in the woods will melt too rapidly which brings up the river making it unfishable. God's warm winds of grace have been blowing on my wife's soul over the last few months melting old falsehoods and mellowing old beliefs, transforming my dear one into a sweeter, kinder, understandable image of Himself. (Romans 8:29) Out of the depths of a tough, rough spiritual winter has emerged a creation that is as fresh as an evening breeze over the Miramichi because of the thaw that comes with God's love.

# 88

## Wood Warmth

He warreth himself, and saith, Aha, I am warm . . .
—Isaiah 44:16

There is a wonderful warmth that greets you when you walk into a building heated with wood, a "primitive perfume" to those of us that love the smell of smoke. Added to the crackle of the wood fire is the fine fragrance that only a wood stove or fireplace can give off. As I sit at Martin Vickers' desk overlooking the beautiful Miramichi River, I am missing such a warmth. Believe it or not, this is the third night at the camp called Squirrel Tail that I haven't needed a fire. It was in the 80s today and 70s yesterday so there was no need for a fire in the Franklin stove in the corner. I still miss the warmth that comes from wood.

My father-in-law, Stacy Meister, and I started coming to this camp on the Miramichi River in 1992. In the early days the camp wasn't insulated so once the sun went down so too did the temperature in the cabin. A black Franklin stove rests in the far corner of the living room. I brought in two arm loads of wood the evening I arrived as has been my habit since I started coming to Vickers' Salmon Pool Camps. I was positive I would have to light the Franklin to ward off the cold Canadian nights that were sure to come.

Stacy loved the warmth from a fire in the evening as well as watching the fire. The multi-colored flairs of orange, red, amber, and gold are a pleasant picture to the pupils of one's eyes and a solace to one's soul. I still, after hundreds of campfires and bond fires and stove fires, can sit and watch a fire until it goes out. I still love the warmth on my cold feet after a wet day in the boat. I still love the heat that gets through to your bones after a frosty day on the river. The first thing Stacy and I always did when we got to the camp, either from home or the river, was to build a fire. Once created it drew you to its warmth. There is nothing quite like the warm hug from a wood heat after a cold day Atlantic salmon fishing.

My fishing partner died three and a half years ago from lung and liver cancer. We got nine trips into the camp together, and I have had six since. In many ways it isn't the same, but in one area it is—the Franklin is still in the corner ready to give me wood warmth when and if I need it. One other thing that hasn't changed; my Lord is still meeting me here. I realized it was God's heat that has kept me warm these last 48 hours. It has been his warm breeze blowing in the window all these nights. The aroma of wood smoke might not be filling the cabin tonight, but the aroma of God's river and surrounding woods is. The happy crackling fire can't be heard in the living room, but I can still hear the tinkling river flowing gently by the window where I write these thoughts. The superb warmth of the fire is not my comfort and contentment tonight, but rather the warm wind of God blowing through the window.

# 89

## Wild Wings

. . . a still small voice . . .

—1 Kings 19:12

I don't think I have ever fished the Miramichi River in the spring and seen more birds then I have on this current trip. I leave this tranquil place in the morning for the hustle and bustle of the city life. This morning stillness was still in control. I woke to a veil of thin delicate clouds. My guide called them "a washboard." I must admit I had never seen a set of clouds like them before. It was as if the valley was posed for the rush of wild wings.

They were everywhere. There were robins on the lawn and ducks on the river. There were fish hawks over the river and cormorants in the river. You would have thought I was in a bird sanctuary, not one of the primer Atlantic salmon rivers of the world. Today, because of the dirty Miramichi, my guide and I travelled eight miles up the Cain's River to find a "clean run" of water to fish. On the trip up the Cain's we met many more fowl. More narrow then the Miramichi, the Cain's provided us an amphitheater to listen to the sound of wild wings.

At first they were barely audible, a mere echo off the steep walls of the canyon where the Cain's ran through. Then from around the corner came the muted notes of a pair of ducks. They seemed surprised to see Jason and me in the front of Buttermilk Brook. They quickly altered their course to the other side of the river bypassing us just a few feet above the river's flow. Their cry only added to the wilderness experience I was having. Combined with the rushing sound of the water over a rocky bottom was the rustling sound along the bank itself. The two ducks created an airborne melody that I still can hear. Then it came! A pause, "a selah" (do you know it-check your Book of Psalms in the Bible); an interlude of intense silence after the ducks had turned the next corner and went out of sight. Without a quack-quack my guide and I were left with the water and the music of wild wings.

Moments later the forest birds that had been shut out by the passing ducks reclaimed their place in the wilderness symphony. You know the sound I am talking about, the chorus of birds that wake you on a spring morning when you have your bedroom window open. It is a most pleasant chorus, and that sound continued until Jason started the Mercury for our return trip down the Cain's. We were escorted periodically down the river by the sound of wild wings.

Have you ever studied the Bible just to notice its many mentions about birds? I have. God created the birds on the fifth day of creation (Genesis 1:20) along with the fish I was fishing for to remind us humans just "what is what." Birds cause us to look skyward. (Colossians 3:2) This is my fifteenth message from the Lord in four days, and I dare say when I get home it will be four months before I hear fifteen more. I have so much thanks to give to the birds of the Buttermilk Brook for the great interlude they gave me on this trip because I have learned much from their wild wings.

# 90

# Sudden Surprise

...and the son of man, that thou visiteth him?
—PSALMS 8:4

It had been another wonderful few days on the banks of the Miramichi River. I had come to land a few retreating salmon from one of the world's greatest Atlantic salmon fisheries, but as usual it was the sudden surprise I remember most, not the salmon.

It was my first spring fishing trip with my good friend from Ellsworth, Maine, Fireman Mike Hangge. I had talked to him for years about this fabled place called Vickers' Salmon Pools. He had gone on a fall trip, but had never been to the riverside to witness the sudden surprises of nature in spring. And sure enough, it happened on the first morning we were there. As we sat at breakfast Mike suddenly said, "Look at that!" Because I was watching the river for any signs of a rising salmon, I had failed to spot the deer as it made its way around the corner of the lodge. As if on holiday the young female paid no attention as it fed on the new grass sprouting from the lawn in front of us.

For the first few minutes Mike and I stared, open mouth and all, at the beautiful white-tailed deer that had disrupted our bacon and eggs. Then it came to us that we ought to get a few pictures of this wonderful bonus to our fishing trip. I grabbed my movie camera, and Mike went for his "Canon." Over the next quarter of an hour we snapped pictures and made footage of the deer as it ate its way across the lawn in front of the main lodge. Not once did this gem of the woods act afraid or concerned. No doubt it was hungry and was going to get in a good breakfast before the busy camp yard was filled with guides and "sports."

Eventually, I ventured out on the front deck to get one final shot, and then and only then did the Miramichi deer turn its head and nod "goodbye" with a wave of its white tail. I watched as it took several huge leaps and vanished across the small stream at the back of the camp yard to the forest beyond. Even after the deer disappeared Mike and I talked of this rare sudden surprise that certainly started our Miramichi morning out on the right foot.

As one reads through the Bible one can't help but notice the times the Good Lord shows up unexpectedly. Unannounced, He appears without an invitation yet in tracing these surprise visits I have noticed the various reasons why God pays these calls on His people:

1. To commune with His man. "And they heard the voice of the Lord God walking in the garden in the cool of the day. . ." (Genesis 3:8)

2. To convey His message. "And the Lord appeared unto him in the plains of Mamre: and he sat in the tent door in the heat of the day." (Genesis 18:1)

3. To correct a mistake. "And he said, 'Who are thou Lord?' And the Lord said 'I am Jesus whom thou persecutes. . .'" (Acts 9:5)

How long does it take for you to recognize a visit from God?

# 91

# Likable Lad

A man that hath friends must shew himself friendly . . .
—Proverbs 18:24

Irv. That was the name given when I first met him on the shores of the Miramichi River. It was my father-in-law's nickname for his favorite salmon guide—Irving "Irv" Vickers.

Irv is a breed all to himself. He has alert eyes that can catch the slightest movement of nature, a fleeing deer or a rising salmon. His ears are also very sensitive to the slightest change in the noises of nature. Despite arthritis in his massive woodsman's hands he is quick to pull an anchor rope or a motor cord, especially when heading out after salmon. The years have taken their toll on him, but he still, even after thirty years, in love with "the river."

Trip after trip Irv and I have developed a friendship much like the one my father-in-law had with him for over twenty years. Stacy died of liver and lung cancer nearly four years ago, and since our last fishing trip together Irv has been my Miramichi guide, that is until this last trip.

I arrived for my tenth spring only to find that my dear friend was sick. He is a puzzle to the doctors, but I could see from first glance that Irv was very thin and very sad. Three months of illness had taken fifty pounds off his strong body frame. The laugh and smile were still there, but the energy level was down. Despite the setback, I enjoyed my three days fishing with Irv's son-in-law, Jason Luce, but my greatest joy was once again spending some quality time with Irv on the banks of the Miramichi River.

As has been our custom since I first visited Vickers' Salmon Pools, Irv took me on a tour of the camp yard to see all the improvements he has made since I was last there. The brand new third camp (Green Machine) was done except for a few touches here and there. The diverting of the springs from behind the camps had been completed combining a half dozen springs into a small stream, a stream the camp owner, Martin Vickers, Irv's cousin, has calls "Irv's Stream." Perhaps the most pleasant part of the time there was a two hour talk on the banks of the river joking and talking about the past trips with Stacy. What a joy it was for me to be in the company of the most "likable lad" in Howard, New Brunswick, Canada.

As I reflect on my gracious and gentle guide, I ponder how this present world only sees wonder in "something special, something sensational, or something spectacular." They are not impressed with a special bond that is made between two strangers. I know of such "a miracle." When Jesus came to make a friend of me (John 15:15), we were strangers, but He still called me "Bear." He knew my nickname, and He used it to call me unto Himself. The world is full of likable lads so make a friend as Jesus made a friend of you and me.

# 92

## Singing Stream

Be still, and know that I am God.
—Psalms 46:10

They call it "Irv's Spring," and it will create, I believe, another salmon hole for Vickers Salmon Pools.

Behind the cabins of Vickers' camp yard are a number of small springs. When I first visited these cabins on the banks of the Miramichi River in 1992, there was enough water flowing from those springs to create a small pond between the main cottage and Martin's cabin. Over the years the water from those springs have only made the yard muddy and served no useful purpose until this year. Upon arriving for my annual black salmon fishing trip I discovered that Irving Vickers, the camp manager, had diverted all the water from those various springs to a single stream on the backside of the third cabin. A small singing stream was created that now flows into the Miramichi River just below the Camp Run.

It is a beautiful little trickle of water that now highlights what was once an open area between the woods in the back and the river in the front. I walked its short course, and I heard a song. All streams make music. Granted, the bigger brooks are louder, but the smaller streams are more soothing to the soul. It is a solemn song that rises and falls, rises and falls, with each pebble and stone in the narrow stream bed. It's never ending melody is the result of an unending supply of water. Some streams dry up in the heat of summer, but a spring fed stream—never!

I had come to enjoy the music of the mighty Miramichi. The low deep rush of the river softly surrounded me as I slept. Without any rapids on that stretch of the waterway the mighty flow isn't loud or overbearing. In contrast Irv's stream has a louder sound than the gigantic river into which it flows. The sound of forest animals and birds combined with the winds of the valley blend together giving a heavenly quality to the symphony, and now a singing soprano of the stream has been added to the choir.

In its crisp notes one finds solitude and a reprieve from the noises of the modern world. Martin has brought cable and telephone into Vickers' yard, but I stay away from these like a plague. I prefer to talk to the animals, and I prefer to listen to the waters—mighty or mini. It is as if you walk back in time when you stroll along the big stream or "Irv's Spring." There is not a note of human activity that can penetrate the singing stream. Only the song of the stream can be heard.

Only at such places and in such positions can we really hear the Father speak, the somber sounds of a stream echoing the audible voice of God. It is the supernatural awareness that God is there, and His voice sounds like a singing stream—"Irv's Spring." When was the last time you heard the voice of God? Have you checked the local brook?

# 93

## Icy Image

He casteth forth his ice like morsels . . .

—Psalms 147:17

This year on the opening day of fishing the Miramichi River was still full of ice. I was not there, but my salmon guide, Jason Luce, was telling me about it as we fished together in the first week of May. Opening day for salmon fishing on the mighty Canadian river is April 15, and usually by that date the river has thrown off its winter coat of white and overcoat of ice. Jason's description of ice-out went something like this:

"I stood on the banks of the river overlooking an icy waterway. Its surface was a dark expanse of packed ice. On the morning of ice-out the ice, nearly two feet thick, had a distinct appearance of an old garment which was pitted and moth eaten. But there was something happening to the ice underneath. A distant rumble like the dull thunder of a coming summer storm began to reverberate down the valley. Then came tumbling down its length a growing roar! The sound of moving ice silenced every other sound around the camps. Then, just as suddenly, another surge of thunder came cascading down the river valley like the sound of heavy artillery in a war. A mighty hand below the ice pack began to move the surface of the upper ice around the corner. Gigantic pressures and great friction began to fracture and crack the once united river ice. Unseen forces were at work on the ice-locked waterway. Added to the power of the water was the power of the sun shining down on the Miramichi. From below and above the icy image of the river was transformed into a rough and rugged sea of ice cubes!"

As I thought of this word picture described to me by my guide, I thought of how much this mirrored the society that I was living in today. Like the Miramichi River my world is caught in an icy grip of apathy and affluence. Cynicism and crime have made our world cold and frosty. The culture has become solidly sinful. Man has become cool to the things of God and cold to anything holy. Selfishness and sordid gains have taken the place of helping the helpless. Locked in sinister sins, the flow of the world has been hid under a covering of hard lasciviousness and lust. The cloak of cruelty has replaced the "robe of righteousness."

Yet, as I look over my frozen, sin-covered world I hear a rumble, a distant thunder. It is the Spirit's trumpet sounding as I hear the moving of God upon my world. The Sun of Righteousness (Malachi 4:2) is shining down on this world, and the breath of His Holy Spirit is still flowing under and through this world. (John 7:38,39) And just as spring temperatures and spring flows break up the mighty ice on the Miramichi so too shall come a day when this world will be freed from its icy prison house of sin. The Son of Righteousness will come and open this world to a thousand years of sin-free days!

# 94

## Red-Breasted Robin

Behold the fowls of the air...

—Matthew 6:26

I have never been to Vickers' Camps in the spring that the robins haven't beaten me there. This is not unusual because normally I don't get to my favorite salmon lodge before the end of April or the first of May, plenty of time for the local robin population to return.

A short distance from the camp yard on the hill a hundred yards from the main cottage there is a small marsh. It is less than an acre in area. It lies quietly tucked in by the camp road to its left and the forest to its right. Here the first birds of the spring like to come and rest. Here the early bird loves to sing its favorite tune as I walk past on my evening stroll to the road.

But spring had come late and moved in slowly this year. Already it was past the time when the trees should have been budded and the snow in the woods should have been gone. The hill up to the marsh was still frosty, and the woodland around the marsh still was drab and dull. The whole Miramichi River Valley was simply waiting for winter to leave. The country seemed bored with all the ice and snow that had come early and stayed late, but there was hope in the area because the red-breasted robin had come back.

It seemed strange to see robins and snow in the same marsh. Robins and ice are an odd combination, yet there they were among the bushes and shrubs of the marsh. Solitary yet sociable, these special winged creatures are often the first real hopeful sign that winter is coming to an end. I didn't know how far these robins had flown to meet me at Vickers' Salmon Pools, but I do know they made my stay at Vickers' Camps that much more pleasurable this year. The robins always bring with them the hope that despite the cold nights and the cool days, there is a change coming and coming very soon! We as humans usually can't sense it, but the robins can.

Their alertness to the change of seasons is a rebuke to me. Paul writes to the saints at Thessalonica, "Therefore let us not sleep, as do others; but let us watch and be sober." (1 Thessalonians 5:6) Paul also wrote to the young man Timothy, "This know also, that in the last days perilous times shall come." (2 Timothy 3:1) Like the robin we can't see the future, but like the robin we can react to the changes in the season. I believe it is time for us to pack our bags and get ready to move on. With each passing sign there is hope in the air that this age, this season, is ready to end. The worst winter in human history is about over, a millennium of spring is about ready to dawn!

Why did God send the robins so early this spring? To tell me that spring wasn't far behind? Why does God send his saints into a cold world? The same reason—to tell a frosty world that there is hope in Christ, and He's not far behind!

# 95

## Whipping Winds

For the wind passeth over it . . .

—PSALMS 103:16

Spring storms are common on the Miramichi River usually accompanied by gusty winds. I have seen and have recorded on my video camera whitecaps on the "river" that would make you think you were on the ocean or a large lake. Any valley is a natural conductor of whipping winds.

At the same time the grim winds whip up the surface of the river into a foam, they blow through the trees along the shore and the bushes along the bank. As the branches bend the wind plucks off the old clinging needles and bits of bark tossing them into the water. Added to the dry grasses and other shore garbage, the Miramichi is soon unfishable because of the collection of wind-swept garbage deposited into its flow. It all seems to be a scene of confusion and chaos, but it isn't. Despite the fact the wind has cramped my fishing it has also started to plant.

Ever since God said, "Let the earth burst forth with every sort of grass and seed-bearing plant. . ." (Genesis 1:12), nature has not changed. Year after year, decade after decade, century after century, and millennium after millennium, God has used the wind to disperse the seeds of the seed-bearing trees. Enclosed in natural capsules, these seeds are blown by the spring winds until they find a landing place. Whipping winds whirl these assorted pods around sometimes for miles. In this sheltered haven a tiny germ of life is ready to burst forth into new life. Flying far on the wings of the wind, these seeds will adorn the forest floor with new growth. The wind is the secret of how wild flowers and wild plants travel so far. We forget that God is not only the Creator, but He is also a Gardener. (Genesis 2:8)

As I have watch for over fifty springs this miracle of nature, I am just now realizing this is exactly how the Holy Spirit works. Likened to a wind in John 3:8, the Spirit takes the seeds of the Church and transports them too far off and distant lands. As I write this devotional my daughter, Marnie, is landing in Togo, West Africa. Her friend, Joshua Alban, is working in the Czech Republic. Here are two young people with American roots, but willing to be blown afar by the Holy Spirit of God. They are willing to be planted far afield to spread the gospel to those who have never heard about Christ. I myself am a blown seed. I was raised on the Blackstone homestead in northern Maine, six generations deep, yet the Lord has blown me to plant His seed in South Carolina, Georgia, New Hampshire, and in the countries of Canada and Australia and India, not counting three places in my home state. "As my Father hath sent me, even so send I you." (John 20:21)

The whipping winds of adversity or the grim gales of difficulties might be blowing you about and breaking you loose from "your comfort zone," but you need to yield to the moving of the Spirit so He can plant you where He wants you.

# 96

## Winter Wait

Trust in the Lord with all thine heart; and lean not unto thine own understanding. In all thy ways acknowledge him, and He shall direct thy path.

—PROVERBS 3:5, 6

I don't mind winter. As a matter of fact I like its imprisonment at times. There is no better day then the day when the snow and storm locks me away in my study. "Forced to stay put" I call it. Rarely does it happen anymore because of all the modern equipment that can move anything and spread enough sand and salt to get you going very quickly. Granted, I enjoy these stranded days early in the winter, but when April comes I am ready to go fishing.

Winter came late in autumn and lasted into early spring. Ever since I moved to the coast of Maine (29 years now), I have enjoyed fall taking a bit of winter and spring taking a bit more. Winter only lasted from January through February, but this year we were paid back with a November 1 to a May 1 winter. Deep snow, thick ice, and cold temperatures seemed to hang on, and even I got "cabin-fever" as April 15 approached, the opening of salmon season on the Miramichi River in New Brunswick, Canada. This had been an annual trip my father-in-law started ten years ago, but this year I had to wait on winter.

I have lived long enough to know that when dates are extended and seasons are lengthened, God has a purpose. I have come to realize that when there is a lot of snow, God knows we will need the stored water. God promised Noah the seasons (Genesis 8:22), and His Son promised that the rain and the sun would fall on us all. (Matthew 5:45) So sometimes we must simply trust Him, and know that He knows what He is doing with the lengthening or the shortening of the season.

Sure enough, now that time has passed I see clearly what God was doing this past winter. May ended up being one of the driest months on record. If winter's moisture hadn't been extended into spring, there wouldn't have been enough water for nature to blossom and bloom. This year in Maine it was the late snows that watered the ground and gave spring a kick-start. Instead of the normal water that comes from the sky to refresh the new plants, it was the melted snow left over from winter that gave spring its first drink.

As a child I memorized Proverbs 3:5–6, and as an adult I have also learned to trust His timing as well. If I had gone to the Miramichi River on April 15, I couldn't have fished because the ice was still in the river. God's delay of three and a half weeks allowed me to spend the most pleasurable time I have ever had at Vickers' Salmon Pools. The weather was literally perfect. No rain, no heavy winds, and mild temperatures. I didn't build a fire in four days which is a first! Waiting is not wasting. It is a wonderful walk into God's perfect timing.

# 97

# River Renewal

While we look not at the things which are seen, but at the things which are not seen: for the things which are seen are temporal; but the things which are not seen are eternal.

—2 CORINTHIANS 4:16

According to the date on the calendar, spring is here, but outside my coastal home the harsh winter of 2000–2001 is still firmly entrenched. I went ice fishing today and, believe it or not, there is still three feet of ice on Branch Lake, the local pond! Few signs, if any, can be seen of the seasonal change that must take place.

I called my friend in Howard, New Brunswick, to see how the Miramichi River was doing. According to his wife, Marsha Vickers, Irving isn't feeling well, and neither is the river. It is still locked in its grim, grayish overcoat of ice. Arctic winds are still funneling down through the Miramichi River Valley and spring in Canada is still six weeks away. The foot hills that line the banks of the mighty river are still covered in a snowy coat measured in feet not inches. With no apparent sign of spring the Miramichi will wait.

Yet deep beneath the ice, the river lives. Like the togue on Branch Lake, there is still plenty of liquid for the salmon of the Miramichi to winter in. Despite the outward appearance, the Miramichi is still flowing, albeit hidden from view. To the natural eye it seems impossible, but to the knowing eye it is alive and well as if no ice or snow covers it. The sun's energy is strengthening with each passing day, and the water from below is warming.

Soon and very soon the melting will begin to change the canopy of white into a covering of blue. The river had resisted the forming of ice many times as the power of its flow and the still warm waters broke up the ice. Eventually, it yields to the arctic cold, and shorter days and winter takes a firm grip on its top. Now, it only waits the renewal that spring will bring.

As I ponder the Miramichi condition on this the first day of spring, I am also reminded of the verse above. The river runs eternal, not temporal. So too does the Spirit of the Living God which is likened to a river in John 7:38,39. Granted, sometimes the believer's life seems to be unmoving. The flow has been stopped by icy sins of deceit and lust. Covered in transgressions and iniquities, the believer is frozen in time unable to move for God. Shame and regret covers like the snow and ice on the Miramichi River Valley. There are no signs that anything can be accomplished again, but this is a devilish lie. Like the flow of the mighty Miramichi the Spirit still runs deep, thawing and melting the wickedness that has bound the believer. Added to that is a sweet warmth of a Savior's love, the combination of Son and Spirit, and like the combination of sun and stream forgiveness will soon cover those old sins. Like the "river" it will flow free again. Are you waiting for such a renewal?

# 98

## Miramichi Medicine

...the balm of Gilead...

—JEREMIAH 46:11

It had been one of those busy, busy, busy years. Go here and go there, go, go, go, go anywhere, and then on top of that try to do everything everywhere; teach that class, visit that patient, counsel that individual, make that appointment, and meet that demand. I was so busy I could only think of one prescription for my weary life, a dose of Miramichi medicine.

Life as a city pastor is non-stop September to April. Rare is the week I don't work at least part of all seven days. In the last seven years I have averaged only 50–60 days off in the entire year. I have discovered to take a day off in the city is near impossible. My wife and I have learned that the only way to get away is to get out-of-town, and the only way to leave town is to leave the country. For me that means Canada and Vickers' Salmon Pools.

It was my father-in-law, Stacy Meister, who first prescribed the Canadian version of the "Balm of Gilead." (Jeremiah 46:11) It wasn't until recently that I read Philip Keller's description of this fabled tree. "Balm of Gilead...What a precious tree! So much beloved by all wild creatures. Its perfume in the spring. Its green and whispering leaves for shade in the summer. It's cool groves where fawns find shelter and grouse chicks grow safely. Its gorgeous golden banners that flutter so bravely in the fall. Its soft, tender, nourishing bark that beaver relish all winter. Yes, balm of Gilead! The tree of life for all seasons. The tree of life that supports all those who share its wild world. The tree of life that uplifts a solitary man on this spring morning!"

What he has just described is the Miramichi River Valley to me. To walk its shores is a balm beyond belief. Each time I visit this place (15 times in the last 10 years) I am awe struck at the sight. Magnificent cumulus clouds overhead dot a brilliant blue April sky. That was how I first saw it, and despite many a miserable day weather-wise that is always how I feel whenever I am there. The glorious reflection of the sun off the river creates a million or more diamond-shaped beams of light off its surface more wonderful then all the diamonds in DeBeers' mines. The air is crisp and clean, and the aroma is pure heaven on earth. It soothes my soul, and it bathes my busy spirit in calmness and quietness. I even have time to talk to my "Boss," something that is sometimes lacking in "His" work. It is a crime that one has to get away, go away, and get lost before he can communicate with the very One that called him into His work.

I thank the Good Lord above for providing me such a "Gilead" just five hours away. It is a place that is a slowing medicine for my soul and a stabilizing balm for my spirit.

# 99

## God's Geese

Behold the fowls of the air . . .
—Matthew 6:26

The spirit-stirring sound drifted slowly downward into the Miramichi River Valley. If I am honest, I would say the noise reached my soul. Have you ever heard it? The wild Canadian geese are on the move again. I have seen them up close and personal on their nests with tiny yellow goslings inside. I have witnessed them in great numbers swimming peacefully on a northern pond, but the most magnificent sights have to be when they take to the wind!

Can you imagine it? Some of these geese fly two thousand miles from the Arctic tundra to some Florida marsh. They never seem to fear the miles or the many problems that could happen along their route. As for me I have only ever seen them in the middle of their flight, somewhere part way between home and holiday or somewhere between their winter homestead and their summer breeding grounds. Granted, some never make it to Canada but stop off in Maine to breed and multiply. It's all good country! But for me to see their famous "V" in Canada makes the mystic more magnificent.

In somber awe I face upward every time I hear their haunting calls from "higher ground." Whether fishing the mighty salmon on the Miramichi or plowing the back-forty on the family homestead, one can't keep his eyes earthbound when a flock of wild geese pass over heaven bound. I know they are not serenading me personally, but in my heart I think they are saying, "See you in the fall!" The enduring image of their precision flying like a squadron of World War II B-17s is an ever present fixture in my mind. I love to see a single goose, but a group of geese is more pleasurable to me. A massive "V" of spring migrants trumpeting in full voice is a natural sound unmatched.

Those of you who have watched such an air show know that the wild goose can fly at tremendous speeds, alone or in formation. If you are privileged to see such a flight, you had better watch carefully because it will soon be over. Crossing from south to north in the spring, or north to south in the fall, the moment is fleeing. Therefore, fishing or plowing must be put on hold for a few minutes to watch one of God's most majestic marvels. And to imagine these grand geese can accomplish this feat without jet engine, onboard computer, or satellite positioning capability is simply amazing. Hour after hour, from dawn to dusk, these great birds fly unaided. Strong wings and great lung capacity combined with stored-up energy propels these mighty migrants on their way with a deep God-given ability to fly a straight and true, dead-on course to wherever they are heading.

Each time I see a single goose, or gander, or a whole flight of geese, I am reminded what a marvelous Creator we have. I like Phillips translation of Matthew 6:26: "Look at the birds in the sky!" Perhaps, those birds are a flight of God's geese.

# 100

# Bountiful Blossoms

While the earth remaineth, seedtime and harvest...
summer and winter...shall not cease.

—Genesis 6:22

There is a marvelous privilege one experiences travelling to the Miramichi River Valley in the spring. It is the opportunity to see nature bursting into bloom!

I love the few, short weeks in spring when "bland" brown gives way to "garden" green. This glorious transition takes place annually, but most people miss it on their rush to summer. I rarely miss the majestic moment because of a five-hour car trip I take at the height of the transformation from my home on the coast of Maine to the Miramichi River in eastern Canada. I am going to fish salmon, but until I get my wet fly wet I enjoy the breathtaking beauty of bountiful blossoms.

Added to a landscape coming alive are the animals that show themselves along the way. I have seen rabbits, eagles, osprey, deer, moose, and bear. There has been the occasional sighting of a fox, or a woodchuck, and of course the robin—springs first ambassador. But stirring them all to make an appearance after a long hard winter is the brilliant blossoms that reappear from ground and forest. Under a blue sky a green carpet of grass destroys all natural fear and is replaced by a God-given impulse to feed.

This year's rebirth was exceptional in my opinion. Maybe it was because the winter was extra-long, and it had overstayed its welcome. But out of the bareness came a beauty that month after month, storm after storm, and snow after snow could not hold down. Unrelenting amounts of snow and ice had blanketed the area from Ellsworth to Howard. Temperatures rarely saw the freezing mark for weeks on end, chilling and freezing the forest and fields from here to there. I have watched this process for over fifty years now, and I sometimes wonder how any living thing can survive in those coldest months of winter. How can that small fragile squirrel along the Union River or that small fragile fir on the front lawn survive? Where do the rabbits hide, and how do the deer survive in the open on those nights the temperature goes below twenty below?

Yet they all survive, or at least most of them. The coming warmer temperatures and a warm rain brings the miracle, and each spring I drive through five hours of renewal, rebirth, resurrection, and restoration. Out of the drab comes delight, and out of the dull comes bright. A beautiful blossom of beauty is seen around every curve and corner on the winding road from Maine to the Miramichi. Each time my eyes see an old spot transformed, I am reminded of the promise Noah was given by God printed above. I travel every year to my favorite fishing hole in the wonder of that promise, and next year about this time I will travel it again—Lord willing.

# 101

## River Runoff

For whom the Lord loveth he chasteneth . . .
—HEBREWS 12:6

Over the last ten years I have seen the Miramichi River in its various shapes. It is not the biggest river I have fished or witnessed in various stages, but it is a river I have seen its many faces. In summer it is nothing more than a wide stream. In fall it can change overnight with a heavy downpour upriver. Once, my friend Mike Hangge and I were fishing the river during the first few days in October. When we arrived, the water conditions were ideal. We managed to hook a couple of fish within the first hour, but then it started to rain. Over the next three days the river was full to overflowing to the point we had to fish from shore. Because the Miramichi River Valley watershed is so extensive, the river's makeup changes with the weather. In the spring another factor comes into play.

It had to have been when I was fishing that a fierce, fiery sun melted the winter snow from the hill country surrounding the valley. The gentle river began to rise with each passing moment. A literal torrent of ice-cold liquid was pouring into the river from every brook, stream, and creek up and down its hundreds of miles of shoreline. As I stood beside the rising current I realized that the good fishing of my first two days would be ending.

Despite my disappointment a thought was given to me. A river runoff is necessary if winter is to leave and spring is to come. This is also true of life itself. How often we are disappointed by sudden changes in our lives.

Pressures at work begin to rise. Stress seems to overflow our lives. The rising tide of problems seem to engulf us. We stand on the shore of our lives and wonder what is happening. Our once productive lives are now covered in dirty criticism and raging currents of dissatisfaction. Two years ago I was in a similar situation. The fishing hole known as the Emmanuel Baptist Church was producing regularly. I was having a wonderful trip through eight years of pastoring. I thought it would continue unabated. Then it happened! Disagreements began to rise. I tried to stop them, but it was like trying to stop the rise of the Miramichi—impossible. I could only stand and watch eight years of work wash away. I was sad and angry, but once I realized that there was some old, dirty snow buried deep in the closets of many at the church that had to be melted, I yielded to God's will. God's fiery conviction began to work. He began to melt away all the anger and bitterness and hate.

I am happy to report that the river is fishable again, and I am back on its banks casting the fly of love into a clear pool. I have learned as with nature, you need a runoff every once in a while to clear the obstacles that are keeping the saints down, and that is only possible when God melts away the "frost."

# 102

## Vespers Vista

> Praise the Lord from the earth ... mountains, and all hills ... beasts ... and flying fowl.
> —Psalms 148:7, 9, 10

A few weeks ago I was in a boat motoring up the Cain's River with my salmon guide, Jason Luce. I was once again fishing the Miramichi River Valley, but because the river was so dirty with a sudden melting of the snow pack, Jason and I had worked our way up the Cain's in search of clean water and perhaps a salmon or two.

The wild wilderness terrain was new to me. Despite fishing the mouth of the Cain's River (where it empties into the Miramichi River) for ten years, I had never gone this far up the river. Now I was motoring up mile after mile into this picturesque river valley. Around every corner and curve was a new sight, a new wonder, a new vista to see. It had rained in the morning, but on this afternoon of exploration we were covered with a clear sky and pushed by a gentle breeze. We had travelled nearly seven miles when we passed another boat. As we left them behind the river was ours, and we entered a vast wilderness cathedral.

Jason finally stopped and anchored the boat at Buttermilk Brook. His hope was that a few late departing salmon would still be there. They had left, but that was okay with me. I began to look around at the steep slopes that plunged to the river's edge to my right. On my left was a fairly flat piece of terrain and around the corner above us several acres of glade. The entire meadow was coming into a spring green. An old cabin sat off the river deposited there by an ice flow according to Jason. The sounds of nature were everywhere, and I thought I had come to "afternoon vespers!"

Scattered in the beauty of the area were stands of pine and fir. The scene was out of a nature magazine that others get to go to, but you only get to see in pictures. Seldom had I ever been to a more pleasant place in my life. Sun-drenched and sun-killed, the combination of the river and the ridge, gorge and glade, was more than I could take in. I was awestruck and silenced by the scene. The most talented landscape artist couldn't have done better if he had a hundred years and unlimited resources. I have seen other places in northern Quebec that could take your breath away, but this was a masterpiece create by the Master Himself. In a thousand seasons and more the mighty creative hand of the Almighty had shaped this spot on the Cain's River into a breathtaking chapel of solitude. The vesper choir of birds was rehearsing for the setting sun. The winds and the water were tuning their instruments for the final act of the day.

On the last drop before we headed back to camp I stood once more to my feet and took a 360-degree turn. I know few places praise the Lord today, but on Buttermilk Brook corner on the Cain's River there is a place that does.

# 103

# Morning Mist

And every plant of the field before it was in the earth, and every herb of the field before it grew: for the Lord God had not caused it to rain upon the earth, and there was no man to till the ground. But there went up a mist from the earth, and watered the whole face of the ground.

—Genesis 2:5, 6

As I finish this series of "Miramichi Messages," I must paint for you one more image of the river I have come to love. We might simply call the portrait "Morning Mist."

One of my favorite authors is Oswald Chambers. He died during the First World War, and his writings are mostly Biblical in nature. It wasn't until I read his biography that I learned not only was he an inspiring writer, but that he was also a poet of exceptional thought. I also discovered that he was a fisherman and loved nothing better than to take his rod and fish for trout in his native Scotland. In that biography I found this poem written by Chambers on September 1, 1893.

> Mysterious morning mist, so dense and frail,
> Slowly stealing, tenderly white and pale,
> Weirdly clinging, concealing in thy shrouds
> Reflections perfect, clear of woods and clouds,
> Rendering the distance indistinct and strange.

> Changing to mystery all within thy range,
> Rifting, lifting, scattering in the breeze,
> Facing, dissolving, dying 'mid the trees,
> Lost in thyself forever as the sun
> Flashing his splendor in the river's run.

I too have seen the "mysterious morning mist" gathered over the Miramichi. I too have watched as it grew in power until it engulfed the entire valley. The "cloud shroud" blocking everything along its banks until nothing is visible or recognizable. Veiled in a white pale blanket, the morning air is stilled and silenced before the mighty mist that now is completely in control of the area. I have watched from the observation deck hoping to see a jumping salmon through the misty dew. When a ghostly figure does rise above the river's surface, one wonders whether a salmon or a sea monster has broken through the morning mist.

I also have thought as I looked out through the picture window of the cabin we now call "Squirrel Tail" that it must be as it was on those first few days of creation. Before the sun had reached its full strength a "weirdly clinging" of water vapor hanging suspended over the "river's run." And then as Chambers puts it, a "lifting," a rising of this "mysterious mist" begins to take place, "dissolving, dying" as the morning sun works its magic and scatters the shroud until there is nothing left but the "splendor" of the stream.

# 104

# Pasture Precepts

He maketh me to lie down in green pastures . . .
—PSALMS 23:2

I am at Doctor Martin Vickers' camp again. This is my sixteenth trip in ten years. Today is April 15, 2002, opening day of spring salmon fishing in Canada. My father-in-law, Stacy Meister, first brought me to these "green pastures" on April 27, 1992. Despite the time of year, despite brown grass and white snow and dirty water in the river, it is still a "green pasture" place for me.

Why is Vickers' Pools a "green pasture" place for me? I believe it takes a number of ingredients to make a "green pasture" place. First, the place must be free from hurry. This is a laid-back-kind of place. No rushing at Vickers' Camps. As I write these thoughts, Marsha and Toby are fixing supper at a "conversation pace." They are the camp cooks, but they have time to visit with "the sports!" Supper will be put on the table overlooking the river not on a schedule, but according to the timing of the quests and the "fish" stories that must be told before supper. Supper will be early tonight because opening day was a shut-out!

Second, the place must be free from friction. I have never heard a hard word at this place. The owner, Marty Vickers, is a quiet, soft spoken, trouble-free kind of guy. The staff, Irving, Marsha, and Toby, is a close family with a gentle English spirit. How can it be a "green pasture" place if the guides and fisherman are fighting? There are seven of us in the camp these first three days of the season, (and of course seven guides), and despite "no fish" on opening day no one is mad or upset. Most come to this camp to get away from the maddening crowd and catching a fish is just a bonus in this place.

Third, the place must be filled with soul-satisfaction. You must be satisfied and contented here, high water or not, dirty water or not, fish or no fish! I have learned in my trips here that the Good Lord has given me this place and whether I catch the "big one" or not, I need this place. I don't come to this place just to fish as you can see from this series of "messages." There is more soul-satisfaction here than in most places I visit. I have learned to be satisfied with my guide, the cooks, and the results of my days on the river. Even the weather, wet and raw, was satisfactory today.

Fourth, the place must be free from tension. In a world, even the world of the Church of God, there seems to be seasons of tension. Times of tension come when the brethren are at ought with each other. Often times it comes when the strains and stress of the world increases. For me, I need a tension-free place in my life.

When you come to a "green pasture" place "He maketh you to lie down." To rest, to relax, and to be recharged is the reason for a "green pasture" place. We need to come apart to such a place before we come-a-part!

# 105

## Materialism Magnetism

a man's life consistent not in the abundance of the things which he possessed.
—Luke 12:15

When you spend four days with a group of fisherman from southern New England, you get a clearer picture of materialism. I am on the Miramichi River for spring salmon fishing. This is the first time I have been in New Brunswick for opening day. I am sharing Vickers' Pools with five other men, three of them from Boston, Massachusetts. All five are middle-aged men with very successful careers, men who have plenty of money to indulge their passion for fishing. I have only spent twenty-four hours with them, and I have already heard more stories than I care to about expensive things.

Let me make this very clear up front. There is nothing wrong or wicked about either wealth or things. The danger of materialism is that we get distracted by both, and both can be "the root of all evil." (1 Timothy 6:10) I was very fortunate to have been raised on a poor family farm in the 1950s and 1960s when our possessions were minimal, our wants were reasonable, and our contentment was exceptional. Nevertheless, I have lived in a prosperous "state" where more is better and less is frowned on. Collecting is still the number one past time of most Americans, and for my five companions they were in the business of "fishing stuff."

Don't get me wrong because I am not "casting the first stone." I too have fallen into the trap of possessing, but I am happy to report that I eventually came back to my roots of "in God I trust." I still live in this possession-made world that rests on the two pillars of buying and spending, and I am still tempted at times. Gadgets, gimmicks, and gaudy things still draw me at times, but I am reminded of what the Lord said about "the deceitfulness of riches, and the lust of other things entering in, choke the word, and it becometh unfruitful." (Mark 4:19) Instead of seeing only to fulfill our need, we want a six-pack of everything and three cars and two houses and a camp and all the "stuff" to fill them all. We have now filled them and are working on the "self-storage" sheds of the world.

As I listen to the tales of the purchases of my fellow-fishermen, I am glad to say all I have was given to me, and I still enjoy fishing with an "old" fly attached to an "old" line in an "old" reel connected to an "old" rod! I am still fishing in the same fishing clothes I wore ten years ago when I first came to this river. I have learned that I don't need a new fly or a new rod to make my Miramichi fishing trip exciting or enjoyable. I am tempted like others by mass media, magazines, newspapers, books, billboards, and flyers to buy more. I feel drawn by the "magnetism of materialism," but I am and will continue to resist the draw. I am more determined than ever after the experience of this trip to unclog my life even further.

# 106

## Squirrel Tail Stillness

He leadeth me beside the still waters.

—Psalms 23:2

It is the end of my second day on the banks of the Miramichi River for the spring of 2002. For 48 hours my friend, Mike Hangge, and I have been boarding with an undertaker, a hair dresser, and a mechanical engineer from Massachusetts. They are three great guys, but very loud, very talkative, and very much I-know-it-all kind of guys. The good doctor, the owner of the tree cabins, has returned home to Maine leaving his camp, better known a "Squirrel Tail," empty. He told me just before he left that Mike and I could move in. We have, and I am back to my favorite room in the complex (Old Ned's Room). It is my most favorite room because it was here my father-in-law brought me ten years ago.

What a difference a day makes. Yesterday the river was dirty and high. We fished in a steady, cold rain, and Mike and I caught nothing. Today, the river was clearer, dropping, and the sun came out a few times. Mike and I hooked into seven fish including three big salmon. Tomorrow looks even better, but on this the third evening on my sixteenth fishing trip to the Miramichi there are not only "still waters" before me, but I am resting in a "still waters" place.

I am one that needs a "still" place to really hear "the still small" voice of God. To meditate, to commune, and to reflect on the things of God I need a "still waters" place. I have come to believe that my Lord wants me in a similar place as David writes about. Rested and relaxed, not hurried and harassed by worldly men who only eat and sleep fishing. I am an avid salmon fisherman without a doubt, but I am more an avid follower of my Shepherd. I am thankful that when I make a mistake like I have on this trip to book dates with a camp full of worldly men that He allows me for the last 46 hours of this trip to be alone and quite away from the crowd. Squirrel Tail cabin is my "still waters" place.

Most try drinking from the troubled waters of the world, or they try drinking from the deep well of sin. Everybody is trying to quench their soul's thirst, but eventually everybody will realize it can't be done at those watering holes. They are like the people Jeremiah spoke about, "For my people have committed two evils: they have forsaken me the fountains of living waters, and have hewed them out cisterns, broken cisterns, that can hold no water." (Jeremiah 2:13) Broken and barren, dried up and parched, these souls act happy and joyful, but they are dying of thirst. I am so thankful that my Good Shepherd knows my need and has led me back to these "still waters." Notice "waters" is in the plural—river and retreat. It is dark as I finish this article, and I can no longer see the river before me, but I have just opened the window in my bedroom, and I can hear the "still waters" just as I am hearing the "still small voice" in my soul.

# 107

# Winged Walk

But they that wait upon the Lord shall renew their strength;
they shall mount up with *wings* as eagles;
they shall run, and not be weary;
and they shall *walk*, and not faint.

—ISAIAH 40:31, MY EMPHASIS

One of the sights I have witnessed on the Miramichi River is eagles, not the American eagle but Canadian eagles. To me it doesn't make any difference their nationality, they are magnificent creatures and each sighting is special. The eagle reminds me that my Christianity is a winged-walk.

When Jesus died on Calvary, and we accept His redemptive work, He sets us soaring. I know many Christians are still crawling, earthbound, but we were saved for the stratosphere. Ours is not an easy-going, powerless flight, but rather ours is a Spirit-filled takeoff. The updrafts and stormy winds are for our uplifting. Each time the Spirit, as a "wind" (John 3:8), brings a challenge or a crisis into our lives, it is for our strengthening. So many of us are like the eaglet sitting on the edge of the nest waiting to fly, wanting to fly, but terrified to just set off into space. We want to stay put like the children of Israel in Egypt. But as with them, so with us, the

Spirit stirs the nest (Deuteronomy 32:11). What does He want us to do? He wants us to "mount up with wings as eagles." He wants us to spread our wings of faith and launch ourselves into the air currents of His grace.

It is time we see the gusty winds of strife as helpful rather than a handicap. Like the eagles along the Miramichi River, it is time we use the "upper winds" to lift us higher. There is a popular misconception today among believers that we are pedestrians instead of pilots. If we are a pedestrian, we can be "cribbed, cabined, and confined," but as pilots we are free to soar. Ours is an upward calling, not a downward cross. Remember, after Calvary Jesus took flight and so should we because the higher we climb the cleaner our lives will be and the more direct our course.

I read this on the banks of the Miramichi. "One day I observed a prairie eagle mortally wounded by a rifle shot. His eyes still gleamed like two circles of light. Then he slowly turned his head and gave one more searching and longing look at the sky. He had often swept those starry spaces with his powerful wings. The beautiful sky was his home, it was his domain. A thousand times he had exploited there his splendid strength. In those far away heights he had played with the lightening and had raced with the winds. Now, so far away from home, he lay dying because he forgot and flew too low." And William Stinger writes, "I am an eagle born to fly; up the stellar highways of the sky. Along the Milky Way where blazes; new dawn, new planets, new days. I am man-born, God-led, sky-bent. Almost omnipotent."

# 108

## Always Ahead

Set your affections on things above, not on things on the earth.
—Colossians 3:2

Another trip to Vickers' Pools on the Miramichi River has come to an end. This was my 44th day of fishing on this wonderful watershed. It is the last night at "Squirrel Tail" Lodge, and I sit before a picture window overlooking the river for one last time. It was a good trip, if not a great trip, for my fishing partner Mike Hangge, a fire fighter, from Ellsworth, Maine, and a parishioner. In two days Mike landed 11 of 29 salmon caught at the camp, including two 32-inchers, his biggest fish caught on a fly. I managed to hook three, but only land two. Mike was 11 for 11! I will never live this trip down because the veteran was bested by the rookie, and I only caught my last two fish when I finally yielded and used a fly Mike had tied himself. Needless to say, in three days I had plenty of time to look up!

    Despite the changing weather (one and a half days of rain, one day of overcast skies, and a half day of sun) the river was wonderful as it always is. I have learned that life is a lot like spring salmon fishing on the Miramichi. The weather is unpredictable, the river is unmanageable, and the fish are moody, but one aspect is always sure—you can always look up because faith grows in the foulest conditions. Monday nobody caught fish, but nobody went home. By Tuesday everybody was hooking into fish, and my friend Mike hooked into six, a record for him. What had happened? The weather warmed, the river had cleared, and the fish had become friendly to our flies.

With the dropping of the water and the rays of sun hitting the water, the salmon of the Miramichi could see better Mike's "Copper Renuos." So it is with life. One day will be a miserable day, and the next a memorable day. Haven't you experienced such days?

Our eyes must be focused above the "rollercoaster" waves of life. We need to learn in life as with fishing that there is another day coming. It will probably be better than a no-fish day, or it could be a six-fish day! God leads us through dirty rivers and rainy, raw days to get us to a brighter day. (Psalms 23:4) Ours is just to follow through the Monday of life to get to the Tuesday. We do this by always looking ahead. (Philippians 3:13) Paul said it, I believe it, and I practice it while fishing or just living. To do anything less would be foolish because there will always be fish-less days, muddy rivers, and cold rainy days, but there will also be a trophy salmon, clearing waters, and sunshine days as well.

We should never yield to gloomy forecasts. A guide told me today that the forecast was freezing rain for tomorrow. I will not be on the banks of the Miramichi tomorrow, but I will be back on the coast of Maine tomorrow. Remember, dawn follows dark, spring follows winter, a rainbow follows rain, and a fish-full day follows a fish-less day. Just ask Mike.

# 109

# Fine Fishing

To the weak became I as weak, that I might gain the weak:
I am made all things to all men that I might by all means save some.

—1 Corinthians 9:22

## THE FEW THAT DIDN'T GET AWAY

How well do I recall those days, when I went forth to fish (witness).
My greatest source of happiness and my constant dream and wish
Was hours spent in fishing when I would simply pray,
Lord, grant me grace to catch a few that won't get away.

For years I've fished the hedges and lanes and many catches knew.
I found the places where they were as all good fishers do.
Each time I'd humbly see a catch I'd prayed at the end of each day,
Lord, thank you for the grace to catch the few that didn't get away.

Each soul was a mighty haul at least in my own eyes.
For every time I told the story I could hear heaven verbalize.
I'd tell the story over and over the action was play by play.
Lord, thank you for the grace to land the few that didn't get away.

Though the task grows bigger and the feet get awful lame,
The end of a fishing trip turns out to be the same.
For in going far, or travelling near, in highway or byway,
Lord, thank you for the grace to catch the few that didn't get away.

# 110

# Grand Goodbye

The salutation of Paul with mine own hand,
which is the token in every epistle: so I write.

—2 Thessalonians 3:17

There was one last goodbye to make. On the first Tuesday of September, 1986, I felt a vacuum and a void in my fisherman's (pastor's) heart. I needed to say goodbye to the parish I had pastored for eight years so I drove through Westfield, Maine, one last time.

Fortunately, everyone I wanted to see was home so I could make a proper goodbye to my second fishing hole.

I travelled again through the highways following a familiar trail I had made for eight years. I was alone. My family had moved to Eastport a month before so the kids could start school, but I was not alone. Canadian geese were flying high overhead honking rudely as they too headed out to unknown places further south.

I raised my head and watched for one more opportunity to share my faith with the folks of this small northern Maine town. Now I was heading for new waters, and I wondered if I would or could ever find another fishing hole like Westfield. I knew her holes so well. I knew her fish so well. I knew her modes and the methods of catching her prize inhabitants. All her habits were known to me. I had learned how to pray in a gale of wind and how to wait patiently in her pools. I wanted to leave, but I didn't want to leave.

How can I tell you what it is like to have a town as a best friend? She's always there, her transparent citizens always carrying a surprise. Sometimes she yielded a soul, sometimes she didn't, but that didn't make me love her any less. Sometimes a neighbor would skitter by, or a mother with her brood would speak to me, or a postman would stop what he was doing just to get caught up. No matter, through all seasons she accepted my heavy voice, my constant preaching, and my continuous sermonizing of her people with my verses, and my dragging her people periodically to church when they really didn't want to be there.

The birds were always flying over her except late into October when the cold winds blew, but I was still fishing for men. Moose came to feed in her fields, and deer were known to stop by. I had learned and seen so much about God as I walked through her lanes. I couldn't imagine not taking my weekly pilgrimage up her abandoned railroad tracks, but here I was turning my back on her for the final time as a resident of Westfield. I knew I had to do it because my family was already in Eastport, but the tug at my heart strings was strong. I turned and looked one final time at her.

The ride to Eastport was slower than I thought it would be. My heart and mind were heavy with thought as I stumbled through what I was doing. I had said my goodbyes, but I didn't feel any better. I would not feel better until I had found her replacement, until I found "new water" to fish.

# 111

## Special "Sports"

And the things that thou hast heard of me among many witnesses, the same commit thou to faithful men, who shall be able to teach others also.

—2 TIMOTHY 2:2

After years of fishing, one of the purest pleasures I have developed is the joy of taking others fishing. Whether planned or unexpected, I have had the privilege of being there when others have experienced their finest encounters with the creature we call "the fish." The same pleasure comes when you share the joy of fishing-for-men.

I have never considered myself a guide, but there was one place I did become the guide of choice. While pastoring a small country church in Aroostook County, I became good friends with Herschel Smith. One of Herschel's great loves was fishing. Being a potato farmer unwilling to wait on "the early and latter rains," he built an irrigation pond in the middle of his farm in Westfield. Not content to use it only for irrigation, he soon stocked it with brook trout and eventually with rainbow trout. For seven years he gave me a free pass to fish his pond whenever and with whomever I chose. Because it was a private pond and Herschel was an avid fly fisherman, his only rule was "fly fishing only."

At first I went alone to Smith Pond. Then as I began to understand the pond, others came along to share in the pleasures of the pond. I began from day one to chart and record the catches I made. Within a few years I had a very good idea where the trout lived, fed, and spawned. While others would often return from Smith Pond with an empty creel, I rarely came back empty handed. From 1979 to 1986 when I left Westfield to pastor a church on an island off the Downeast coast of Maine, I fished Smith Pond 118 times and caught 923 fish. In the same time my "sports" caught another 290 fish. From August 27, 1979, my first day at Smith Pond, to October 14, 1986, my last day fishing the pond, I was only shut out 11 times. I did return to Smith Pond after I left Westfield 26 more times, and I caught another 144 fish and my "sports" caught another 62 fish. We were only shutout three times. These totals make Smith Pond the greatest fishing hole I have ever fished (that is until I discovered Malcolm Branch Brook, a natural creek where I have caught thousands of brook trout over the year, another book in it). In 144 trips to the pond, I and my "sports" came back empty-handed only 14 times while landing 1477 fish. That is an average of over ten fish a trip! Because it was a private pond, I could fish it from "ice-out" to the first freeze. My record was in 1985 when I fished Smith Pond 34 times from April 27 to November 8. I caught over 300 fish that year with my "sports" netting 125 fish.

Though I haven't had as much success fishing-for-men as I have had fishing for fish, I have had over the years the privilege of helping many a would-be fisher-of-men get started. Whether through preaching, teaching, or personal mentoring, spiritual "sports" are the best part of the job.

# 112

## Teaching Tactics

...and he gave some...teachers...

—Ephesians 4:11

When I was a lad, I shanked an angleworm around a fish hook and threw them both into the brook. That was about the extent of my fishing technique. I waited for a fish to bite, and, if one did, I dragged it up on the brook bank as fast as I could. Fishing mostly small trout stream in northern Maine, my equipment always outweighed my quarry so I usually won. It wasn't until I started to fish with my father-in-law, Stacy Meister, in Canada that I learned that there was more to fishing than what I just described. Over the last twenty-five years I have learned fishing tactics and techniques from one of the most knowledgeable fisherman I have ever met. Stacy always took time during our fishing to fish for men. Stacy had accepted the Lord late in life, but was a gifted soul winner and a bold man in his witness.

Stacy was the man who taught me the importance of knots. Fishing knots that hold securely without slipping or seriously weakening your fish line are essential to successful fishing. Who of us hasn't lost a good fish because we were careless with tying on our fly. Stacy taught me that the choice of the right knot is especially important with synthetic line and leader material as they tend to slip easily. Stacy taught me to cut off old knots and tie new ones periodically when fishing, especially if you have been catching a lot of fish. We have the tendency in the excitement of the moment to keep on fishing while our knots become weak. Since all knots fray and weaken with use it is important from time to time to check them and retie them often. Stacy taught me the improved clinch knot, the Lark's head knot, the double surgeon's knot, and the blood knot, to name a few. What knots are to the fisherman, Bible verses are to the fisher-of-men. Stacy taught me to learn them well.

Stacy was also the man who taught me the importance of taking care of my hooks. "Hooks catch fish." I can still hear him say it. "All other fishing tackle serves only to get the hook to a fish's mouth." I learned with artificial bait or a hook all dolled up with feathers and fur, you must, like with knots, be constantly checking your hook. I will never forget the time while fishing Atlantic salmon on the Penobscot River in central Maine with Stacy, I had three solid strikes by a good size salmon. In the excitement of the moment I never imagined the reason I couldn't hook the fish was that the point and barb of my number two salmon fly had been broken off who knows how many casts before. The Penobscot River is a rough body of water on flies, and a periodic check of your hook is essential. What hooks are to the fisherman, your testimony is to fisher-of-men. If your testimony isn't sharp, your witness won't be either. Our life must always live up to our lip!

# 113

# Spiritual Season

Preach the word; be instant in season, out of season, reprove, rebuke, exhort
With all longsuffering and doctrine.

—2 Timothy 4:2

What is there about spring that makes it so special? If you're like me, it's trout fishing! That's what spring is all about, a time to continue trout fishing. After a long Maine winter of dreaming about trout fishing, it's time to start casting bait, natural or artificial. It's time to look up some old trout friends. Like that big brown trout at Branch Pond you lost last January just before you got him through the ice hole. How about that fat, old bookie you released by the Dead Head on Smith Pond last May? Perhaps, it's time to check on that huge rainbow you hooked in your favorite pond, but lost on its fifth jump. Then there are those heavy togue off Sandy Point on Alagash Lake. Yes, spring is the time of the year to look up some old friends.

    What is there about summer that makes it so special? If you're like me, it's trout fishing! That's what summer is all about, a time to continue trout fishing. After a successful spring with nymphs and streamers, it's time to begin dry fly fishing for rising trout. It's time to see if you can place a #14 in front of a swirling rainbow. It's time to see if you can cast a #16 Royal Coachman as far this summer as you did last summer. It's time to see if you can choose the right Mayfly pattern to duplicate the hatch coming off your favorite trout fishing hole. Yes, summer is a time to try out a new dry fly fishing pattern.

What is there about fall that makes it so special? If you're like me, it's trout fishing! That's what autumn is all about, a time to continue trout fishing. After a productive summer with dry flies, it's time to cast wet flies for spawning trout. It's time to return to the old fishing holes that trout like to haunt each fall, and to return to the hole you call Channel and to the countless painted brook trout that lie there in October; to return to the brook call Goddard and the brilliant colored trout that gather there in early September; to return to the pond created by Herschel Smith where red-bellied, white-tipped trout congregate in its upper pools each November. Yes, autumn is the time to revisit some old fishing holes.

What is there about winter that makes it so special? If you're like me, it's trout fishing! That's what winter is all about, a time to continue trout fishing. After a marvelous fall with weighted lines and stoneflies, it's time to go ice fishing on Branch Pond with Irving Braley, Buster Ingles, and Harold Parker. Yes, winter is the time to visit with old friends in an ice shack fishing for togue.

Too often we forget that fishing for men, like trout fishing, is for all seasons. There is never a time, never a season that we ought not to be preaching the gospel of Christ. (2 Timothy 4:2)

# 114

## Boy Barry

And said, Verily I say unto you, Except ye be converted, and become as little children, ye shall not enter into the kingdom of heaven.

—MATTHEW 18:3

For as far back as I can remember I have always been happy doing something out-of-doors. In my life I have been very fortunate with few illnesses or physical shortcomings. Being raised on a farm in the north Maine woods offered me numerous opportunities to walk in the woods and stroll by the streams. Trying to keep me cooped up in a house was like corralling a wild stallion. It didn't make any difference if I was catching bull frogs in the nearby frog pond, or trying to capture a young heifer in the back pasture, or fishing for trout in Salmon Stream, I loved the outdoors and still do. As long as I was outdoors that was all that mattered to me.

Always being a boy at heart has gotten me into trouble on an occasion or two. Like the time I convinced myself that Dad's warning about running in and out of the cellar while putting in wood wasn't really dangerous. A scar still visible at the back of my sixty-nine-year-old head is a testimony that Dad was right, and the boy in me was wrong. The boy in me often convinced me that it wasn't really necessary to be home in time for supper, and that nobody really care, which they did. A few years ago my father and I got in deep trouble with the women of the family when while fishing our favorite trout stream I forgot that the family had planned a night out for Reno's pizza. Guess who didn't show up until after dark. They were kind because they brought us home some extra pizza, but the boy in me had done it to me once again, and this time it was me who led Dad astray.

To this day I would rather watch a squirrel gathering acorns or a robin build her nest than the attractions of an Amish Village. Recently on a trip to visit my brother in Pennsylvania, my family was all over me for taking a video of a robin gathering building materials instead of them enjoying their long-deserved vacation. The same problem occurred when we stopped at an Amish wood crafting place. Out back was a rainbow trout pond. We have more footage on rising and feeding trout than we do on where my brother lives. That boy in me just doesn't want to grow up. Someday I am going to have to sit him down and explain that he is too old to be acting like a ten year old. You notice I said someday.

If there is anything I have learned from my upbringing, both physical and spiritual, it is the truth that our Lord wants us to be "children" all of our lives. He never wants us to lose the childish excitement that brought us to Him. Oh, we are to mature spiritually without a doubt, the teachings of Paul are clear on this, but it is a maturity without losing the "child in us." The song writer had it right when he titled his church hymn *A Child of the King*. If you lose the child, you lose "the wonder of it all."

# 115

## Hallowed Holes

For this cause left I thee in Crete . . .

—TITUS 1:5

We thank you Lord for the gifts of special places these fish have taken us. To the brook called Beaver located deep in the woods behind my father's farm where our first trout was taken. It wasn't big, but to a boy it was a trophy bar none. To that special hole at the mouth of Bull Brook. To a lake called Portage located near the northern Maine town of Portage and to its mouth a river called Fish where on shining smelt our first land lock was caught and where Stacy introduced me to the "salmon." To the river call Chalifour in Quebec Province where a northern pike's explosive leaps gave us the taste for big fish. To a lake we called Number One located in Mistassini Park, Canada, because of the huge pike we caught there year after year. It still is number one to me! To a pond we call Walleye and to the tasty fish caught there that made our taste buds jump. To a river called Penobscot located in central Maine which showed us that bass fishing could be fun and for the numerous Atlantic salmon we have caught in her salmon pools, B-Pool, Guerin Pool, Wringer Pool, Second Pool, Eddington Pool and the runs we called Church and Wringer. To a pond we called Smith located in the small Aroostook County hamlet of Westfield where rainbows of grand size are caught with weighted line and jerking, jigging nymphs. To the pool called Hospital located near the Eastern Maine Medical Center where at the going down of the tide our Pink Ent took the salmon just feet from shore that no other fly could hook. To the hole we call Channel and to the countless painted trout in brilliant fall colors that lay there in October. To the bar we call Mouse and to the many giant pike caught there, and to the time we held Stacy's rod on his trophy pike's first run. To the Pool they call the Lower Davis located on the border of New Brunswick and Quebec we give our greatest acclamations, and for the two Atlantic salmon caught there in consecutive years, totaling fifty-nine thick pounds, totaling eighty-six silvery inches, totaling seven spectacular jumps, totaling a dozen twisting runs, totaling one and one half miles of the beautiful Restigouche River, and totaling two hours and forty-five minutes of the most exciting fishing we have ever had. To a river called the Miramichi where black salmon fishing became a passion, and to the first trip there where in three days we caught more Atlantic salmon than we had in thirteen years. To her runs we called Camp, Grilse, Home, White Cottage, Stacy, Beaver, Bank, and Cain, and the over one hundred salmon we have caught.

As the Lord has led me to many fishing holes, He has also led me to many a "spiritual" fishing hole. I remember well my time in Perham, Pembroke, Westfield, Eastport, and Ellsworth. Special in those holes were the pools at Epsom, Birchwood, Colliers, Southern Acres, Sonogee, Courtland, Seaport, and Hancock. And for the years the Good Lord left me there!

# 116

# Tremendous Trips

For the kingdom of heaven is as a man travelling into a far country ...
—MATTHEW 25:14

Ever since 1975, I have been taking fishing trips with my family and friends. At the compiling of this log, I have taken 140 trips with at least a few more planned. As with fishing days, fishing trips vary. Some were very successful while others were a "wash." Sometimes you can take that literally. Despite foul weather and few fish, a fishing trip will always produce a highlight or two, but then there are those special times when everything seems to go perfectly.

I have always been an amateur historian so it is not surprising that I have kept a trip journal on all these trips. Ever since my first trip to Canada with my father in law, Stacy Meister, I have jotted down the time and place, the fish and fisherman, the weight and length, the weather, and when in a small notebook I keep in my fishing vest. When I return home from my fishing adventures, as I did recently from my one hundred and fortieth trip, I compile my notes into the various journals and logs I have been keeping since the mid-seventies.

If a fly-in fishing trip into the back waters of northern Quebec Canada was my last fishing trip, and a weeklong trip into Quebec with a group of Boys Brigade boys was my first trip, it was an overnight trip to Beaver Brook with a couple of cousins was my second! Camping out overnight under the stars of northern Maine by a babbling brook gave me my first taste of the joys of fishing for a few days in a row. I had been fishing ever since I was small, but my second overnight trip showed me the privileges of being on a stream at first light, and the advantages of fishing until dark without the wasted time of hiking out before dark. Ever since those early days, I have always enjoyed getting away and staying away for as long as possible. On one of my last trips with Stacy I almost convinced my father-in-law that three more days on the Miramichi were just what the doctor ordered. My primary fishing trip partner was fighting a battle with lung and liver cancer. Of the 140 trips I have taken 43 of them was taken with Stacy before his death in 1997. We had to come back, however, to my brother's college graduation and a banquet given in honor of Stacy for a lifetime of work to bring the Atlantic salmon back to northern Maine. Despite the nice graduation and the recognition, both Stacy and I would have preferred to still be on a fishing trip.

As I think about these many fishing trips of the past and hopefully the many fishing trips of the future, I am reminded that as a Christian I am always travelling on a trip. As the song writer puts it, "This world is not my home I am just traveling through. . ." The Bible verifies this concept with verses like this, "Dearly beloved, I beseech you as strangers and pilgrims. . ." (1 Peter 2:11) We are always on a tremendous trip and an opportunity for fishing for men is around every corner!

# 117

# Fly Fishing

Behold, we count them happy which endure.
Ye have heard of the patience of Job . . .

—JAMES 5:11

What is it about fly fishing that causes a normal human being to stand in a body of water hour after hour and cast an imitation of an insect onto that body of water knowing full well that his chances for success are very limited?

When I first started fishing with my father-in-law, Stacy Meister, he warned me that fly fishing could become addictive. He never warned me of just how addictive it could become. What I would never tolerate in other forms of fishing, I put up with rather easily in fly fishing. I found that I loved the long hours of no action because of the sudden and unexpected thrill of the strike. One fish caught on a fly is worth one hundred fish caught any other way. Raised a worm fisherman, it was only after I met my wife to be and her registered Maine guide father (and a kindred spirit) that I became a fly fisherman. For twenty years Stacy showed me the fine points of fly fishing, whether salmon or trout, and now I will even fish for bass with a fly. Fly fishing has become my hobby as well as my pastime. I still on occasion participate in other forms of fishing (It is very hard to cast a #16 in the middle of January to an eight inch hole drilled in a frozen pond!), but if I had my way, I would fly fish the year around.

For me fly fishing first of all means challenge. There is an intimacy with a fish and a fly that no other form of fishing can supply. Fly fishing seems to be the natural way to catch a fish. Shiners for togue in the winter and night crawlers for bass in the summer are natural, but an artificial fly resembling a hatching insect strikes me even more so! Maybe it is the challenge that not any fly will do. I have stood in the waters of the Miramichi River in Canada for three days, cast every fly pattern in my possession, and still fail to hook a salmon even though I was casting over fish each time. I have stood waist deep in the heavy waters of the Big Eddy on the West Branch of the Penobscot River in central Maine all day, casting flies and changing flies, and my margin of defeat was not the size or the type, but the shade of color I was casting. Fly fishing is a challenge, but so rewarding when you finally discover all the right factors, and you hook a fish on a fly. The hours are not wasted but only add to the conquest.

Fly fishing is divine business because only when the Good Lord grants you grace to be there at the right time with the right fly will you hook the right fish. I too have learned that when you fly fish, you have to pray. You have to put your faith in something, and for me that something is Someone. It takes the same patience and purpose to cast the "gospel fly"—the pattern we call "God's love."

# 118

## Master Maker

*O come, let us worship and bow down; let us kneel before the Lord our maker.*
—Psalms 95:6

I met Stacy Meister for the first time when I went to his home on Maynard Street in Washburn, Maine, to take his oldest daughter Coleen on our first date. (We just celebrated our 50th date anniversary.) Little did I know on that spring evening the contact I had made.

Our relationship grew slowly as I was off to college within a few months. Four years away in South Carolina followed by five years away establishing a church in New Hampshire hindered our getting together except on the rarest of occasions. We had discovered that we had a common interest in fishing, but during those nine years of separation we only lake-fished together in Maine and Quebec, Canada. However, in the summer of 1978 my family and I moved back to northern Maine and settled in my hometown of Perham only seven miles from Stacy's house. Within a day, June 29, 1978, to be exact, Stacy had me fishing on the Aroostook River, and this time I had a fly rod in my hand and a hand-tied Meister Mosquito on the end of my line.

It wasn't the first time I had been exposed to a fly fisherman. My dad, Wendell, and my Uncle Hartson were avid fly fishermen. I had often gone fishing with them in my childhood, but I was too impatient to learn how to fly fish and pretty much stuck with worms and night crawlers. Stacy, however, encouraged me to try this new sport. He had all the equipment because he not only made his own flies, but his rods as well. On that first night out I landed three six-inch brook trout, and I was hooked. Since that day in 1978 I have kept records of every fish I have caught on a Meister Fly. As I begin finish compiling these "fly stories," I have just passed the forty-first anniversary of that fly fishing trip. This year's fishing season I passed the 9,000th mark, and I have added a few more, so as for now my grand total of fish caught on a fly is 9271. Until 1997, all my landings had been on a Meister fly, but since his passing I still caught fish on his flies, but have added the flies of Mike Hangge and Gab Garland (a very young teenage who has just started tying, but if he keeps at it will become an expert at it) and L.L Bean to my arsenal.

Stacy left me with thousands of flies, but now I am unable to go to him for a special fly. I have had to find a new fly tier. My friend and parishioner, Mike Hangge, now ties what I need, but I will continue to fish with Meister Flies as long as I live because Stacy will always be the Master Fly Tier in my book. He was an artist in his combination of feathers and furs, of thread and tinsel, of beads and yarn. Too prove this point, despite the 22 years since his passing on my last fishing trip to Canada; I was catching trout on flies Stacy had made in the 1980s and 1090s.

As with Stacy, the Lord is a Master "Maker." I believe the greatest crime of the evolutionary thought is that this title is being taken away from God. Whereas Stacy worked with God-made things, the Lord began with nothing (Hebrews 11:3) and created this wonderful world and all that is contained in it, including the fish (Genesis 1:20). He is, and will always be, the Master Maker for me.

# 119

## "There" Truth

For where your treasure is, *there* will your heart be also.

—MATTHEW 6:21, EMPHASIS ADDED

How many good Atlantic salmon fishing stories have you heard? Perhaps a better question is how many have you told? However, the best question is how many good salmon stories have you experienced? The difference between the first two questions and the last is, simply speaking, BEING THERE:

You have to be there to hear the roar of a salmon river cascading through a granite gorge as you stalk the unpredictable Atlantic salmon.

You have to be there to feel the pressure tug of the mighty waterway on your waders as you cast for ocean-wise salmon.

You have to be there to taste the fur and spruce spiced air as you motor slowly across your favorite salmon river in search of the one that got away.

You have to be there to enjoy your first feed of elk steak and onion hash as you watch a tidal pool rise and fall.

You have to be there to smell the edge of salty breeze and fresh water joining as the tidal waters meet and the king of ocean and stream flashes "silver in the sun."

You have to be there to see a calm pool erupt as a titanic swirl signals that an Atlantic salmon has taken your Silver Rat.

You have to be there to touch a tired salmon as you move it gently back and forth in a river's swift water to restore its precious life.

You have to be there to experience the satisfaction of fishing over salmon all day without a hit, but in the fleeting moments of daylight you catch the best salmon of the season.

You have to be there to savor the thrill of turning over your rod and reel to your only son after you've hooked your first salmon of the season.

You have to be there to know the joy that comes from catching the most elusive game fish in the world and then returning it back into its watery domain.

You have to be there to appreciate the sheer pleasure that comes from simply casting a fly after an Atlantic salmon with only a hope of ever catching one.

You have to be there to view the special places and people that are only seen where salmon are found and where salmon stories are believed.

Truly, it is when you add BEING THERE to a good salmon story that it becomes at least to you a great salmon story, and I've been there.

Such is the principle behind the verse highlighted above. If your heart isn't in His service, you are really not "THERE." And if you're not there, neither will the "treasure!"

# 120

# Fishing Friends

Ye are my friends, if ye do whatsoever I command you.
—John 15:14

I have always been a very friendly guy, but the making and needing friends is something I never spent much time pursuing. Don't get me wrong, I think having friends and being a friend is a wonderful pursuit, but I am by nature a loner and to have friend's means to be around people. My calling requires me to be near people most of the time so when I get a chance to get away it usually is away from people. However, over the years I have made certain friends while fishing. These friendships have only grown and matured with each fishing trip together. I have had the privilege of being there when they have experienced some of their finest encounters with the fish species. Out of these memorable memories comes this 'angling admonition'!

What is it that draws a rich man to a poor man, or one cousin closer to another? What is it that causes a friendship to develop despite distance and denomination? In these 'angling admonitions' I have introduce to you a father and a father-in-law; a cousin and a car salesman; a butcher and a brother-in-law; a truck broker and a teacher; a nephew and a nursing home manager; an eleven-year-old and an electrician; and a sower and a surveyor. There is but one common denominator between this preacher and these professional people, a love of fishing. It is what drew us together, and it is what keeps us together. It is what fostered our fishing friendship. It might have started with a simple hello on the banks of a river or sharing a secret method of attracting trout out of a particular pond. Maybe it was sharing a special fly or a private lodge on a Canadian river. It began by being born into the same family or going to the same church. The seed of friendship was sown and over the years as it was watered with companionship and comradeship, a growing relationship was the result. Interestingly, age had no restrictions either. The stories you have read and will read are about men of all ages. Some are younger, others older, and some the same age. When fishing age is rarely a factor because the love of fishing overcomes all natural barriers. If you can bait a hook, cast a fly, or land a fish, that is all it takes to bring kindred spirits into a bonding that time and troubles can't break.

I still have trouble with the concept that the Almighty God wants to be "friends" with us. I feel this was what God was doing each day as he walked with Adam and Eve in "the cool of the day." (Genesis 3:6) He was making friends. Jesus did the same thing as He walked the highways and byways of Galilee, He was making "friends." (John 15:15,29) I believe Solomon was talking about Jesus when he mentioned in one of his proverbs of ". . .a friend that sticketh closer than a brother." (Proverbs 18:24) Is He your friend?

# 121

## Fireside Five

Not forsaking the assembling of ourselves together, as the manner of some is; but exhorting one another: and so much the more, as ye see the day approaching.

—Hebrews 10:25

The smoke from the campfire drifted slowly upward, and the cracking fire casts an amber glow over the five fishermen drawn around it by the cool night air. The blue, green, and white tents stand out among the stunted spruce as a fiery sun sets slowly over an unknown mountain in the west. At the same time the silvery moon comes up over the ridge to the east and casts its shining shadow over the entire scene. One of the figures stands and throws another log on the fire which makes the sparks fly higher and higher. From a distance the only sound to be heard is the blending of the rushing river by the campsite, and a pair of loons calling loudly from across the bay.

The five men seem to be saying nothing as they sip Stacy's "swamp water" tea from their mugs and gaze admiringly at the beautiful campfire before them. However, before long the silence is broken by the wind blowing heavily through the trees. The moon quickly disappears behind a massive dark cloud. The group of five appear to be unmoved by the changing weather conditions. Suddenly, a flash of lightning to the south is followed by a sharp clap of thunder overhead. Nevertheless, the thunder and lightning are lost in the grandeur of the north country. The quiet five, deep in thought, hardly react to the quick shower that comes and goes as the moon makes another curtain call over their favorite camping and fishing spot.

The light from the fire dances in their eyes as thoughts of other days fishing in the north woods come into their memory. Thoughts, specifically of those special Stacy catches, come to mind, the kind that real fish stories are made of. The strike that was never followed up, but given to a son-in-law; the run that never ended, at least in Stacy's mind; the one that got away... As time moves on and a campfire is built facing the north, Stacy sits in front of it, gazes into it just right, and a fish story begins to emerge. After a few years, the tall tale takes on a life of its own. The fish grows bigger and longer. With each recall the fish takes more and more time to bring to the boat or bank. And with each passing campfire the legend of Stacy's fishing experience becomes more and more famous, until there is only one place the story is believed—around a blazing campfire in the outback of the great north woods.

The evening lengthens as the moon rises higher in the dark sky, and the river quiets down to a restful night's sleep. It is at that moment a word is heard from the circle of five saying, "Boys, let's pray and thank the Good Lord for another opportunity of being together in His great creation, and let us look forward to the day when He shall appear.

# 122

## Gauntlet Game

For we wrestle not against flesh and blood, but against principalities, against powers, Against the rulers of darkness of this world, against spiritual wickedness in high places.

—EPHESIANS 6:12

As my father-in-law, Stacy Meister, and I drove down Route Two from his home in Washburn, he told me of his brother's attempts to restore the salmon to the mighty Penobscot. It had been a difficult job with all the obstacles and pollution that were then in the river because of the modern advances made along the river's banks. It had taken a generation of policy change and restocking, but the salmon had returned in 1979 after a long and dangerous trip to the shores of Greenland. The first Atlantic salmon of a new generation had evaded deep sea fishing nets, seals, and numerous other enemies to return to the river of their stocking. Stacy had gotten a call from his brother, and it was time we joined the fishermen from all over the Northeast migrating to the Penobscot in search of the returning Atlantic salmon.

Our first stop that morning was the Bangor Salmon Pool where the first fish of the season had been caught. It was love at first sight. I have fished many salmon rivers since, and while the Penobscot never became my favorite, it will always be special because it was my "first love" in salmon streams. The tide was out when we got there so we had plenty of places to fish. Casting our flies into Ryder's Ledge Pool and Peavey Pool as well as The Pond, the gauntlet had been thrown, but no salmon took up the challenge. After a couple of hours we moved up river to the famous Edenton Pool. The spray from the river pouring over the Veazie Dam could be felt on my face as I stepped down to the banks of the Penobscot for my turn down through the run. There were a few fellow fishermen ahead of me as I began to cast my first "Thunder and Lightning" into the flow along the shore. It wasn't long, however, before I heard for the first time "fish on!" The echo of those two little words was just coming off the face of the dam when I turned my head to see the fisherman ahead with a bent rod. I watched my first struggle between salmon fisherman and salmon with delight. What a heart-pounding thrill! I hadn't been entertained like that before. The fresh Atlantic salmon jumped twice against the heavy ten foot rod and the swift current of the river in front of the rod rack. Ten minutes later a sparkling seven-pound salmon was netted. It was enough to make my number one wish from then on to be the capture of one of those fabulous fish.

As the salmon of the Penobscot ran the gauntlet of fishermen along the shores and in the surf, we run the gauntlet of principalities, powers, princes, and politicians of this world, and their one goal is to catch us.

# 123

## Angling Anglers

Fear not; from henceforth thou shalt catch men.

—Luke 5:10

I believe there is a distinction between fishing and angling. There are fishermen and there are anglers. Fishing is simply the pastime of catching fish by any means possible. Angling is choosing to catch fish in a specific manner. Ever since I received my first "Meister" fly rod, I became an angler, not simply a fisherman. I had been fishing since I was a lad, but in 1979 I really began angling. I like Steven J. Meyer's definition the best which is *"to use artful means to obtain an objective."* The objective is to catch a fish, and the artful means is by a fly attached to a fly rod.

Artfulness contains in its meaning objects of beauty. To the angler there are no two more beautiful objects in the world than a finely crafted rod and fly. Consider if you will my favorite fly rod. It has a name: Meister, named after my father-in-law, Stacy Meister, who created it. My first "Meister" was built in the fall of 1979 to replace an eight-foot trout rod I had accidently left on top of my father-in-law's pickup while on a fishing trip to central Maine after Atlantic salmon. We never did find the tip end. How many hours Stacy spent on it I dare not say, but for seventeen seasons it has passed every fish test I gave it. It has been semi-retired twice, only to be put back into service in an emergency. Twice it has had to be returned to Meister's expert hands to replace guides worn out by so much use. Its last accomplishment was in landing a couple of heavy duty black salmon on the Miramichi River near

Upper Blackville, New Brunswick, Canada. It had been taken along on the ride only as a backup for my newest "Meister," a nine foot salmon rod with a two-inch butt. It was given to me at Christmas in 1996 so I wouldn't take my son's salmon rod black salmon fishing as a backup for another "Meister" handcrafted for me in the winter of 1980–81.

As with the right equipment to catch the Atlantic salmon, you need the right methods to catch men for Christ. I have come to believe that we are to use Biblical methods to win people to a saving knowledge of Jesus. An old deacon of mine said many years ago, *"What you win them with you win them to!"* Paul stated very clearly that "It pleased God by the foolishness of preaching to save them that believe" (1 Corinthians 1:21). Today, many in the Church are trying to save their friends through concerts, conferences, and the current best sellers on the Christian book chart. Don't get me wrong. Music, books, and motivational speakers have their place, but God's method for saving souls has not been changed in 2000 years. As I am not about getting a new rod and fishing a new fly, we as Christians don't need to look for "another gospel" (Galatians 1:6), "another Jesus," or "another spirit" (2 Corinthians 11:4). And we don't need another form of preaching either.

# 124

## Slippery Salmon

Behold, ye have sinned against the Lord: and be sure your sin will find you out.
—Numbers 32:23

Here is a "true" fish story that illustrates Moses' precept highlighted above.

I was catching most of the fish on this particular trip so I decided to give the salmon a chance. Leaving my heavy rod at camp, I used my lightweight trout rod. Sure enough, I could land 33-inch salmon with that "Meister," too! The only problem was it took three times the time to land the fish. After hearing for the second time, "Aren't you ever going to land that fish so the rest of us can go fishing?" I figured I would return to the quick landing rod I normally used. That afternoon I was quickly back into the salmon while Stacy had been shut out going on the third day. He had hooked a salmon early in the trip, but had lost it when his hook let go. He hadn't had a hookup since, and we were in the final hours of our three day trip to the Miramichi River in New Brunswick, Canada.

I had just dropped my 2-ought Copper Renuos into Stacy's Run and was pulling the line back when the big salmon hit. Little did I know it was going to be the last fish for my big "Meister." The dark salmon fought hard against the swift current flowing through Stacy's Run (named after my father-in-law), but within ten minutes I had it to the boat and Irving had the big salmon net around it. It was a beautiful 32-inch salmon just starting to change into its silvery ocean color. Deciding I should have a picture of the nice fish, I asked Stacy to get my camera and take a picture. He had already gotten the fight on my movie camera so as he put down the video camera I laid my rod on the side of the boat. Taking the salmon from Irving, I had to turn around so Stacy could take the picture from the back of the boat. As I pivoted around, the big salmon slipped from my grasp. He went straight into the air and landed directly on the butt end of my rod just above the handle. There was a crunch and then a huge splash. The salmon had returned to the Miramichi, but not before smashing my "Meister." I had never lost a rod before in an accident, not stepping on one, not slamming one in a door, and not sticking one in the ground while walking through the woods. When was the last time you ever heard of a guy breaking his favorite salmon rod with a ten-pound salmon?

The rod is still proudly displayed over its original catch (a 46-inch Atlantic salmon) on a wall across from my office desk at the Emmanuel Baptist Church in Ellsworth, Maine. It is also displayed to remind me of the carnal sin I made that day on the Miramichi. Stacy had rehearsed in my ear for years to take care of the rod first, but when I failed to heed his warning, it cost me my favorite Atlantic salmon rod! So it is with God's warning about sin. One moment of unguarded thought or action could cost you more than a fishing rod.

# 125

## Comparison Concepts

Simon Peter saith unto then, I go a-fishing.

—John 21:3

I have fished ever since childhood, but I only began fishing-for-men in 1970 (I just finished my 50th year in that ministry (2019) and the Good Lord has been good to me in allowing me to lead at least one soul to Him every one of those years!). Over the years I have noticed a number of similarities between fishing for fish and fishing for men. These are my top seven comparisons:

A fisherman goes where the fish are. Matthew 28:19 *"Go!"*

I have never caught a fish in my fisherman's study. A fisherman has never caught a fish from his fishing boat while sitting in his backyard. Fish don't come to you, you go to the fish. Jesus' command to fisher-of-men is to "go." Jesus went to Samaria to catch the woman at the well.

A fisherman actively tries to catch fish. 2 Timothy 4:2 *"Instant!"*

I have talked to a lot of men who claim to be fishermen, but I have learned over time that they really like to canoe, or talk, or cook. This fisherman fishes! I know men that have all the equipment, but they never go fishing. I am ready to go fishing the minute the opportunity arises, and so ought we when fishing for men.

A fisherman likes to catch fish. Luke 15:10 *"Joy!"*

The man who says he goes fishing just for the fun and catching fish is a bonus is not a fisherman. The fisherman's greatest joy is when he has a fish on his line. I go fishing to catch fish, and I witness to others that they might come to a saving knowledge of Christ. Anything else is a waste.

A fisherman takes his fishing seriously. Romans 9:3 *"Accursed!"*

I work hard at fishing. I am serious and intense when I fish. I do everything in my power to catch a fish every time out. I don't fish to eat, I fish to fish. (James 5:20) Soul-winning is also serious business. The life of an eternal soul is in our hand. Fishing is a hobby, but fishing-for-men is a profession. (Ephesians 4:1)

A fisherman knows that different fish require different fishing methods. 1 Corinthians 9:22 *"Means!"*

I don't fish bass the same way I fish salmon. Even spring salmon fishing is different than fall salmon fishing. Jesus dealt differently with Zacchaeus than he did with Nicodemus. Adapting is the key to fishing and fishing-for-men.

A fisherman always knows that fishing is difficult at best. Matthew 10:16 *"Midst!"*

Fish always have the advantage. You can be shut out anytime. (Luke 5:5) You don't always catch fish on every cast. The key is to keep at it.

A fisherman knows it takes time, effort, and practice to be a top-notch fisherman. 1 Corinthians 15:58 *"Steadfast!"*

Keep casting. Keep fishing. "Throw out the lifeline across the dark waves, there is a brother whom someone should save!" Be known for goin' fishing'!

# 126

## Hampton Harvest

And Jesus said unto them, come ye after me, and I will make you to become fishers of men.

—MARK 1:17

I have been a fisherman most of my life, but it wasn't until 1970 that I became a "fisher-of-men." Having moved over the years from fishing hole to fishing hole, I have discovered some productive spots and favorite places to fish for fish. The same has been true in my spiritual fishing. Over the last fifty years I have cast the Gospel fly called "Christ's love" into many a "deep [Luke 5:4] pool," but without a doubt the most successful spiritual fishing "hole" has been a Canadian "pool" called Hampton Bible Camp.

In 1987 I was asked for the first time by the new director of Hampton Bible Camp, Dwayne Gray, to share a week of messages to a group of 10 to 13 year olds. I had fished in Canada for many years, but this was only my second spiritual fishing trip to the land across the border. On July 5 I arrived with my family to minister to the kids of this CSSM horse camp. (Yes, you can even fish in a "pool" filled with horses!) At that stage in my life being a camp pastor was not a new experience. I had conducted services in half a dozen other camps, but hadn't been very successful in seeing much of "a catch for Christ." In six days I shared 19 messages and 10 young people came to know the Lord Jesus Christ as their personal Savior. I was thrilled, and Heaven rejoiced. To lead ten people to Christ in the fishing hole called "church work" had taken me years to achieve, yet within a week I had a limit I had never experienced before!

Since that opening week, I have returned to "fish" Hampton every year except in 1994 when just before I was to head out for my favorite "fishing hole," I had a kidney stone attack. So for 21 "seasons' (my last year was 2009 when the camp director left and the new one never called me back), I have returned again and again to cast the Word of God into the hearts of the campers who make Hampton their home for a week in the summer. I kept fishing records (50 years, 982 days, 11,409 fish), both literally and spiritually, and in 21 years fishing 126 days, I have made 512 Gospel "casts" to 1592 kids of which 211 young people responded positively to the presentation. And to think the old fishing hole would be playing out is far from the truth. As a matter of fact, last summer (2002) was the best trip I have ever made to "the Hampton horse pool" when in 24 casts to 106 campers, the Lord landed 25 into His "net" of salvation!

My most thrilling "catch" at Hampton took place one night when I was tired from a difficult day in the "deep." The camp seemed harder than usual, and I was beginning to think there was little interest when a knock came to my door. It was one of the lady counselors saying that her room of girls wanted to meet me down in the chapel. What happened there in the next hour will forever be my best day "fishing." One by one, I led each girl (8 total) to the "net," and Jesus, "the true Fisherman," landed each of them safely!

# 127

## Fabulous Find

We have found Him...

—John 1:45

The thought for this 'angling admonition' began over ten years ago even if the actual writing has only been over the last two years. I still recall the first day my father-in-law, Stacy Meister, brought me to Vickers' Salmon Camps nestled on the banks of the mighty Miramichi. The location left nothing to be desired. It was down a short, dead end woods road. Its path was narrow and muddy and snow was still in the woods, and a thick screen of trees and shrubs lined the roadway down to the camps. The two cottages were tucked away on a small shelf overlooking the river. Unknown and unnoticed by most who drive by, this hallowed hideaway has become one of the very special places I have discovered in my Christian pilgrimage where I "find Him."

As the early followers of Christ sought and found Jesus, we have found it necessary to "find Him" again. Lost in the Christianization of Christianity, our Master has been lost in the rite and rituals of religion. No longer is He sought after because what most seek is a formal religion that conforms to their lifestyle and needs. Little do they realize that it is imperative to develop a personal relationship with the Almighty. I have been preaching this concept for over 50 years now, that the only way to have a friendship with the Almighty is to find Him in His Son the Lord Jesus Christ, and may I underline "the only way?"

To do that you must get alone and find a closet, a quiet place where it is just you and Him. Don't get me wrong, there are other places besides Vickers' Camps, but on the night I write this it is just Him and me. I have the main lodge to myself. The doctor, the owner, and his doctor friend are across the yard in the small camp. The other two fishermen here are in the new cabin by Irv's Spring. Irving, the caretaker, and his wife Marsha, the cook, have gone home after a long day watching after the needs of the five of us. I am alone with Him and the flowing of the low river over its rocky bottom. The rustling of fall leaves by the wind announces the unexplainable presence of Him.

Few are the places in this world that bring such an intimate interaction with Him in my life. Here I sense Him. I am, despite the familiarity, drawn to this place. Here, alone with Him, I am exhorted, edified, and encouraged. Here I hear His "messages" clearly, and my hand can't write fast enough to get it all down. Sixty-two years ago I found Him for the first time when I was sitting in the front row of a junior church in my small county church in Perham, Maine. It thrills me to think that after nearly six and a half decades that I am still excited each time I "find Him" as I did tonight, sitting in a chair beside me in the living room of Vickers' Lodge.

# 128

## Writing Water

Write the things which thou hast seen.
—REVELATION 1:19

For more than ten fishing seasons I have been coming to the shores of the Miramichi River in Canada. I am again sitting in the main lodge at Vickers' Salmon Pools overlooking New Brunswick's premier salmon river. Tomorrow I will start to finish what I began in early spring, my eleventh season on "the river" which has been planned as "the first and the last." I fished the first three days of the season (April 15–17), and I will fish the last three days of the season (October 13–15).

One of my favorite writers, W. Phillip Keller, once wrote in his book *Still Waters*, "Writing is a tremendously demanding discipline." That might be true for most writers, but for me, on the banks of the Miramichi, this is not true. Each time I come to this inspiring place, I am inspired to write something. From time to time it is important I come to a place like Vickers' camps to hear clearly the "messages" the Lord gives me. I am alone in the main lodge as the night darkens and the anticipation of the first cast draws near. Until then, I am drawn to pen and paper to write like John. This is not labor for me, but a labor of love. The trip to this place through brightly colored lanes of orange, yellow, and red, I am filled with the sights of a splendid autumn and my impressions of a colorful Creator.

If you have gotten this far in "Angling Admonitions," then you know that I am a fisher-of-men who loves to fish. I love everything about fishing, from the hunt to the thrill of the release. I love the places fishing takes me and the unique oneness that I have with God while fishing. I have tried to share in these "messages," the deep devotion I feel when I am alone with God in the middle of the Miramichi surrounded by a few salmon. I hope that I have also recalled for your enlightenment the exciting exhortations I have received while fishing. God's sermons seem so clear to me near water or while I travel to some distant waterway.

As I travelled the 260 miles to Vickers' Salmon Pools, I experienced again a release. I know that might sound funny to some, but "release" is a word I have chosen with great care. The miles passed quickly in my old 1982 Omega as I viewed one after another the brilliant maples. Decked out in their best fall garb, I exchanged the drab of the city for the heavenly brightness of God's wonderful fall masterpiece. Just a quick glance and they were gone, but around the next corner was another spectacular example of God's handiwork. I never spoke or uttered a word, but my heart leaped for joy to think I knew personally the Artist. Open spaces lined with a rainbow of colors, highlighted by stately maples, underlined by the blue waters and it's known as the Miramichi River Valley. I wrote it down so you too might know my Creator and His wonderful creation, and what you too can experience every time you go looking for a soul to catch!

# 129

## Daybreak Dawn

Jesus Christ the same yesterday, and today, and forever.
—Hebrews 13:8

I rolled over and noticed the red numbers of the camp clock. It was 6:47 AM. Another Miramichi morning was just beginning. It was the third dawn of a late season trip to the New Brunswick river. On the first morning of my salmon fishing trip the fog was so thick I could barely see the river just twenty-five yards from my bedroom window. The next morning it was raining liquid ice through a chilly northern gale. On the morning of my third day I awoke to a cold, clear, crisp daybreak. A cloudless night had resulted in a very heavy frost. It was so white it might have been mistaken for a light dusting of snow. Despite the frosty start, an awesome, breathless sun was breaking clear of the ridge on the other side of the river.

There are those still, sacred, special moments in which it is just you and God. The other camp residents hadn't stirred yet, and Marsha and Irving hadn't arrived either. The presence of God was near, very near. There was barely a breath of air as the few remaining leaves swung slightly on their stem. It is the middle of October and each move could be their last, but not today. It was time for the fall foliage to fall, but there are always a few stubborn, steady leaves that hang on unmoved by white frost or Arctic winds. Tomorrow might be different, but on this the last Atlantic fishing day of the 2002 season, the leaves would hang on for another day. and so would I.

There is an overwhelming feeling of stillness, a quiet interlude unmatched by any other time of the day when you are on a river. Because of the location of Vickers' Camps, there isn't even a sound of distant cars. There is nothing in the camp yard to disturb the stillness for about an hour or so. The cooks will come and so will the guides. The fisherman in camp will stir for breakfast, but now it is my time with my Maker. Morning moments before dawn when the Eternal seems so near, it is time for me to know that He is God and to hear His sweet, soft, still voice say, "Morning Bear."

As I look out the big picture window in my room, I see the gently flowing river. The water is low so each distinct rock formation at the bottom of the river can be clearly seen. The endless, timeless river doesn't seem to change, just like my God. I had a fellow sportsman comment about the view yesterday on how it doesn't change, and I replied that it hadn't since I first came to its shores in 1992. The same can be said of my God. He is the same every morning. I sit alone watching the daybreak over the Miramichi, and I realize that He came on vacation with me. I know He is there, but I also believe He is here. I cannot in my finite mind comprehend the enormity of the presence of God, but I do know He is here, near, and dear to me.

# 130

## Huge Hen

> ...and cast an hook, and take up the fish that first cometh up...
> —MATTHEW 17:27

I know that there are a number of species of fish swimming up the Miramichi River, but I care for none of them except the Atlantic salmon. I travelled 265 miles from home to fish for salmon. If I have learned anything about salmon fishing in 23 seasons, it was that, like Peter in the verse above, it depends more on the Lord than on the lure!

    A case in point is the special salmon I caught today. I am once again sitting on the couch in the master bedroom of Vickers' main lodge located on a knoll overlooking the Miramichi. It is October 14, Canadian Thanksgiving Day, and darkness has once again blotted out my view of the waterway. On this the next to the last day of the 2002 fishing season I am the only man in camp to have landed a fish. Over the last few days of the Atlantic salmon fishing season, despite a half dozen men in camp, it was the Good Lord who allowed me to catch the last salmon of the season.

    After hundreds of casts over tens of salmon, a huge hen grabbed my fly over Beaver Bar just before five o'clock, only a few hours ago. Because the river is so low, only a foot and a half of water was flowing over the bar when the fish hit. The second the salmon took the #4 fly it made a mighty swirl that could be clearly seen by me, my guide, Kenneth Sullivan, and the boys down river. In the mad rush to get away with her prize, the salmon burst through the barrier of water breaking clear of her watery dominion.

Into the raw, windy air she leaped, not once, not twice, but three times! Her tarnished silver sides arched high into the afternoon sky trying desperately to throw the double hook buried in her jaw. Each time she cleared the river, the hook tightened its grip. Ripples radiated across the pool each time she reentered her world, leaving widening rings marking clearly her location to me and my guide.

As if I was watching one of those outdoor television shows, I kept my eye on her flashy, darting form as I steadily pulled her closer and closer to Ken's open net. Each time she saw our shadows (because the sun was setting behind us) she would rush back into deeper water, and her shining sides would reflect the drying rays of the sun that reached down through the clear, cool water. In the swift, smooth swish of her tail I saw the power that had gotten her to Vickers' Pools. Little did she know that her magnificent journey was not coming to an end. As she tired, I drew her closer to shore. After nearly a quarter of an hour she came too close, and Ken had her in his net.

She was a gift to me, a prize of God's grace, and she had nothing to fear because after her eggs were stripped by the Miramichi Salmon Club she would be returned to swim and spawn again. (The huge hen was 33 inches at 13.7 pounds!) Whether a 'soul' or a 'salmon', one must never forget that both come from the Lord, Oh, we play a part but we can never take credit for either, for they are all of God mercy and grace!

# 131

# Two Thanksgivings

and be ye thankful.

—COLOSSIANS 3:15

In 2002 I will celebrate two Thanksgivings. I have always thought that America skips over Thanksgiving day to get to Christmas. The last Thursday of November I will recognize and celebrate America's traditional Thanksgiving, but this year I also had opportunity to celebrate Canada's Thanksgiving as well. On the same weekend we honor Columbus, the Canadians are celebrating their Thanksgiving Day. Instead of being home this year, I was fishing the Miramichi River at Vickers' Pools when this Canadian holiday happened, and for my first Canadian Thanksgiving I have something very thankful to be grateful about.

I have just come off the river with my host, Marty Vickers, and my guide, Kenneth Sullivan. Ken and I met this spring for the first time when he guided me for three days of spring salmon fishing. I have known of the doctor for ten years, but it has only been in the last few years that I have had opportunity to fish with him. On this my sixteenth fishing trip to the Miramichi River I had a chance to fish with the doctor on the last three days of the 2002 season.

For the first day and a half the fishing had been difficult at best. That doesn't mean there were no fish in the river because there were plenty. (I saw nearly 140 rolls and rises in the first two days!) Despite fishing over fish, nobody was hooking fish. (I think the salmon had spawning on their minds!) That all changed for one salmon around 4:45 PM on October 14, Thanksgiving Day in Canada.

I had fought a heavy "up river" wind through the Upper Run. (Vickers' Pools are divided between the Upper and Lower Pools.) Taking the advice of an old guide, Irving Vickers, I had tied on a fly that had never seen the river. (It was an original fly pattern tied by my father-in-law many years before.) It was a large fly (#4) for fall fishing, but it was just what was needed. I was fishing my father-in-laws' rod and reel, a heavy 10-foot rod with an English reel. (Stacy had passed away in the fall of 1997, and his wife had passed them on to me.)

The combination of a heavy fly, a heavy leader (12 lbs.), and a heavy rod allowed me to cut through the gusty wind as I approached Beaver Bar. (Beaver Bar is at the bottom of the Upper Run, the last pool in that section of the river.) I made one cast into Beaver Bar and a bright hen salmon engulfed the new, old fly. For the next 10–15 minutes I fought the salmon for control of the "bar." Her thirty-three inch frame came out of the water three times before Ken netted her, and we placed her in the Miramichi Salmon Club box. (The Club collects late fall salmon for their eggs and sperm.) Pictures were taken and a film was shot of the process, and I had my largest fall run salmon to date. Now, that is something to be thankful for on Canada's Thanksgiving Day, even if you are an American. We forget sometimes Paul's admonition: *"In every give thanks: for this is the will of God in Christ Jesus concerning you."* (1 Thessalonians 5:18)

# 132

## Mellow Moods

Peace I leave with you, my peace I give unto you . . .

—John 14.27

Perhaps, the most significant and meaningful impact that Vickers' Salmon Pools has on my soul is in providing a restful peace. Even after a day like today, when I saw 72 salmon jumps (some jumped literally beside me and some directly in front of me), rolls, or swirls, yet failed to hook a single one, I am at peace, content just to be here. Repose and restoration linger here despite the frustration one feels at times not being able to tempt a fish to bite. Harmony and a healthful atmosphere fill this place. The Miramichi River Valley is full of mellow moods.

    This stretch of New Brunswick, Canada, has for over ten years had me in its spell. I am one with this place whether fishing in the river or feasting at the lodge. I had my first deep fried turkey tonight. Last night it was two-inch steaks. The fishing has been pitiful, but the meals have been plentiful. Despite the fact I am rubbing elbows with mostly medical doctors, four at last count, I am one with them because of our common love of Atlantic salmon fishing. There is something very unique about such a place, a place where you belong, a place you're treated like family, a place where peace abounds.

    Some would thank Dr. Vickers, the owner, for this, and I have, but all afternoon as the warmth of a mid-October day engulfed me and my fishing companions, I thanked God in verse and in song for this interlude from life's "haste and waste." The older I get the more I am thankful for a quiet, peaceful few days away from a busy, buzzing, backwater town. I find peace here, and I am convinced that ten years ago when my father-in-law first brought me here, he had no idea I would still need it five years after his "departure."

This afternoon I fished mostly through Stacy's Pool. Besides the salmon I saw a flight of ducks shoot up river winging low over the surface of the waterway. I saw a pair of eagles late in the day cruising up river no doubt in search of supper. These only added to the peaceful scene, and it reminded me again of the verse printed above. The Heavenly Father does take personal interest in our serenity as much as a father-in-law. Each time I come here I am constantly reminded that God cares for us both bodily and spiritually. I am embraced here with His presence and engulfed with His love. His peace "that passeth understanding" can be as simple as an afternoon standing in four feet of 45-degree water watching a peaceful river full of salmon flow by. Sensations of this sort produce "mellow moods" in my entire being. Standing in the soft afterglow of a fallish sun followed by the moon glow of a half-moon puts me at peace with myself, my world, and my God. I would encourage anybody to find such a place for themselves. And is not that the reason we share our faith, so that a restless world will find the same peace we enjoy in sins forget, on our way to heaven, and the Spirit of peace in our hearts?

# 133

# Delightful Day

This is the day which the Lord hath made; we will rejoice and be glad in it.
—Psalms 118:24

From a foggy daybreak to a starry evening, my 45th day on the Miramichi River is one worth recording, not for the fish I caught (because I hooked none of the 72 fish I saw), but simply because "this is the day which the Lord hath made."

For years I have been numbering my days (Psalms 90:12) as the Psalmist suggests. Today was number 18,851. It was a day of contrasts to say the least. It was cold in the morning and warm for October in the afternoon. It was foggy before noon and clear after lunch. It was windy before dark, but at dusk the wind died down. The river was rough with the wind up, but smooth as glass when the wind calmed down. At times I could see the mirrored image of the breathtaking beauty of the fall foliage reflected off the water, and at other times the reflection was distorted. There were times when I thought there wasn't a fish in the river. It was a day the Good Lord decided to create for its diversity.

Have you ever pondered a single day the Lord has created for you? Maybe for everyone else, but have you considered it as a day just for you? According to my deacons, today, October 13, 2002, is Pastor Appreciation day. I have been a pastor nearly thirty years and have been much appreciated by most of the people I have labored among. I am thankful that my church gave me this day off and my wife freely let me go on vacation alone, but more than that I rejoice in this day as a day the Lord has given me because it includes time spent alone with Him in my private room in the main lodge at Vickers' Camps. I am sitting before a huge picture window that overlooks the sleeping stream. It is dark and hard to see, but I know what I am looking at. I am reading W. Phillip Keller's book *Still Waters*, a book about a lakeside camp he turned into a home. This is not home for me, but each day I am here is like being home, and home is the greatest feeling in the world.

"This is the day the Lord has made for me." I am thankful for each moment as I finish its minutes. I will finish this day as I do most of my days now, reading His Word and falling asleep praying praises to Him. A few years ago I started a pattern in my God-given days. "Soon after night" I wake and my first thoughts are "Morning Lord," and He says to my heart, "I have another day for you." Then "soon after noon" I acknowledge Him again and pray. Finally, "soon after nine" I say, "Goodnight Lord," and thank Him for the grace to finish another day in His service.

The next time the Lord gives you a day as He did for me today to meditate and ponder, why not take some of that day and do as the Psalmist suggests, ". . .rejoice and be glad in it. . ."

# 134

## Rejoice Reflections

Rejoice in the Lord always; and again I say, rejoice.

—Philippians 4:4

I am writing, but I am also watching. It is 1:30 PM, and I am waiting for my guide to return from lunch so I can go back fishing. I will fish Johnson Rock this afternoon. It seems to be the hot spot right now at Vickers' Pools on the Miramichi River. Two men from Portland, Jens Jorgensen and Fred Robinson, have caught three fish there in two days. Jens got a 32 and 30-inch salmon and Fred landed a 38 incher, one of the largest fish of the season. As I wait I watch for any sign of salmon in the pool, and as I watch I write, and as I write I rejoice in all three.

 I rejoice in the sound of the wave action on rock and sand, and the rhythmic splash of water each time a salmon comes clear of the waterway. The calming noise of water on rocks, rocks piled up in mounds by Irving and Marty to make breakwaters for the salmon to hide behind against the strong flow of the Miramichi. Their hope is the salmon will stop long enough for a fisherman to get a fly in front of them. Now that is something to rejoice about!

 The same river that gives me salmon sightings and stone sounds also gives me a place to meditate and ponder the greatness of God. Despite the fact I didn't hook a salmon this morning, I had a wonderful first morning. It was foggy and cool. I was standing in 45-degree water. I rejoiced all morning over insulated waders, wool socks, and warm clothes. It was cold, yet to me it was paradise. It was so serene and still it was heavenly. Some people picture Heaven as a crowded city, but I believe Heaven will be like a morning in an engulfing fog fishing for salmon in the "River of Life." (Revelation 22:1) In this I rejoice.

I rejoice in the privacy and seclusion of Vickers' Camps. Despite the fact there are five other fishermen in camp, it is still very private. I am alone as I write on the river's bank. This morning during peak fishing tine, 9–11 AM, I counted 13 other fishermen on both sides of the river, yet I was alone, lost in the thought of the goodness of God that gave me a Sunday off to be here. As my church in Ellsworth, Maine, was worshipping in their sanctuary, I was worshipping Him in the stream. I sang hymns and thought of sermons. I rejoice that we can worship Christ anywhere!

Finally, I rejoice in the beauty of the maples around the river. They are my favorite fall tree because of the wonderful colors they paint. Foliage of flaming yellows combined with hot orange and crimson make the banks of the Miramichi almost as appealing as the silver-sided salmon in its waters. Then there are the red sugar maples, the most magnificent of them all. Recently, I sent my daughter in Pennsylvania a few such leaves from a scarlet version of this classic tree so she too could rejoice in God's colors.

# 135

## Climate Change

Thou, O God, didst send a plentiful rain . . .

—Psalms 68:9

As I went to bed last night there was no sign of what was in store for me when I awoke to my second morning on the Miramichi River. The moon was high and half, but bright and clear with every heavenly star twinkling. I fell asleep about ten, and because of a hard day on the river, I slept like a baby. I didn't hear the rain when it began.

Long, long before the breaking of the dawn there was a stirring in the fall leaves outside Vickers' main camp where I was sleeping. It started out a gentle breeze, but soon the wind turned into a cold northern gale. The first drops hit the river unnoticed by any of the fishermen in the camps, but soon the rain turned into a torrent as a mid-October storm blew in up the river unexpectedly, and, to be honest, unwanted. I have fished in the rain and cold before on this river, and I knew what the wind and the rain would do to casting a light fly after migrating salmon.

I left the camp alone for the upper pools. The other five fishermen and two guides decided to wait a bit before they came into the storm. I walked along the shore alone in a steady autumn rain. Soon the odd drop of water was getting through my insulated rain suit. I had my insulated waders on so the only place water could penetrate was near my face. It was a raw rain, but my fisherman's heart was already thinking that this might be just what the salmon needed to change their appetite. The day before had been a warm

Indian summer day, but nobody in camp hooked a fish. Maybe, just maybe, a climate change would change the fish.

The ancient sound of falling rain increased as I stepped alone into the top of the first pool. Water was bouncing off everything as I began to cast my small double "Copper Killer" into the flow of the river. It was not long before I noticed the first rise of the day at "split rock." The "dimple" produced the first salmon swirl. It was exciting to think that the rain had at least stirred up the local salmon population, and at least for the moment I had them all to myself. The rain was now denting the river with large holes. It was then from far down the river I saw the trees along the shore change. A furious gale was working its way towards me. Combined with the wet rain and arctic wind my hands were frozen. I knew that the climate on the river had changed, and it was time to adapt.

I fished the rest of the morning in terrible conditions, but as noon approached the rain stopped and the wind became manageable, but I was still looking for my first hookup of the trip. Late that afternoon a beautiful hen made my trip worthwhile. Despite the wind and rain, the change in the weather had affected the salmon, and I landed the only fish caught that day. When the Good Lord changes the climate in your life, look for a hidden blessing in the upheaval.

# 136

## Windy Wind

I would hasten my escape from the windy storm and tempest.
—PSALMS 55:8

This was a day in October when the wind came winging in on a gale.

I left the warmth of Vickers' Lodge for an early morning fishing trip in a cold pouring rain. Being very well dressed for the weather, I didn't mind the walk up the bank of the river or the walk back down through the river. There was little wind so I figured despite the rain I could still fish affectively. As I started down through the upper pool, I notice that the tops of the trees on the ridge were beginning to move. The Miramichi River sets in a small valley about two hundred feet below the ridge line to the east of Vickers' Salmon Pools. It took the wind a few minutes to work its way down to my level, but when it did, it changed my fishing dramatically.

Watching down river I could see the front coming. A cold front was expected with a stiff northern wind to follow the rain. The gusty winds would throw my fly "up river" instead of down river where the salmon were laying. It makes fishing tough, but not impossible. I did have to switch to a heavier rod and leader and a larger fly, but in the end that would work to my benefit as I caught the last Atlantic salmon of the season at Vickers' Pools.

The events of this day on the Miramichi reminded me of the verse printed above. This is what most people do when the wind and water comes in on a gale. I must admit that I sought shelter in the guide's hut a couple of times that morning, a place to get in out of the rain and wind and a place to dry off and get warm. Standing in the wood-heated hut though would not fulfill the purpose of my last season fishing trip to the Miramichi which was to catch a salmon. Whatever the weather, a fisherman must be in the river casting his fly if he is to ever land a salmon. This precept is also true in life.

James writes, "My brethren, count it all joy when ye fall into divers temptations. Knowing this, that the trying of your faith worketh patience. But let patience have her perfect work, that ye may be perfect and entire, wanting nothing" (James 1:2–4). I have learned over the years in life and in fishing that some of life's greatest blessings come with a rainy wind or a windy rain. Unexpected and unwanted, you find a joy somehow in the middle of it all that you will never forget and are always thankful for. The powerful northern wind had pushed the storm in, but it had just as quickly pushed it out so that by the time I found my fish for this trip, it was a clear, sunny day. Granted, it was tougher to throw a fly, yet, as in life, we adapt and become more patient. Patience and perseverance will in the end be rewarded as it was on that day on the Miramichi.

# 137

## Several Senses

...which neither see, nor hear...nor smell?

—DEUTERONOMY 4:28

My first morning of fishing is over on this Pastor Appreciation Sunday. One of the reasons I am on the Miramichi River is the generous gratitude of my flock in Ellsworth, Maine. When they discovered that I had made plans in the spring to come in the fall, and that the dates actually fell on this Sunday to thank pastors, they were even more excited to give me the four days off to go fishing. It was their way to say thanks, and they know how much I enjoy coming to this piece of God's colorful earth.

From a foggy start, the sun has come out and for the middle of October it is actually warm. As I write these thoughts I am sitting on a bench on a bluff overlooking the banks of the Miramichi River. The water is low. Every major rock in this section of the river can be seen. If you look carefully, you can see the path the salmon have to take to navigate this part of the Miramichi, and the salmon are running. I saw 36 of them this morning alone, not counting the 12 I saw yesterday afternoon after I arrived at Vickers' Camps. Besides the rolls and rises, I did witness a hookup as a man on the far shore tempted a bright salmon to bite. The fish ran straight at me before exiting the river and throwing the fly. What a sight!

The sounds, sights, and smells are spectacular, and it is of them I would write this noon hour. Unlike the idols described by Moses in the verse above, I bring my senses of sight, smell, and sound when I come to the Miramichi.

As I write I hear I hear the buzzing of insects in my ears. Despite the lateness of the season, the Indian summer day has brought out the last brave bugs of the year. Rarely do they survive to October, but on this day they can make a final flight. Bugs bother most folks, but I am by God's wonderful waterway, and a few blackflies and mosquitoes can't dampen my joy.

Next, I hear the babbling brook before me. (Yes, water really does babble!) It is the sound of water over rocks. It is one of the most tranquil noises I know. It calms the nerves, and it relaxes the brain. Then there is the light breeze blowing through the colorful leaves of the trees. Sight and sound combined at this time of the year excite both senses at once. I am also sitting under a Canadian flag which is singing its own song as it flaps in the breeze.

The smells of autumn are also everywhere on the shores of this waterway. The smell of dry grass and dry leaves are pleasant smells I remember from my childhood. It is not a decaying smell to me, but a sweet aroma that speaks of harvest and a successful planting season. I just hope that I will have a successful harvest on this river this fall. I have seen salmon, and I have heard salmon, but I haven't gotten close enough to smell one yet. (But I did the next day!)

# 138

## Providential Provision

Notwithstanding, lest we should offend them, go thou to the sea, and cast an hook, and take up the fish that first cometh up; and when thou hast opened his mouth, thou shalt find a piece of money: that take, and give unto them for me and thee.

—Matthew 17:27

I too have caught fish with something in their mouth, but never money! In one of the most amazing "fish stories" of the Bible, we have a tremendous insight into the person of Christ. In the debate over paying taxes, I see these marvelous truths about Jesus:

1. The piety of Christ. Piety means devotion to religious duty and practice. It was for this reason, I believe, that Jesus dropped the privilege of being the Son of God and paid the Temple tax. By rights Jesus didn't have to pay because it was His temple, but he wanted Peter to learn a lesson we still need to learn. In the first century the "fish" was the symbol of Christianity because taking the first Greek letters of this phrase "Jesus Christ God's Son Savior" spells fish in the Greek language. The "fish" Peter caught on that day was symbolic of what kind of Christian we ought to be. What kind of devotion do you demonstrate?

2. The power of Christ. I see two things in this "fish story." First, Christ's omniscience. He knew which fish had the coin. How many fish were

there in Galilee Lake? Yet Jesus knew one had a coin in its mouth. Only God can know such things. Second, Christ's omnipotence. He made the fish bite Peter's hook, probably not the only hook or net in the water at that time. Jesus was in control of the actions of a single fish. Only God can do such things. Jesus told His disciples that He had been given "power" (Matthew 28:18), and that power included control over the "fish" of the Sea of Galilee.

3. The poverty of Christ. Jesus didn't have enough money in His pocket to pay the tax. Once again we have an illustration of Christ's poverty. (2 Corinthians 8:9) He became poor for us. He had no place to lay his head, and He was homeless for us. (Matthew 8:20) Think with me for a moment of the pattern clearly seen in the gospels. Christ borrowed a boat to preach from because He owned no boat. Christ borrowed a lunch from a small boy because He had no food to share with the people that had come to hear Him speak. Christ borrowed a donkey to ride into Jerusalem because He owned no animal. Christ borrowed a room to celebrate the Passover with His disciples because He had no such place. Christ borrowed a tomb to be buried in because He had no grave site. It is, therefore, not surprising He had to send Peter fishing for the Temple tax.

# 139

# Special "Ships"

*They that go down to the sea in ships that do business in great waters.*
—PSALMS 107:23

Fishing and boating go hand in hand. Though I do a lot of wading, some of my best fishing trips have taken place in a boat. There is a spiritual connection to this practical reality in fishing. Isaiah 57:20 tells us that humanity is like a "sea." Psalms 107:23 tells us that there is a "business" to be done in the great sea. I believe the two are connected when you consider the "ships" that are necessary to "fish" for men. Consider the following if you will:

1. Discipleship. Luke 14:26,27,33. Part of discipleship is witnessing. (Matthew 28:19) What are we supposed to "make" in the world? Disciples! Disciples catch disciples. Discipleship is an all-out commitment to Christ.

2. Fellowship. 1 John 1:6,7. We speak of fellowship with the "saints" and our Savior, but we are to have fellowship with "sinners" as well. Jesus spent the bulk of His time in the world in fellowship with publicans and sinners. How are we to reach them if we don't fellowship with them? Note, we are to fellowship with them, not have fellowship with their unrighteous works. (Ephesians 5:11)

3. Friendship. Proverbs 6:3; 17:17; 18:24. Again we are to be careful with this "ship" because of the warning of James 4:4, but we must show

ourselves friendly if we are to win people to Christ. Christ is again the perfect example as He showed Himself friendly to the woman at the well and the publican of Jericho. Friendship evangelism is perhaps one of the most successful methods in witnessing. Friends have led friends to Christ throughout the history of the Church.

4. Stewardship. 1 Corinthians 4:2. Do you give your money to reach others? Most would say yes. I believe that stewardship in witnessing is more than supporting the missionary. It is about giving of your time and talents to this great fishing endeavor as well. Part of going to the sea in ships is having you on board. Many pay for the fisherman and his fishing boat, but few get on board and fish themselves.

5. Scholarship. 2 Timothy 2:15. To spiritually fish you need to know the Bible. You need to know how to "rightly divide the Word of God." You need to have the answers for a dying world. (1 Peter 3:15) We are promised that "the Word" will not return void. (Isaiah 55:11) Our words will fall on deaf ears, but the Word of God has power (Hebrews 4:12) to break through spiritual deafness and spiritual blindness (2 Corinthians 4:4) and touch the soul. Are you using properly these "ships" in your fishing-for-men?

When was the last time you went "fishing" in one of these "ships?" From these "ships" souls can be caught.

# 140

## "Deep" Disciples

Launch out into the deep . . .

—LUKE 5:4

One of my favorite fishing stories of the Bible is now much clearer in its meaning. Ever since I heard a message by Dr. David Jeremiah on television, the truth of this fishing trip by Jesus has taken on a new explanation. What was Jesus really fishing for when he commanded Peter to "let down your nets for a draught?" David Jeremiah suggests that Jesus was really fishing for "disciples."

In this fishing trip into the "deep," Jesus was looking for certain characteristics in these Galilee fishermen that would make them fishers-of-men (Luke 5:10). Consider what Jesus found in the "deep."

1. Disciples who responded positively to the Lord's command. " . . . Nevertheless at thy word . . ." (Luke 5:5) Despite the fact Jesus' order was not logical and far from reasonable to the experienced fisherman, Peter, not yet a disciple, was still acting like a disciple.

2. Disciples who were ready for the unexpected. " . . . And they beckoned unto their partners . . ." (Luke 5:7) Despite the fact Peter didn't expect to catch any fish, he and Andrew were ready to react when they "enclosed a great multitude of fishes." (Luke 5:6)

3. Disciples who were responsible to do what they could do themselves. "... And filled both the ships..." (Luke 5:7) Jesus found the fish, and it was the responsibility of the fishermen to land the fish. Jesus will only do for you what you cannot do yourself. The rest is up to you.

4. Disciples who recognized their unworthiness. "Depart from me; for I am a sinful man, O Lord." (Luke 5:8) God's disciples in the Old Testament had the same attitude. Consider Isaiah (Isaiah 6:5) and Moses (Exodus 3:11).

5. Disciples who relied on God and not themselves. "For he was astonished, and all that were with him..." (Luke 5:9) Note the "they" of this story (Luke 5:6,7,9,and 10). Jesus wasn't just after Peter, but a stringer of disciples. Peter, Andrew, James, and John all realized that without Jesus' help they would never have caught such a haul.

6. Disciples who refocused on their real job. "... Henceforth thou shalt catch men." (Luke 5:10) Remember, these men had been following Jesus for a while (John 1 and Matthew 4), but a follower is not necessarily a disciple. It was this fishing trip that turned the four men into disciples, but Jesus discovered on this trip that they already had the qualifications to be a disciple.

7. Disciples who renounced all other things. "... They forsook all, and followed him." (Luke 5:11) Jesus would say later in one of his messages on discipleship, "So likewise, whosoever he be of you that forsaketh not all that he hath, he cannot be my disciple." (Luke 14:33)

"Deep" disciples have these characteristics.

# 141

## Patient Pastor

... but patient ...

—1 Timothy 3:3

One of the qualifications of a pastor is listed above. Most people struggle with patience, as I do, but recently I was reminded of the patience the Lord gave me when He called me into His work. I have been a pastor for nearly fifty years, and despite the fact I fought my calling to the pastorate, the gift of pastor/teacher (Ephesians 4:11) was granted me at my conversion and with it the characteristics of that office. One of these characteristics is patience.

Sometimes we don't realize that when the Lord calls us to a certain work, He gives us the virtues needed to fulfill that calling. Sometimes I struggle with patience over certain things, but deep down I am very patient because of the Spirit that dwells within. A case in point came to light quite a few years ago. I have been ice fishing with Buster Ingles and Harold Parker on Branch Lake for lake trout since 1996. The 2003 season began on opening day, January 1, with perfect weather and plenty of ice. An avid record keep, I have recorded time and size and weight of every togue caught since 1996. A look in my record book revealed that I had not landed a lake trout since January 26, 2001. Buster and Harold had landed numerous trout, but I had been shut out most of the 2001 season and all of the 2002 season. In that time I had also kept track of how many hours I had fished without landing a fish, and I was nearing the 100-hour mark!

The season started good, at least for the "boys." Buster was nearly 80 and Harold was over 80. In the first nine days of the year I got to fish three times, but was skunked all three days. In the meantime Harold and Buster were landing over a dozen togue. Plus, Harold landed the largest landlocked salmon I have ever seen caught through the ice and the largest pickerel he had caught out of Branch Lake. Added to those totals were two huge brown trout. Then frigid weather set in. For three weeks I waited through sub-zero days and gusty Arctic winds to return fishing. Finally, on January 29, I got back to the lake, but once again I was shut out. I had passed the 113-hour mark, and now it had been over two years since I last caught a togue. As a matter of fact, even the "boys" were shut out on the 29th, their first no-fish day in eight days ice fishing.

The very next day we returned to the lake, but moved from Mile Rock to the Narrows. Within a half an hour I landed a four-pound togue. The wait was over—114 hours, 2 years, and four days of patience, a record wait for any togue! However, in a greater fishing wait, I am still waiting the day I will bring Harold and Buster to Christ's fishing net (the tragedy is that both eventually died without my knowledge of them coming to the Lord, but the Lord knows those who are His. (2 Timothy 2:19) Waiting in witnessing is waiting on the Lord!

# 142

## Productive Pools

*. . . the fish pools of Heshbon . . .*
—Song of Solomon 7:4

Fishermen just love to talk about their favorite pools, the special places where they have caught the "whopper." Over the years I too have made a list of some very memorable "fish pools." Let me give you my top ten:

1. Beaver Brook, Portage, Maine—my first real fishing hole and its sweet brook trout.
2. Number One Lake, Mistassini, Quebec—a place of monster northern pike.
3. Smith Pond, Westfield, Maine—a farm pond with numerous brook trout and rainbow trout.
4. Penobscot River, Veazie, Maine—my first Atlantic salmon hole.
5. Lower Davis Pool, Grog Island Lodge—where I landed two huge Atlantic salmon, a 46 incher and a 40 incher!
6. Big Lake, Princeton, Maine—the fabled "Anchorage" and the large smallmouth bass off shore.

7. Miramichi River, Howard, New Brunswick—out of Vickers' Salmon Camps and the mighty black salmon.

8. Malcolm Brook, Pinkham Road, Maine—full of shore lunch bookies, where I have caught more fish than in any other fish hole.

9. Branch Lake, Ellsworth, Maine—an ice fisherman's paradise if lake trout are your prey.

10. Alamoosook Lake in Orland, Maine where smallmouth and largemouth bass can be caught in great numbers and great sizes.

As in the natural world, so too in the spiritual world of fishing-for-men. Solomon remembered the "fish pools" of Heshbon, those that wrote of Jesus and his fishing trips remembered the "fish pool" at Sychar (John 4:5), or the "fish pool" at Bethesda (John 5:2). Would Philip ever forget the "fish pool" at Gaza (Acts 8:26)? Would Peter ever forget the "fish pool" at Caesarea (Acts 10:1)? Just like I will never forget these "fish pools." Let me give you my top ten spiritual fishing holes:

Cider Hill Nursing Home, Athens, Georgia, where I led Mary Huff to the Lord, my first catch as a fisher-of-men.

Otis Lake Campsite, Quebec, Canada, where I led Claude Laves and his best friend to the Lord on an outing with the Boy's Brigade.

The McQueen Home, Allenstown, New Hampshire, where my first deacon and I led a mother, Simone, to the Lord, and where over the next few years all six of her children came to a saving knowledge of Christ.

Calvary Baptist Church, Westfield, Maine, where I started an Awana ministry and led my first clubber, Julie Fulton, to the Lord, and over my time there (1979–1986) I saw 68 people come to the Lord.

Hampton Bible Camp, Hampton, New Brunswick, where I have had my best success fishing for the Lord. In 21 fishing trips from 1987 to 2009 I have seen 211 campers make a profession of faith.

Awana Ministries from 1984 to 2020 where I have been casting the Gospel fly to three-year-olds to twelve-year-olds. In 834 clubs I have shared in scores of catches for Christ with the faithful fishermen and fisherwomen of Calvary Baptist and Emmanuel Baptist.

The Churches of Andra Pardesh India where in a six-day spiritual fishing trip I saw 54 people come to the Gospel net the most in the shortest time in my Gospel fishing career.

Living Water's Christian Camp where for the last five years (and I have just be asked to return for the 2020 camping season) I have not only been casting the line of love at 6–13 year olds, but have also been teaching them to fish. Many come from the cities of Maine and most have never been fishing before. It is exciting to witness their catching their first fish, but what is even more excited is the kids who have come to know Jesus as Savior.

Edayappara, India during an evangelistic crusade in the courtyard of the Kangazha Baptist Church when Shibu Simon's grandfather (80 years old) responded to my message and got saved. The cherry on the top was the very next day I had the privilege of baptizing George in Big Stream.

Erumely, India where after I cast the truth of "Forgiven Forgotten, Forever," the very first Muslim ever to be converted through the IGBC of Kerala, India got saved; my most unique catch of my spiritual fishing ministry.

# 143

## "Fishers" Fraternity

I will send for many fishers, said the Lord.
—Jeremiah 16:16

I do not know whether this verse is a prophecy or not, but when I came across it in Young's Concordance I was taken with the similarity between this "Thus saith the Lord" and Jesus' call for fishers-of-men.

As Jesus walked the shores of the Sea of Galilee looking for disciples, He came across a set of brothers, "and they were fishers" (Matthew 4:18 and Mark 1:16). Jesus' words to them were very clear, "Follow me, and I will make you fishers of men" (Matthew 4:19 and Mark 1:17). The four friends left their nets and became the charter members of a "fishers" fraternity that continues to this day.

I believe there is a brotherhood in fishing. I have been a fisherman for over fifty years now. I have travelled with friends to far off fishing holes, and I have travelled to far off fishing holes and found friends. A few years back I took a trip to Howard, New Brunswick, for the last three days of the Atlantic salmon fishing season in Canada. Usually I go with Mike Hangge, but this Ellsworth fireman had other duties during the middle of October. I arrived at Vickers' Camps to find a half-dozen men already enjoying the fine autumn weather and the excellent hospitality of Irving and Marsha Vickers. I had only met Marty Vickers, the owner, and the staff of the lodge before yet it wasn't long before our conversations spoke of long-lost friends.

Such is the bond that develops between strangers that fish the Atlantic salmon. What I have found about salmon fishermen is also true about trout fishermen or bass fishermen. There is a "fishers" fraternity, and it is linked by a common love and joy of fishing. We speak the same language, and we enjoy the same pleasures. The conversations are all about fishing and how to fish or subjects relating to fishing like flies and reels and rods and presentation and line and pools and weather conditions and, of course, telling "fish stories!"

Over the years I have wondered why the Christian community isn't like the fishing community. We have all been called to be fishers-of-men. (Matthew 28:19) Jesus called and is still calling "many fishers," but we don't act like a "fishers" fraternity. I have been a pastor nearly fifty years, and in that time I can count on one hand the number of individuals I have gone spiritually fishing with yet in the same time I have pastored hundreds upon hundreds of individuals claiming to be Christians. In each of the four churches I have pastored I have organized and directed a "witnessing" or "soul winning" group. I have taught classes numerous times on "how to" and "what-to-do" but only a handful have actually "gone fishing" with me. Jeremiah's verse is contrasted by the reality of Jesus' statement to his disciples, "But the labourers are few." (Matthew 9:37) Despite the few in the Church that actually fish for men, I have also observed that in the world there are relatively few fishermen, or women, so the true is true of both groups, so I am blessed to have gone first with the few, like Stacy Meister, Fred Boone, Shagu Simon, and the best I have ever meet, a lady named Pam Diveto!

# 144

## Sweet Species

We remember the fish which we did eat.

—NUMBERS 11:5

I am a fisherman (my wife would say an avid fisherman), but I am not much of a fish eater. Most of the fish I catch I return to be caught again, hopefully by me! If I do land a fish or two and decide to keep them, I will give them to a few friends who enjoy fresh water fish. A case in point happened a number of years ago. I landed two lake trout on Branch Lake while ice fishing with a couple of fishing buddies. One weighed 3 pounds 10 ounces and the other weighed in at 2 pounds 14 ounces. The reason I know their weight is a fancy digital scale we keep in the ice shack to weigh all our fish. For years my two fishing friends, Buster Ingles and Harold Parker, have been keeping statistics for the Maine Department of Inland Fisheries & Wildlife. We measure every fish landed and record its weight in a special book. Coming from the "old" school of thought that all fish landed become a fish fry, I had to keep my togue or the "boys" might never take me fishing again. So now who do I give them to?

    The first fish went to the Carter family who live on the upper end of the lake. They come to my church and love togue. We had already left a four pounder on their door earlier in the season, but my first fish of the season was readily accepted. Now, what about the second fish? As I drove home from Buster's house, I thought who I might give the second togue to. As I pulled into town the thought hit me that maybe Mike Hangge was working at the fire station. Mike is a dear fishing friend and a fantastic cook. He loves to prepare meals for his crew at the fire station. Turning off Main Street I soon came to the Ellsworth fire station located under City Hall. Sure enough, as I walked into the hall leading to the main office there was my friend talking on the phone. After finishing his conversation I asked if he was interested in "fish" for supper. He readily accepted the togue and promised he would save a piece for me. I don't care for togue, but another species in the trout family I am not so quick to give up.

Mike and I love to fly fish for brook trout. One of our favorite spots is a small stream located deep in the northern Maine woods. To fish it properly you must have a canoe. Mike and I fish Malcolm Brook for only one reason. It is not for the moose which we see just about every trip up the stream. (One year we paddled within feet of a baby moose.) It is not for the size of trout located in the brook because they rarely exceed ten inches. So why do we fish this wilderness creek? The answer is simple—a fried trout shore lunch. On our way up the stream we select the ten (a two-man limit on Malcolm Brook) best trout of the morning. At high noon we find an open space along the banks of the brook, and Mike prepares the trout with all the fixings. The Eastern brook trout is the sweetest fish of its species!

Such is the sweet taste to one's soul when you bring someone into the Gospel net. Paul speaks of this sweet savor in 2 Corinthians 2:15–16. That sweet savor in heaven is called rejoicing in Jesus' classic parable on the 'lost' (Luke 15:7, 10). Have you as yet tasted the sweet savor of winning someone to Christ?

# 145

## Picture Proof

... the Lord prepared a great fish ...
—JONAH 1:17

In 1982 I was pastoring a small church in northern Maine. While there I had the privilege to fish the Restigouche River in Quebec, Canada, because of the husband of a member of the church. Herschel Smith owned an Atlantic salmon lodge, Grog Island, on the lower end of that mighty river. Between 1980 and 1982 I took six trips to the river staying each time at Smith's lodge. Each trip was memorable for the huge salmon that were landed on light line and small flies. The two largest Atlantic salmon I have caught to date (I'm writing this in 2003) were caught out of the Restigouche River. The largest was 46 inches long and it weighed in at 37 pounds, and the second was 40 inches long and it weighed in at 22 pounds. I have pictures to prove both catches, and the larger of the two is hanging on the wall across from my office desk at the Emmanuel Baptist Church in Ellsworth, Maine. However, the best fish story of my Restigouche trips is one told by my fishing companion on my last trip.

Herschel was selling Grog Island Lodge, but before he did he called to ask if I wanted one more trip before the papers were signed. I told him I would like to go, and he asked if I would take Calvin Gallagher alone. Calvin was a young fisherman who had always wanted to fish for Atlantic salmon. He also came to the church where I pastored and the Smiths attended. Calvin quickly got three days off, and we headed up through New Brunswick to cross the Restigouche into Quebec. Calvin was like a school boy when we arrived. He couldn't wait to fish as he saw the huge salmon mounted on the lodge walls, some as large as forty pounds. Calvin vowed he would land one of these massive fish, no matter what!

However, the fishing that year had been slow. The water was low and warm, and the few fish that were stopping in front of Grog Island were not very aggressive. Each trip onto the river brought numerous sightings, but no hookups. We fished four hours in the early morning and four hours late into the evening. It was the second week in July and the afternoons were hot. We were shut out until the evening of our last day. Calvin had hooked a salmon on the morning of the second day, but failed to land it when the double hook he was using came loose. Calvin vowed again he would land a fish one way or the other.

As Calvin and his guide worked their way through the Lower Davis Pool, Calvin spotted a large dorsal fin just above the surface of the river. The guide explained it was a dying salmon that was drifting down stream. Before the guide could say anything Calvin reached over the side of the square-stern canoe, grabbed the salmon, and threw it into the canoe. He then pounced on it and subdued it. Calvin had his fish, and I have the picture proof of the only Atlantic salmon I know that was hand-caught by God's grace! As I recall this story in my mind it reminds me of the determination it that at time in our witnessing for our Lord. Failure should never be an excuse not to press on, keep on, and go on in our request to win someone to Christ.

# 146

## Dragonfly Distraction

The fowl of the air, and the fish of the sea . . .
—PSALMS 8:8

What a beautiful day, and it is made even more beautiful because I am fishing!

I am surrounded by nature that is teaming with activity and full of life. The pond is quiet, no fish yet, but the air is filled with scores of streamlined insects darting about, zinging and sagging, diving and hovering, rising and falling with the gentle breeze. In the midst of all this activity a number of dragonflies appear. They are not birds ("the fowl of the air"), but they are big enough to be called a bird. I have seen hummingbirds smaller!

I know why the dragonflies have appeared over the isolated trout pond in northern Maine—mosquitoes. The morning started out cool so the mosquitoes were hiding, but with the warming of the late spring sun they are hovering over Matthew's Pond by the thousands now. So far they haven't found me, but it is only a matter of time, that is, unless my friends, the dragonflies, can clear the pond of this north woods pest. Like Super Cobra helicopters the dragonflies soar gracefully through the gathering swarms of mosquitoes. The single-engine mosquito is no match for the jets of the dragonfly. As my trout fly lies quietly on the surface of Matthew's Pond, I am spellbound by the gracefulness and speed of these marvels of God's creation.

It was then I noticed on the side of the canoe I had borrowed from the boats along the shore a strange and ugly creature. It was grayish-black in color, and it labored just to get to the top of the rail near my seat in the back of the canoe. It was homely and repulsive to look at. As I watched the insect's back split open, bit by bit a perfect replica of a dragonfly appeared. Its wings were pressed closely to its body as it struggled to gain balance and its distinct form. With each passing moment the warm sun and the light breeze dried the creature. After about a half an hour its wings were dry enough to fly, and in an instant it was off to join its family in an attack on the local mosquito horde.

Later in my study I learned that the creature known as a dragonfly develops for nearly a year in its subterranean home before reaching its goal. It changes from a repulsive nymph to one of God's most graceful insects. This dragonfly distraction reminded me of these verses from the pen of Paul, "So also is the resurrection of the dead. It is sown in corruption; it is raised in incorruption. It is sown in dishonor; it is raised in glory: it is sown in weakness; it is raised in power." (1 Corinthians 15:42, 43) The great difference between us and the dragonfly is that the dragonfly will soon die, but on our resurrection day we will "fly away" to live forever in our "new body" in a glorified state unmatched by anything on this planet!

# 147

## Shore Stroll

He causeth his wind to blow, and the waters flow.
—Psalms 147:18

The day had turned hot, and the fishing had turned cold. It was midday on Matthew's Pond, and I decided after six hours in a canoe to paddle to shore and stretch my legs.

Near the landing on the opposite shore was a blow-down that made a perfect seat and observation platform. As I sat and saw the beauty around me, I thought of my Great Maker. The wind had picked up a bit so there was the lapping of water against the shore combined with the music of a breeze blowing through the canopy of fir, spruce, and pine over my head. The conditions were perfect for a "shore stroll."

The shoreline was thick with underbrush as I made my way to a huge boulder near one of my favorite fishing holes on the pond. Suddenly my attention was directed heavenward as a group of three crows passed directly overhead. Their call alerted every creature that they had arrived and were now in charge. Their arrival, however, brought a quick and instant response from the local nesting society. From out of nowhere a squadron of tree sparrows were unrelenting in their quest of chasing the invaders off. This aerial display went on for about ten minutes until the crows got so annoyed with the little birds they flew away cawing all the while.

The trip to and back from the granite boulder was an adventure in itself as the birds and the local forest creatures announced my presence with every step of my stroll. To me there is nothing more breathtaking then wind, water, wildlife, and wild flowers. The forest floor leading to my destination was covered with the delicate flower of late spring. Truly, the Psalmist was right when he wrote, "The heavens declare the Glory of God; and the firmament sheweth His handiwork" (Psalms 19:1) Solomon was also right when he wrote, "The flowers appear on the earth; the time of the singing birds is come, and the voice of the turtle is heard in our land." (Song of Solomon 2:12) The only thing I didn't see or hear on my "shore stroll" was a turtle, but I have in the past, and I will no doubt hear one on a future fishing trip.

Returning to my log recliner, I laid down for a brief nap. It was then I had a close encounter with the neighborhood squirrel. As I lay down and closed my eyes to listen to the midday melody of water, wind, and wildlife, I was run over by a squirrel. It seems it was one of his paths through his forest glade, and not noticing I was resting on his log highway, he literally ran across me. It was a fitting conclusion to my midday break. Walking back to the canoe to continue fishing, I smiled at the special interlude the Good Lord had given me on His shore.

# 148

## Lucifer's Lures

Surely he shall deliver thee from the snare...

—PSALMS 91:3

On a table in the basement of the parsonage of the Emmanuel Baptist Church in Ellsworth, Maine, is an old green tackle box, the first such fish box I ever had for tackle. I can't even remember now when I got it or if it was given to me, I have had it that long. It is scratched and faded in color, but oh the book of memories it opens when the lid is lifted. This tackle box isn't just a place to store hooks and line and sinkers and lures and tackle and reels and spoons and other fishing equipment. It is also a wonderful object lesson to the "snare of Satan."

In my ministry of teaching God's children the principles and precepts of the Bible I love to use object lessons as illustrations to God's great concepts. One winter I was teaching a group of AWANA kids about the devil's devices for snaring them and trapping them (2 Corinthians 2:11). One Monday night I showed them my old, green tackle box and explained the different lures found there and what they were used to catch. Then I told them of "Satan's snares." This was my "Lucifer's lures" outline:

1. The Lure of Lying (John 8:44). The great liar is very clever in getting us to lie.

2. The Lure of Lust (1 John 2:16). The lust of the flesh and the lust of the eyes are only topped by the pride of life.

3. The Lure of Liquor (Proverbs 20:1). The world has been deceived into thinking that drinking can be controlled.

4. The Lure of Laxity (Proverbs 27:1). Laziness is a great sin against "six days shall you labor."

5. The Lure of Legality (Galatians 5:1). The sin of legalism has run the average Christian into non-service.

6. The Lure of Lasciviousness (Mark 7:22). This is the sin of "excess," a sin rampant in our society today.

7. The Lure of Lewdness (Acts 18:14). There is no longer any shame in our society.

8. The Lure of License (Galatians 5:13). License to sin is allowed in our "if-you-feel-like-it's-okay" country.

9. The Lure of Loftiness (Psalms 131:1). Pride was Lucifer's downfall, and he has caused many to fall with him.

10. The Lure of Lukewarmness (Revelation 3:16). The Lord says that "lukewarmness" is the sin of the Church today.

Let us never forget this admonition from the pen of Paul: "And that they may recover themselves out of the snare of the devil, which are taken captive by him at his will." (2 Timothy 2:26) It has been amazing to me that over the years as I have gone fishing to get away from the office and the ministry, that I have gotten so many lessons from that old, green tackle box. The spiritual lessons learned have now filled a book!

# 149

## Beelzebub's Bait

Keep me from the snares...

—PSALMS 141:9

A week after I taught my AWANA kids about the "lures" of Lucifer (Isaiah 14:12), the next Monday night I showed them the "baits" of Beelzebub (Matthew 12:24) and how he tries to snare us with his special baits. This was my "bait" outline:

1. The Bait of Backbiting (Romans 1:30). Backbiting is one of the great sins the devil tempts us with in relationship to our relationship with others.

2. The Bait of Backsliding (Proverbs 14:14). When the devil realized that he could no longer get our souls, he came up with a way for us to become useless for God's service.

3. The Bait of Banqueting (1 Peter 4:3). Partying has become the number one pastime of many young people. When was the last time you went to a party honoring to Christ?

4. The Bait of Beauty (Proverbs 31:30). We live in a society where "beauty" is king. Looks and how you look is how you are judged today.

5. The Bait of Betrayal (Luke 22:3). Satan gets no greater joy than the happiness he gets when somebody betrays the Lord. A small betrayal is just as bad as a Peter betrayal.

6. The Bait of Bitterness (Ephesians 4:31). The bait of bitterness is very harmful to the one being bitten. The focus of that bitterness isn't as bad as the hook in us.

7. The Bait of Blasphemy (Matthew 15:19). To blaspheme God is a characteristic of the devil and those that follow him. Don't be a part of this terrible sin.

8. The Bait of Boasting (2 Timothy 3:2). Boasting has become popular and acceptable in our society, but there is only one thing we are to boast in. (See Galatians 6:14)

9. The Bait of Brawling (2 Timothy 3:2). Fighting has also become popular in our society, yet God teaches us to love.

10. The Bait of Breakers (2 Timothy 3:3). "Trucebreakers" is a sign of the "last days" (2 Timothy 3:1), and it is just another device the devil uses to snare us.

As I finished my lesson on the devil's "bait," I taught the "clubbers" the words to this old church hymn:

> Yield not to temptation, for yielding is sin. Each victory will help you some other to win. Fight manfully onward, dark passions subdue. Look ever to Jesus, He'll carry you through. Ask the Savior to help you, comfort, strengthen and keep you. He is willing to aid you. He will carry you through.

Remember, to defeat the devil's devices, Lucifer's lures, or Beelzebub's bait, all you have to do is, *"Resist the devil and he will flee from you."* (James 4:7)

# 150

# Fatal Flies

*The wicked have laid a snare for me: yet I erred not from thy precepts.*
—PSALMS 119:110

Besides my old green tackle box, I also showed my AWANA kids a very special fly box. Most fly boxes are small, containing a few special flies for a few special fish. My special fly box is a small suitcase that can be opened from both sides. When you open each latch, you discover row after row of colorful flies for every kind of fly fishing imaginable. The super-fly box was created by my fly tying father-in-law, Stacy Meister, as a display when he went to the Fish and Game shows in the State of Maine. It contained samples of his hand-made trout and salmon flies. When he died in 1997, my mother-in-law gave me the case. The fly case was also filled with a treasury of memories of the numerous days my father-in-law and I spent fly fishing together. Reflected in the hundreds and hundreds of flies were cloudless days, sleepy lagoons, babbling brooks, shore side lunches, and leaping salmon. The special case has also become another object lesson for my warnings to the kids of the devil's devices to tempt us, snare us, and hook us into his wicked and evil ways.

After I taught the kids about Lucifer's "lures" and Beelzebub's "bait," I taught them of "fatal flies." This was my "fly" outline:

1. The Fly of Flattery (Proverbs 26:28). How the devil likes to "butter-us-up" so that we like him will become proud. Flattery will be fatal if we listen to his whispers.

2. The Fly of Falsehood (Proverbs 14:5). The devil by his very nature can't tell the truth. He deals in falsehoods whether bold-face lies or half-truths.

3. The Fly of Fainting (Proverbs 24:10). How the devil loves for us to give in and give up. We will reap if we faint not.

4. The Fly of Faithlessness (John 20:27). We know that only things done in faith will please God (Hebrews 11:6) so it is not surprising that the devil would tempt us to doubt.

5. The Fly of Fear (2 Timothy 1:7). The author of fear is the devil (Hebrews 2:14,15), and what is fear but a way to destroy your faith and trust in God.

6. The Fly of Fighting (James 4:1). Fighting within and fighting without is a constant tactic of the devil to keep us out of step and without peace with God.

7. The Fly of Filthiness (Psalms 53:3). Whether on television or in the words of a song, it is wrong.

8. The Fly of Foolishness (Proverbs 17:12). The fool is Satan's greatest conquest.

9. The Fly of Fornication (Matthew 15:19). A sexual relationship before marriage is the devil's great temptation.

10. The Fly of Forwardness (Proverbs 2:14). This is the sin of stubbornness, willfulness, and contrariness.

# Postlude

## Both Boats

And when they had done this, they enclosed a great multitude of fishes: and their net brake.

—LUKE 5:6

The ultimate aspiration and continual anticipation of any fisherman is to catch the "large linker" or the "huge haul!" Large size or large statistics are the dream of every serious fishermen I know. The worst result of a day of fishing is being "shut-out," and yet this is exactly what happened to some of the most experienced fishermen of Lake Gennesaret. All they could do now was to clean their fishing equipment and wait for the next fishing opportunity. Or was it?

Peter and Andrew were washing their nets when Jesus came by after a shoreline walk with a crowd in tow. Sensing the need of the multitude, as He always did, Jesus asked Peter for the use of his fishing boat so that he might use it as a preaching platform. Deciding he didn't have anything better to do, Peter pushed the boat off shore and sat in the back of the boat while Jesus delivered a message to the lakeside crowd. Interestingly, Luke doesn't record the title, the text, or even the theme of Jesus' message. Under inspiration of the Holy Spirit the "fish story" was more inspiring and instructive than the sermon of the Savior!

Because God is no man's debtor and neither is His Son, even when it comes to the loan of a fishing boat, Jesus told Peter to go fishing. Peter was instructed to move into deep water and cast his nets for "a draught." (Luke

5:4) (Note: plural nets and single draught.) How many "draughts" had Peter and his friends taken the night before? Rare has been the occasion that I have caught a fish on the first cast, but it has happened. Jesus only needed "one draught." Remember, Matthew 17:27 and Peter's fishing expedition for tax money. But Peter, the experienced fisherman, knew the odds of catching fish in the daytime and possibly high noon. He reminded the Lord of the experience of his friends and himself the night before, but to humor the Lord he would try. For years I have not liked the way the grand Church hymn *Stepping in the Light* starts. "Trying to walk in the steps of the Savior, trying to follow our Savior and King. . ." Ours is not to try, but to trust. How many of us are only serving the Lord to humor Him? How many of us are witnessing just to say we have, but really don't expect to "catch" anything? Peter went fishing, but without much enthusiasm or excitement or expectation. Much like Jonah on his way to the fishing hole of Nineveh!

If I have learned anything about fishermen over the last fifty years, no fisherman likes unsolicited instruction. Most ignore you when you tell them of a fish sighting or a taking fly. Veteran anglers like Peter are more often turned off by an amateur's advice, but this was Jesus so Peter moved offshore to cast his recently cleaned net into the dirty Galilee. Why do I know of Peter's doubt? Compare Jesus' instruction of "nets" (Luke 5:4) and Peter's letting "down the net." (Luke 5:5) It is also here we discovered that either Andrew joined them or he was already in the boat. (Luke 5:6,7—notes the "they.") Resisting the critics onshore and the doubt in his own heart, Peter does half-heartedly and half-way what the Lord told him to do. However, instantly, the net is full of fish; immediately, the net begins to break; and suddenly, the doubting fishermen are struggling to hold on to the catch of the year, or maybe a lifetime. Despite the miracle in progress, Peter and Andrew realize they can't pull in the "haul" alone. Yelling for help, Peter and Andrew are soon joined by their partners, James and John, and eventually they fill "both boats with fish!" (Luke 5:7)

My last admonition in this series is to simply follow the Lord's leading when it comes to casting the Gospel net. He knows the best time and the best place because He knows where those souls are that will respond positively to the presentation. How long have we toiled in vain, but at His gracious word we should let out the net again. How long have we labored in vain? Hear these final words from the pen of Paul: "Therefore, my beloved brethren, be ye steadfast, unmovable, always abounding in the work of the Lord, forasmuch as ye know that your labour is not in vain in the Lord." (1 Corinthians 15:59)

www.ingramcontent.com/pod-product-compliance
Lightning Source LLC
Chambersburg PA
CBHW071335150426
43191CB00007B/739